INNOVATION CAPACITY

INNOVATION CAPACITY

Christine Meyer, Inger Stensaker,
Rune Bjerke, Anne Cathrin Haueng

FAGBOKFORLAGET

First Edition 2023 / Printing 1 2023

ISBN: 978-82-450-4571-0

Graphic production: John Grieg, Bergen
Cover design and typeset by the publisher
Coverillustration by Mathilde Lid, Melkeveien Designkontor AS

Enquiries about this text can be directed to:
Fagbokforlaget
Kanalveien 51
5068 Bergen
Tel.: 55 38 88 00
email: fagbokforlaget@fagbokforlaget.no
www.fagbokforlaget.no

Vigmostad & Bjørke AS is Eco-Lighthouse certified, and the books are produced in environmentally certified printing houses.

Miljøfyrtårn®

Preface

This book came about due to a burning desire to convey research-based knowledge on radical change and innovation in an established firm in an engaging way to students and practitioners. Our aim is to move beyond the narrow conversations among academics where we only communicate through scholarly papers in largely incomprehensible language (at least for anyone outside of academia).

The book is based on RaCE[1], a research program at the Norwegian School of Economics (NHH), which aims to explore and theorize how established companies can become more innovative. We believe in Darwin and selection, and that innovation often happens through newly established, eager businesses, but we also believe that established firms can become more innovative and survive in a rapidly changing environment. However, this is not easy, and many established firms struggle to balance exploitation and exploration. This makes it all the more interesting to take a closer look at established firms' efforts to innovate and renew themselves.

Our professional foundation lies within strategy, organization and management. We have previously conducted research and written about change capacity as a muscle that organizations can develop to handle a high pace of change. In this book we build on our previous insights from change capacity, while turning our focus to changes that aim for renewal and innovation. In particular, we are concerned with the strategic choices established firms make, how they structure the organization to reach their strategic goals, and how they exercise leadership. We draw on existing research within the fields of strategy and management to shed light on the problems and challenges managers face during innovation and renewal. The purpose is not to give a complete picture

1 RaCE = Radical Technology-Driven Change in Established Firms, a research project at the Institute for Research in Economics and Business Administration (SNF)/Norwegian School of Economics (NHH) funded by the Research Council of Norway in partnership with Deloitte, DNB, Laerdal Medical, and Telenor.

of all the research that exists in the field, but rather to carefully select what we find most relevant and interesting.

To ensure that the book is also relevant for practitioners, the two professors in the team, Christine Meyer and Inger Stensaker, are accompanied by two experienced practitioners, Rune Bjerke and Anne Cathrin Haueng. Rune has experience as a senior manager and CEO in several companies, not least in DNB, which is a corporate partner in the RaCE project; Anne Cathrin has been a senior consultant and partner advising major firms in both the public and private sector and was employed in Deloitte (another RaCE corporate partner) when this book was written.

Another key feature of the book is the inclusion of many current and relevant cases. These cases serve to illustrate the theoretical frameworks about how established firms can renew themselves and innovate.

The book is much more than a product of a four-way collaboration drawing on our own knowledge of research and practice. In the spirit of open innovation, we have reached out and asked for help and contributions to the book, and the response has been overwhelming, particularly when it comes to contributing to the cases. While some of the cases are based on extensive data material collected through our research project, other cases have been developed for this book through conversations with managers and/or based on publicly available documentation. We would like to thank all the managers we have interviewed for the cases, our master and doctoral students, the people who have read through individual chapters and those who have commented and reviewed the whole book. This book would not have seen the light of day without your amazing support and encouragement.

Given the number of people involved, this has been a truly innovative and creative project, and the result is a book that none of us could have produced singlehandedly. We have learned so much along the way, and our hope is that you will too.

Bergen and Oslo

Christine Meyer, Inger Stensaker, Rune Bjerke, Anne Cathrin Haueng

Table of contents

Part 2
Innovation within organizational boundaries. 71

A foggy landscape

"Where will DNB be in ten years, Rune? Tell us about your future dreams and how you envision the bank, and we will follow you." These kinds of questions and challenges had been on my mind for a long time, nagging away at me and creating nightmares rather than dreams. In short, I did not have the answers. I hesitated. My words were vague and I spoke in general terms. Was I a man without vision? Was I unable to spot and understand the trends and developments well enough?

A leader is supposed to show the way. The course must be set out in the strategy documents and employees expect that management has a superior understanding of what is going on. Leaders should be the best at sensing the environment – not only the competitive landscape but also threats and opportunities, today and into the future. Maybe my doubts were a sign that I did not have the right capabilities as a senior manager.

After almost a decade as a senior manager, I was more confident. My future vision was clearer, but alas there was no epiphany in sight. On the contrary, what I did see was that the horizon was short, that visibility was poor, and that complexity was growing. No one can clearly see ten years forward in time – not even five. However, my personal growth as a senior manager and increased confidence made it easier to answer more honestly and sincerely. The truth is that no senior manager can know where the business will be in ten years' time. When challenged about future predictions, I began responding with "I have no idea." It is demanding enough to make estimates for the year ahead. Annual budgets have long since been overtaken by more flexible beyond budgeting practices.

Today's reality is that the pace of change is growing faster and faster. Change can strike with tremendous force or can emerge in seemingly small steps that lead to big movements. New and old competitors are constantly attacking parts of the value chain in unexpected ways, and the concept of disruption has shaken several industries to the core. "But what I'm absolutely sure of," I added, "is that if we're not at the forefront of development, we'll be left behind. We have to be in the top 10% most innovative companies in our industry. We must lead the way in the development of new services and products. We have to understand the customers' changes in needs and expectations, faster than most. And we must be better at adopting new technology and new channels to make production processes easier. If we manage to do that, we don't need to be so concerned about epiphanies."

As a senior manager I wished I had a book that could have guided me in my endeavors to build innovation capacity in the organizations I managed. Fortunately, I have now been part of writing such a book. My greatest wish is to help current and aspiring managers and consultants navigate in a foggy landscape and take measures to prepare the organization for the future – into the unknown.

Rune Bjerke

Part 1

Introduction

Chapter 1

Innovation capacity

What is innovation capacity? Why is it so hard for established firms to become innovative? These are the questions we will attempt to answer in this chapter. Like many instinctively intuitive terms, it is much easier to recognize innovation and innovation capacity when you see them than to clearly define what they are. The meanings of the terms are often influenced by our backgrounds. It's like the story of the blind men who were asked to identify an animal solely by touching an elephant. Each of the men found different parts of the elephant; the trunk, the tail, different parts of the body and legs, and each gave a completely different, albeit correct, description of what an elephant is.

We will begin this chapter by briefly discussing why it is so difficult for established firms to innovate. Next, we will examine different ways to define and classify innovation and explain our position in this book. Once we have defined innovation, we can approach the subject of innovation capacity. We will start with the companies' *dynamic capabilities* and combine these with the *complementary capabilities* needed to develop and scale products and services. On top of this there must also be *collective engagement* to create the drive and desire to enter unknown waters.

Innovation in established firms

The starting point in the development of innovation capacity is that businesses need to balance current business and future opportunities (O'Reilly & Tushman, 2004). If all one's resources are spent on efficiency and improving current business, the firm may lose its competitive edge or fall behind in the future. Competitors have found new, better ways to deliver products and services to customers, new players have entered the market with completely new business models, and new technology has broken ground in working smarter and getting products and services into the market faster.

With an increased pace of change and higher demands from customers to innovate faster and more frequently, there has been a growing recognition that companies need to allocate resources for innovation alongside their daily operations. This is not like a contractor who can build a house from the ground up. This renovation has to happen while you're still living in the house. Performing innovation activities in the middle of operations isn't easy, primarily because acute issues will always take top priority, but also largely because operations and innovation require completely different management and leadership principles and cultures. While making a mistake can be catastrophic in operations, making mistakes will be a natural part of an innovation culture. In order to innovate, you must give up control and not overwhelm innovation groups with comprehensive demands for reporting and fast results.

For this reason, leaders must keep two thoughts in mind at once: one, how to drive efficiency and improve daily operations and the existing product portfolio, and two, how to innovate and create new business opportunities.

Established firms have generally developed good procedures for driving continuous improvement by improving efficiency in production processes. However, innovation may pose more of a challenge, particularly if the new innovations threaten the existing business. Established firms tend to develop an immune system that strikes down business opportunities that are radically different, or that challenge what already exists. Because they become so skilled at improving efficiency, they also develop a structural and cultural inertia, making it difficult to change and renew the business. The potential revenue of new business opportunities is also highly uncertain, making this skepticism understandable and rational. Often, all revenue will come from the established firm area, and there will be significant uncertainty about whether, and when, income can be expected from the new area. However, an established firm that does not renew itself will, in the longer term, face completely different challenges, and risks becoming extinct. As such, most will agree that even established firms must build capabilities to innovate.

What is innovation?

There are countless definitions of innovation, some more appropriate than others. Matt Ridley (2020) states that innovation is one of the world's least understood concepts – while still being one of the most important drivers of growth. Economists have long struggled to explain something that cannot be attributed to labor and capital and have simply characterized it as an unexplained residual factor. Fortunately, newer growth theory now accounts for innovation as an independent factor by including knowledge production. However, the concept of innovation is still poorly defined.

Ridley states that innovation – like evolution – can be described as a process in which we constantly discover new ways to reorganize the world, ways that are not likely to emerge on their own but that are useful. Useful is indeed a keyword here. There are numerous examples of innovations that flop because they are far too advanced and expensive or because they are too incomplete. Nobel laureate and economist Edmund Phelps shows how innovations are often inspired by other contexts and countries, therefore defining innovation as a new method or product that becomes a new practice somewhere in the world. For example, the mobile payment solution Vipps was not something the Norwegian commercial bank DNB invented from scratch. When DNB developed Vipps, there were already a number of digital wallets in Europe, including Danske Bank's Mobile Pay.

In practice, it is a little difficult to distinguish what should be considered an innovation and what is better described as an improvement. The boundaries are fluid, which also makes it difficult to measure the extent of innovation in a business, let alone a country. Our goal is not to operate with sharp distinctions but to examine innovations from a strategic perspective and focus on innovations intended to go beyond incremental improvements in existing products and processes. Therefore, the organizational solutions we discuss in this book assume that to (radically) innovate, businesses must implement structural measures either within or outside their organizational boundaries.

There are many different types of innovations. We are concerned with both product and service innovation, as well as process innovation. The latter is about the way new products and/or services are developed. In this book, we will draw on three different frameworks for classifying innovations. Each provides insights into what can be characterized as disruptive or transformative innovations as opposed to the less radical ones, where one can largely build on what has already been done. What may be considered disruptive, transformative and/or radical will often vary in different innovation frameworks. The key point is that this type of innovation will be far from the current core business.

Disruptive innovations

Clayton Christensen coined the term disruptive innovation in his 1997 book *The Innovator's Dilemma*. Christensen's precise definition of disruptive innovations is that they either start at the lower end of the market where customers had a low willingness to pay, or open up new markets that did not previously exist. In his 2015 Harvard Business Review article (Christensen, Raynor & McDonald, 2015), he stated that the term had become a victim of its own success and that inaccurate uses of it had rendered it practically vacuous.

In the last book Christensen wrote with two colleagues before his death (Christensen, Ojomo & Dillon, 2019), he elaborated on his previous definition of disruptive innovations by putting them into a sustainability context, the goal being to combat global poverty. In this book we will distinguish between three types of innovations: efficiency innovations, sustaining innovations, and market-creating innovations (see Figure 1.1).

Efficiency innovations enable businesses to do more with fewer resources, but do not create a foundation to acquire new customers. Many car manufacturers are skilled at this type of innovation, such as replacing the work force with robot technology. This type of innovation, which can be performed within existing operations, is not the primary focus of this book.

Figure 1.1 Different types of innovation (inspired by Christensen)

The second category, sustaining innovations, includes innovations that are aimed downstream toward the customer and seek to improve deliverables, particularly for existing customers who require better performance. Examples of this can be found in the various new and consistently improved versions of online and mobile banking, or the development of products in an environmentally friendly direction. The vast majority of product and service innovations will fall under this category.

Last but not least, there are innovations that can be characterized as being more disruptive and are aimed at creating new markets and attracting new customer groups. This type of innovation will typically seek to attract customer groups that currently do not consume the product or service, either because it is too expensive, too inaccessible, or simply because it is a completely new product or service that the customer has not imagined. In other words, there is no market yet, and the market must be developed. Examples of innovations that approach completely new customer groups include the Ford Model T, which made it possible for completely new groups of Americans to buy cars, as well as microloans, which built a foundation for impoverished people to start their own businesses. Alibaba's establishment of a B2B (business-to-business) web platform can also be characterized as a disruptive innovation. This innovation opened the global market for small and medium-sized businesses in China. Alibaba is a case study that we will take a deeper dive into when we come on to ecosystems in the third part of the book.

Christensen's classification of innovations thus says something about where and how value is created through new development. Established firms face a dilemma, because the better they are at listening to existing customers and meeting the needs of the customers they have today, the greater the danger will be that they fail to spot possible disruptive innovations.

In this book, we will use Christensen's terms regarding disruptive innovations in a somewhat broader sense than he himself defines them, and we will include radical innovations that do not necessarily come from the end of the market with a low willingness to pay. Such a broader understanding of disruptive (or frame-breaking) innovations is in line with innovation researchers such as O'Reilly and Tushman (2016).

The innovation landscape map

Christensen's framework will form the foundation for the discussion of innovation capacity in this book, but we will also draw some inspiration from Pisano's (2019) innovation landscape map. The innovation landscape map distinguishes between innovations that require new technological expertise and new business models (Pisano, 2019). The strength of this framework is that it explicitly deals with the established firm to assess what needs to be changed, and it matches the basis for the various organizational solutions we outline in Parts 2, 3, and 4. Furthermore, Pisano's innovation landscape map more explicitly indicates that the innovations may also entail changes to business models. For illustrations of the different types of innovations, see Figure 1.2.

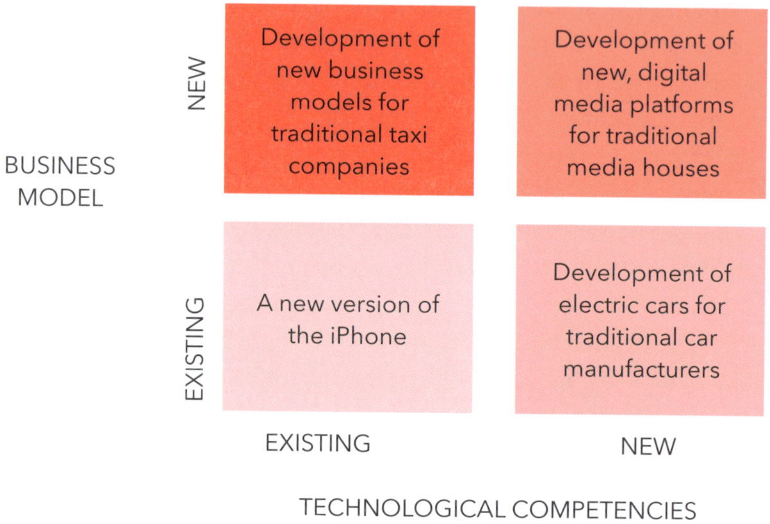

Figure 1.2 The innovation landscape (adapted from Pisano, 2019)

Some innovations will be of such a quality that it will not be necessary to change one's technological expertise or one's business models. Examples of this are when Intel releases a new processor, or Apple launches a new version of the iPhone. Other innovations require changes to business models without necessarily requiring new technology. When Uber entered the taxi market as a new player and challenged existing taxi companies, it put pressure on the business models of the established companies. Very few went as far as developing ride-sharing services, but many developed new web platforms and offered payment in advance. There are also many innovations that require changes to the businesses' technological expertise without demanding changes to business models, such as efforts by established car manufacturers to develop electric cars. For established car manufacturers, it has been much more difficult to develop new technology than it has been for companies like Tesla, which was able to start with developing electric cars right from the start. Last, but not least, there are innovations that require changes to both business models and technological expertise, such as when digital technology reached the media companies and advertising income dropped like a stone. It has taken a long time for media houses to develop new, sustainable business models.

The cases we present in this book fall within the three quadrants that require changes either to business models, or to technological expertise, or both. Innovations that fall within existing business models and technological expertise will not be central – as a rule, they tend to be more incremental, and can be implemented within existing operations.

Innovation portfolio

The two latter categorizations from Christensen and Pisano are useful for specifying what types of innovation are being discussed in a single, specific example, as well as what changes will be needed at the established business. However, they say little about the composition an established firm should have for their investments into innovation. It is therefore relevant to bring in a different, yet related perspective on innovation developed by Nagji and Tuff (2012), which involves the suggestion that businesses should develop a portfolio of different innovation investments.

The portfolio perspective looks at the entire established firm and maps all innovations to create an overview. Innovations may then be classified based on how close or far away they are, relative to the company's existing business. Here, we can distinguish between innovations that take place at the core, or in adjacent areas, or completely at the margins of the company's current business, depending on how far one moves away from existing products and markets. The further you go toward the periphery, the further you move away from the existing product portfolio. The thinking behind this innovation framework (Nagji & Tuff, 2012) is that the business should have a portfolio of different innovation initiatives at different levels, but with most innovation staying close to the core business.

The challenge for the majority of businesses, in the authors' view, is that you place all innovation inside the core, forgetting to also invest in adjacent and transformative innovations. This leaves the company ill-prepared for disruptive innovation. Nagji and Tuff (2012) refer to a common distribution in which 70% of the innovations take place in the core, 20% in adjacent areas, and 10% in transformative initiatives, but they also state that these proportions will vary for different companies and industries. The key point is to have a conscious relationship to investments in different types of innovations. Among the different solutions we outline in the book, some will primarily aim to innovate in adjacent business fields, such as the ambidextrous solution. Other solutions, such as innovation at the edge, will be based on innovations that may be transformative for the organization.

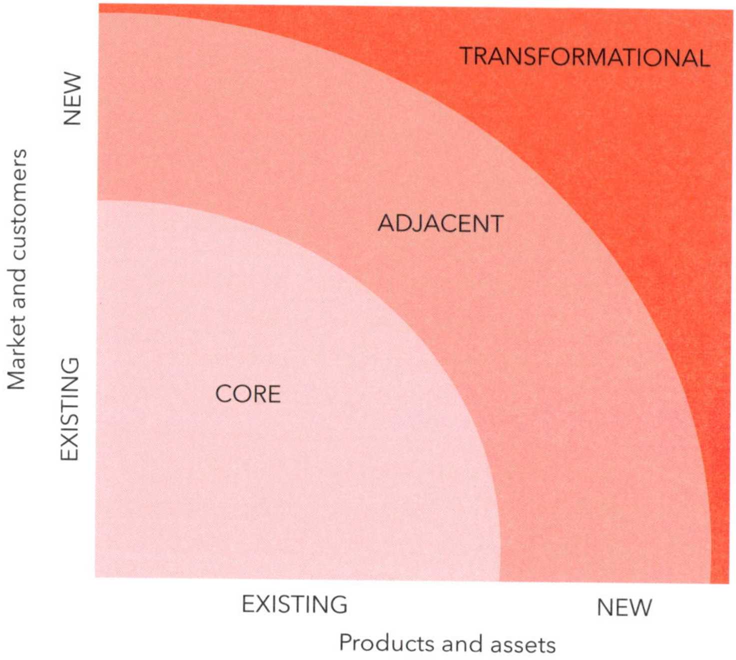

Figure 1.3 The innovation portfolio (Nagji & Tuff, 2012)

In short, when we discuss innovations in this book, we remain at the strategic level. Although efficiency improvements may be important and may create value, we are more concerned with downstream innovations that create new value for the customer, as well as disruptive innovations that attract completely new customers and create entirely new markets. We will take with us the consideration that innovation may create a need for both new business models and new expertise at the business. We will also take with us the portfolio considerations, which make visible how companies often work with several different types of innovations at once – some of which will (and should) be further from the core than others.

Now that we have explained what types of innovations we wish to include, the next question is what is meant by innovation capacity.

Innovation capacity

Building innovation capacity is akin to building a muscle that makes us more capable of innovating than if we had not built such a muscle. It can be compared to winning a ski race. If you are well trained, you will be more likely to take home the gold, but at the same time there's no guarantee that you are going to end up on the podium. Going through hard training is a prerequisite, but is not enough. There must also be some talent behind it. Yet even that is not enough. Many have both talent and are well-trained, but they don't have the drive and the passion to throw themselves into the contest and put in that extra effort needed to win.

Finally, innovation capacity is about succeeding not just once, but over and over again. Luck or coincidences that lead you to victory or an unexpected breakthrough may seem like flukes, but is that accurate? "The more I train, the luckier I get" is one of the most quoted statements among Norwegian sports legends. Kjetil André Aamodt said it after winning a gold medal by one-hundredth of a second.

Transferring this to organizations, we need some capabilities to develop innovation capacity, and we will draw on the theory on dynamic capabilities. Next, we must ensure that we can scale up innovation by having employees with the right expertise (e.g., linked to new technology) allocated to innovation tasks and that there is a system around them that supports the development of innovations. Often, such complementary capabilities take time to develop, and it is not simply a matter of employing many new technologists and hoping for a miracle to occur. Furthermore, there is a need for collective engagement among the employees who drive this development forward, and that they do not give up as soon as they face some resistance.

Figure 1.4 shows the three components that make up innovation capacity:

1. Dynamic capabilities
2. Complementary capabilities
3. Collective engagement

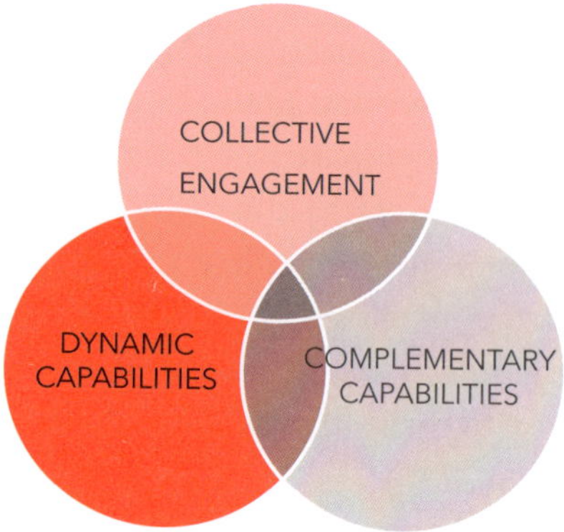

Figure 1.4 Innovation capacity

Dynamic capabilities

To manage their business in increasingly volatile, uncertain, complex, and ambiguous conditions (also known as the VUCA conditions) (Teece, Pisano & Shuen, 1997; Teece, 2020), business leaders need to build dynamic capabilities in their organizations. Dynamic capabilities are distinguished from more ordinary capabilities, which are primarily intended to achieve efficient daily operations in the existing business. The dynamic capabilities are aimed at future occurrences, and how the business can survive in competition or best handle its future mission.

The dynamic capabilities can be divided into three different pillars: sensing, seizing, and transforming. These capabilities build on each other and follow a logical sequence; see Figure 1.5.

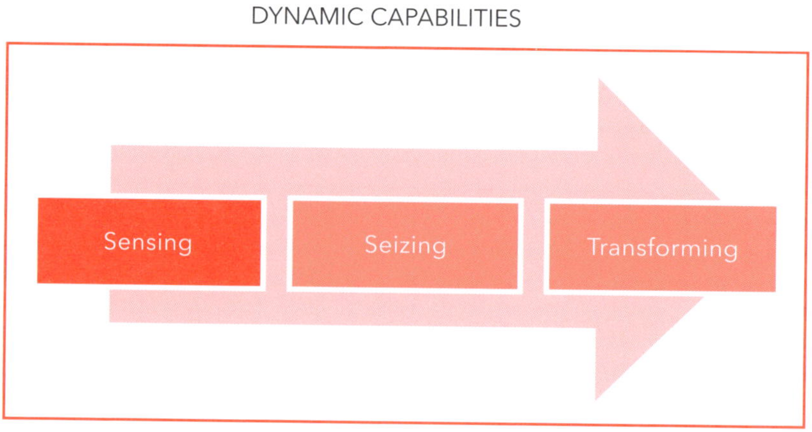

Figure 1.5 Dynamic capabilities

Sensing

Sensing opportunities is about identifying technological opportunities, customer needs, and strategic challenges. In order to detect developments in the external environment, the organization needs to develop strong peripheral vision and pick up on weak signals that are of relevance to the business, such as new regulations that are waiting in the wings, socio-political changes, and technology trends.

Professor Rita McGrath (2020) wrote an entire book about the need for businesses to pick up on weak signals to discover shifts before they happen, calling this capability "seeing around corners". Through continuous and systematic monitoring of one's surroundings, senior management can prioritize what they seek to deal with as well as identify new opportunities.

In large organizations, there may be many different environments that extend their antennae out into their surroundings and that may potentially sense what is happening in the world around them. On the one hand it is an advantage that so many have their feelers out, but for senior management to do a good job of prioritizing, there will be a need to gather this knowledge and systematize it as opposed to letting it stay dispersed among various entities. However, taking a position on how broadly one should be sensing is not simple. Sensing too broadly can easily lead to a lack of focus, whereas excessively narrow sensing may result in a failure to pick up on weak signals in one's surroundings. Although we often discuss sensing as something that is done outwardly, toward the environment, sensing can also mean identifying needs in the market that are not yet known. This has been Apple's trademark in their radical innovations. Apple has created needs as opposed to picking up needs in the market. In the case study on Norwegian broadcaster TV 2, which we will be returning to in Part 4, ideas arose within the organization itself in response to TV 2's own needs. The services were then spun out and developed further because they also covered the needs of other media actors.

Sensing also requires expertise among those who are doing the sensing. DNB's New Tech Lab, which has been given the mandate of sensing and developing radical innovations, has established an office in Silicon Valley. The goal is not to perform innovation tourism but to acquire knowledge on what movements are happening and to be perceived as a serious player with whom it is worth sparring. The New Tech Lab has a role within the DNB group to keep up with what is happening in the market, and has also developed its own innovation pulse, DNB Tech Radar, which aims to keep everyone at the bank up to date on the latest trends. However, New Tech Lab is not satisfied with simply sensing what is happening in its surroundings in the short-term. Instead, it is also attempting to look into its crystal ball and imagine a future where for example, we no longer need a mobile phone.

Seizing

However, it is not enough to just sense and understand what is happening or what might happen. One must also be able to seize the opportunities in timely ways. This second dynamic capability pillar – to seize opportunities – says something about how quickly an organization can utilize ideas that emerge internally and/or externally from their surroundings. At TV 2, a key figure gave employees the time and space to develop their ideas internally. At Nokia, management sensed and understood the technological shift in its surroundings toward smartphones, but were unable to seize the opportunity and turn this knowledge into developing its own smartphones. Interestingly, this was related to the decision-making culture at Nokia. There was a gap between middle management and senior executives, and the decision-making culture had developed to become a culture of fear in which middle management didn't dare to tell the senior management how the company was actually doing (Vuori & Huy, 2016).

There are different ways to seize opportunities, and even if you sense and discover promising ideas, it is rare that an established firm can quickly incorporate new ideas into its own organization. For this reason, incorporating innovations into one's own organization is hard work and often places demands on flexibility, management, and decision-making skills. Furthermore, the timing needs to be right. Sometimes management makes a good choice and gets the timing right for the market, but it is also easy to make the product or service available before the customer base is ripe for it.

Transforming

The third dynamic capability concerns transforming the business. This means that you can set up the various elements in the organization (see Chapter 2 for a visualization of the different elements) to build innovation capacity. This way, the transformation takes the next step from sensing and seizing opportunities to working with all the organizational structures and processes in the organization. This may entail managing counter-acting forces as well as changes to the internal culture in order to create a more dynamic organization that is open to the outside world and better suited for adaptation.

Companies with well-developed dynamic capabilities will be able to sense and seize opportunities before their competitors and change the organization without undermining their regular operations. In some cases, this may mean cannibalizing current revenue streams. Well-developed dynamic capabilities may also be a strength with regard to the surroundings by being better suited to shaping and affecting players as opposed to simply being affected. However, this is not sufficient for building innovation capacity. Complementary capabilities will be needed to develop and scale the innovations to a level that makes the new innovations competitive or useful to the organization.

Complementary capabilities

While the dynamic capabilities ensure that the business can identify and seize new opportunities, the complementary capabilities will be aimed at developing and scaling the innovations. The complementary capabilities can typically be characterized as more ordinary capabilities, but they are applied in the innovative part of the businesses to develop and scale the innovations. They will also incorporate new capabilities that will become ordinary in the future (such as those related to technology) that so far, the established firm has not developed.

In his groundbreaking article on complementarity, David Teece (1986) claims that it has long been a mystery that the businesses that are first to bring products and services to the market are often not the ones who are first able to realize the profits, while number two or three in the sequence of innovators succeeds instead. One explanation for why this happens is that the first innovator lacks complementary resources or capabilities. This may relate to marketing, production, customer support, or other complementary capabilities that are needed to scale up the production of the product or service. Start-up businesses usually lack complementary resources and often underestimate their value, and this is one of the main reasons start-up businesses fail (Eisenmann, 2021). Access to complementary resources may therefore be a reason for a start-up to seek collaboration with established firms. In ecosystems, a lack of complementary resources may limit growth and create bottlenecks. In the case study of Alibaba, the establishment of businesses with complementary skills in payment and logistics operations for the company's e-commerce platforms were completely essential to achieving growth in the ecosystem.

There are several ways for an established firm to work on scaling. Firstly, it is possible that the business *already has* many of the complementary resources needed to scale the product or service. One of the reasons DNB succeeded in launching Vipps was that the bank had a professional marketing system. Just four months after its launch, Vipps had a million users. However, DNB was also aware of the fact that it needed to recruit new technical expertise to boost the volume of its innovations. For this reason, the bank hired a whole host of technologists at once. Over a few years, DNB went from 14% of all new hires being technologists to 50% having a background in technology.

In the industrialization of the offshore windmills in the Ørsted case study, which we will be returning to in Part 2, complementary resources played a key role. In order to create a product that could compete with other energy sources, Ørsted had to reduce the cost of its offshore windmills, and management set a highly ambitious goal of reducing the cost to 100 euros per megawatt hour. In order to achieve this, it had to crack the code of going from large, industrial single projects, in which it had expertise from constructing major coal power plants, to the industrial production of offshore wind farms. For this reason, it hired a new manager with experience from the car manufacturing industry in Sweden.

Another way to scale up is to *acquire complementary capabilities externally*, either through sourcing agreements or through different types of partnerships. For example, if the scarce factor is technical expertise, the established company can boost innovation capacity by cooperating with a more technically oriented business that has IT developers. How quickly this may get up and running depends on issues such as the trust between the parties, as well as the different parties' skills in collaboration. However, as we will demonstrate in the case study concerning the compensation scheme in Part 3 of this book, it is possible to achieve this quickly if the conditions allow. However, the majority of these complementary capabilities do not allow themselves to scale overnight, and must be developed in the organization. To develop complementary capabilities it may be necessary to train one's own employees in new methodologies and tools and to upgrade their expertise. Many need to invest in new technology that supports modern work processes, and organizational and decision-making structures must be adapted to react more quickly and at a faster pace. Newly hired employees also need time to adapt to a new organization, and vice versa.

The Norwegian Tax Administration is a good example of an organization that has been building complementary capabilities ever since Bjarne Hope's period as its director general from 1995 to 2006. Hope brought an entirely new mindset into the Tax Administration. He was the first leader with a technological background to be hired as director general of the Tax Administration and he steered it in a far more user-oriented direction. Hope sensed the right direction for the Tax Administration at an early stage and through his management of the government body he seized the opportunities present in new technology. By systematically investing in complementary skills and developing expertise in the implementation of major IT programs and projects, the Tax

Administration got a solid head start on the other public agencies. Many other public agencies visited the Tax Administration to learn how it had succeeded in its technological modernization programs. For the Tax Administration, the complementary capabilities it has developed over many years imply that it can quickly utilize new and completely modern technology, whether this might be artificial intelligence, handling large volumes of data, or other matters. This expertise was also highly useful when working on the Norwegian compensation scheme for the private sector when the Covid-19 pandemic struck.

The example of the Tax Administration illustrates the patience and systematic efforts behind the development of innovation capacity. The administration has a long-term perspective for its investments in technology. Investments that are made can either restrict or allow opportunities at a later point in time. This is often called path dependence. For example, choosing Microsoft over Apple will lock consumers in to the opportunities Microsoft gives them, and vice versa. Often, path dependence is considered to be highly negative in the sense of being locked in. However, path dependence can also be something positive that creates future opportunities, as the example of the Tax Administration shows. Newer research has therefore recommended distinguishing between the two types of path dependence and renaming positive path dependence path creation (Garud et al., 2010).

Path dependence or path creation also shows how important it is to incorporate time as a key variable in investment decisions. Your investments into expertise and technology today may put you in position to capture opportunities and technologies that become available many years in the future. It isn't possible to know what the opportunities will be from today's vantage point, but by investing in expertise and technology, one can facilitate increased innovation capacity in the future.

Collective engagement

Alongside skills and scaling, innovation capacity consists of an X-factor that spans across the cognitive and the concrete and what can be found in human emotions, namely collective employee engagement. We have opted to view this as a separate category alongside the capabilities, although many of our fellow researchers would likely define this as part of the employees' capabilities. Collective engagement allows employees to put emotional energy into innovation projects, which will contribute to their willingness to go the extra mile that innovation requires. In his book *The World is Flat*, Thomas Friedman (2007) asserted that it was no longer enough to have a high IQ to win the innovation arms race. Instead, it was more important to have passion (or PQ, passion quotient) and to be curious (or CQ, curiosity quotient). With this book and many lectures, Friedman convinced many business leaders that there was a need to look beyond the individual's expertise and intelligence.

> I have concluded that in a flat world, IQ – Intelligence Quotient – still matters, but CQ and PQ – Curiosity Quotient and Passion Quotient – matter even more. I live by the equation CQ+PQ>IQ (Friedman, 2007).

Although individuals may be important, engagement is not only found in each individual. Engagement is contagious, and you can be pulled along and stimulated by others around you being full of fire, eagerness and passion. In other words, what we are focusing on here is collective engagement; which must not be confused with believing in yourself. Although faith is said to move mountains, excessive self-confidence (particularly where this rolls over into complacency) will also create barriers for learning and innovation. Furthermore, success and high self-confidence are precisely one of the reasons it is so challenging for some established firms to deliver innovation.

Excessive faith in "what we've always done" is not a good recipe for building collective engagement for innovation, but experiences of succeeding in innovation may create a positive kind of self-confidence that will drive further innovation. In some of the cases we will be describing later in the book, a collective engagement for change emerged because employees saw results and perceived that organizations – which in some cases were described as traditional and perhaps a little set in their ways – succeeded in significant innovations, such as the Norwegian banks DNB with Vipps and Fana Sparebank with Himla Eiendom.

Collective engagement can be created by leaders and can become a part of the culture, but is also easy to destroy through reporting requirements, requests for tangible results, and failed incentives. Collective engagement must therefore be tended like a plant, and leaders must thoroughly consider how they will build collective engagement and keep it going over time.

"Leading from a platform with sincere enthusiasm is grossly underestimated by many leaders" says Trond Bentestuen, former CEO at the Norwegian supermarket chain Rema 1000 and group director at DNB. He notes that organizations with enthusiastic or highly engaged employees deliver extraordinary results. Norsk Gallup regularly performs a working environment survey of Norwegian businesses. In 2018 it found that on average just 12% of Norwegian employees were actively engaged in their work, while 25% were actively disinterested! Thus, over 60% of the employees were little engaged or a little uninterested. Equivalent numbers in larger, global surveys reveal the same trend. An important question will therefore be whether uninterested employees show weaker job motivation than those that are passionate. If so, this will affect both productivity and improvement efforts at the businesses. How leaders perform their leadership responsibilities is important to the culture of a company but also to the degree of engagement at the workplace. Systematic efforts to see, confirm, and motivate employees will over time be highly important to the employees' engagement. The more there are people who give a little extra, the higher the odds will be for you to achieve extraordinary results – also in innovation. A leader's emphasis on control and micro-management versus coaching and encouragement may also affect the degree of engagement. The same applies to the managers' leadership style, their participation in the company's social life, and the degree of imagination and creativity applied in leadership.

On the other hand, pushing too hard in management tasks may be counterproductive. After all, if everything is always celebrated, the positive effects of celebrations may evaporate over time. In this sense, it is important for leaders to be aware of the impact of collective engagement and how it can be created.

The point of departure

The most important thing about investing in innovation capacity is that it allows participation in the innovation race, and therefore also increases the odds of succeeding in value creation. However, the development of innovation capacity cannot be viewed in isolation from the context of each organization. Here there are two pertinent questions:

1. What kind of uncertainty does the business face?
2. How far has the organization come in establishing innovation capacity?

When there is great uncertainty and it proves difficult to determine the correct direction for the organization, it may be risky to choose highly specific courses of investment. Instead of opening opportunities for the future, one risks closing future opportunities by tying up resources in investments that are likely to fail. Therefore, the solution in such situations may be to build up skills, structures, and processes that can be used for many purposes. For instance, such generic skills, structures, and processes may be to learn more innovative working processes, facilitate faster decision making, hire newly educated employees with general technical expertise and project managers, etc.

The establishment of generic skills, structures, and processes will also be appropriate when the established firm has a low innovation capacity. In such situations, there will be a need to change, and to challenge established structures and processes. There are many ways to do this, and we will be returning to these in the following chapters.

Another way to develop innovation capacity is through options. Real options means investing in projects with low or manageable downside risk, i.e., testing the potential for value creation in the longer term. Depending on the degree of uncertainty, investments can be made in scouting or positioning options (MacMillan & McGrath, 2000). In the first type of options, *scouting options*, the aim is to look out for opportunities to see what is moving in the market. In other words, this can build capabilities in sensing opportunities. A typical example of this is when large, established firms buy their way into start-up companies to gain knowledge and experiment with new business opportunities. This will generally involve small investments and may encompass many different start-up companies.

Positioning options are about placing a few calculated bets on what might happen in the future. Though these are similar to scouting options, they usually involve larger and fewer investments. These options will gradually become more relevant as the veil of uncertainty begins to lift. This will make it easier to narrow down the range of possibilities and identify a possible strategic direction for the organization. It will still be risky to put all your eggs into one basket, but the business can approach this issue through a portfolio of options in which bets are placed for several alternative applications to be in position, such as when it is made clear what technological standard will become the dominant one. Several shipping companies are investing in position options to position themselves for alternative fuels, whether it is hydrogen, ammonia, liquefied natural gas (LNG), biofuels or others. There were also option considerations behind Vipps's investments into both QR (quick response) codes and NFC technology (near-field communication, allowing two devices to communicate wirelessly over short distances). QR is dominant in China, while it has seen limited adoption in Europe and the United States. However, this may yet change, as was observed in restaurants during the Covid-19 pandemic.

Where companies have succeeded in establishing innovation capacity, the challenge is to sustain this capacity. There are plenty of examples of established firms that succeed in building up innovation capacity, but where the spark disappears from the organization over time (Pisano, 2019). A typical progression will be an initial establishment phase in which senior management puts innovation on the strategic agenda, holds enthusiastic speeches, enlists the communications department to spread the good word, initiates programs to teach employees new and modern working processes, sets aside lots of money for innovation projects and hires a new leader to be the spearhead of the innovation efforts. Then time passes and gradually the organization enters a new phase. The CFO starts demanding results of the innovation investments, the innovation projects take a long time – longer than estimated – some projects fail, and the people working on daily operations start complaining about the restricted funding they are being allotted for their priority product and service upgrade projects. After a while, owners and boards also start requesting results, and patience is put to the test. Slowly, the spark disappears out of the organization – and the innovation investments are taken over by more immediate and acute needs.

Moreover, it can be just as challenging to sustain innovation capacity as to develop it – and owners need to be patient to sit through the whole process of transforming a large, established firm into something more innovative. The way we define innovation capacity, the muscle must be kept active throughout the entire cycle, and it must give opportunities for repeated innovation. Everyone can be lucky and get a fluke once, but those who build innovation capacity are setting up the organization for a future that will place demands on continuous renewal and innovation.

Innovation capacity and organizational solutions

We have now described *what* innovation capacity is, and in Parts 2, 3, and 4 of this book we will outline different organizational solutions for *how* organizations can build innovation capacity. This is shown in Figure 1.6 on the next page.

In Chapter 2 of this book we describe different solutions for what organizations can do within their own organizational boundaries. This includes the ambidextrous solution (Chapter 3), innovation at the edge (Chapter 4), agile working methods and organization (Chapter 5), as well as transformation of the core (Chapter 6). In Parts 3 and 4, we look at solutions that cut across organizational boundaries. Part 3, which includes collaboration with start-up companies, partnerships, and ecosystems, looks at outside-to-inside innovations, while Part 4 examines innovations that start within the business and spin off.

Before we move onto the specific solutions for building innovation capacity, in Chapter 2 we will elaborate somewhat more about the how, and introduce a cogwheel model with nine organizational elements.

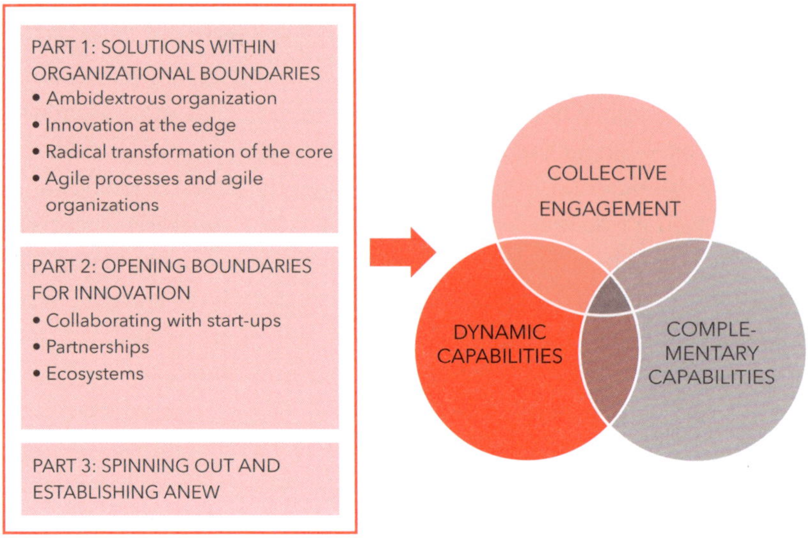

Figure 1.6 Different organizational solutions that can provide innovation capacity

Chapter 2

How to develop innovation capacity

In Chapter 1 we outlined three key components of innovation capacity: dynamic capabilities, complementary capabilities, and collective engagement. In this chapter we examine how established firms can set up their organization to develop innovation capacity. We introduce a cogwheel model to visualize how managers in established firms can implement different organizational solutions that contribute to innovation. We will bring these cogs with us in the later chapters, where we will describe each individual solution. First, however, we go through the cogwheel model in its entirety.

The model we sketch in Figure 2.1 shows how the organization consists of many different elements that interact with each other. The model is inspired by McKinsey's 7S model, which shows that if the intention is to implement a strategy, in this case an innovation strategy, then one must consider how all the organizational elements interact simultaneously. Consequently, one of the key messages of this book is that managers must thoroughly think through what they need to tune and change in order to build innovation capacity.

In Figure 2.1, we have presented nine organizational elements as cogs to visualize the connection between them. If you adjust one of the cogs, it will have implications for the others.

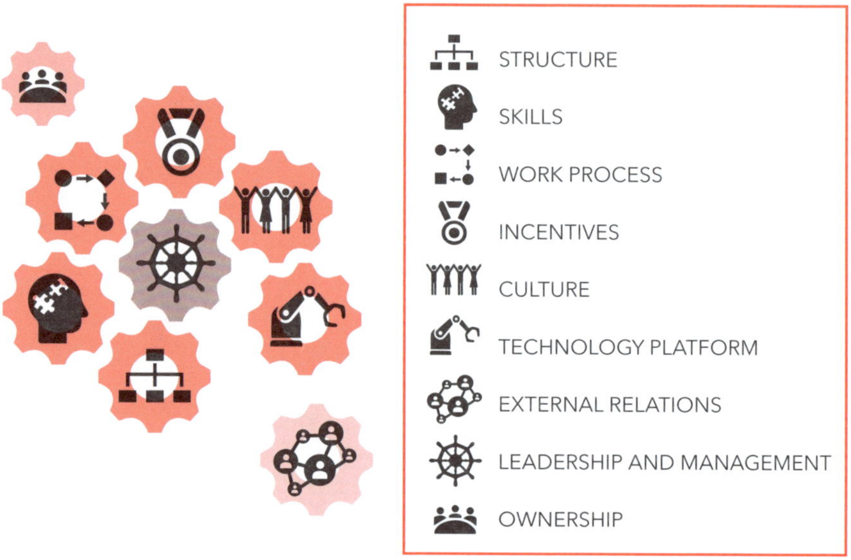

Figure 2.1 Innovation cogwheel model

The terms for the different cogs are generic, but the contents of each cog will guide the establishment of capacity. Managers can adjust the cogs by:

1. Adjusting each individual cog
2. Adjusting the interactions between them

Managers can affect each individual cog, such as by changing the skill composition, or by changing the organizational structure from an organization divided by function to an organization composed of agile teams. However, it won't help much to change a cog if the other cogs are pulling employees in completely different directions. This is not a new insight, but an insight from McKinsey consultants Peters and Waterman in 1980.

The essence of McKinsey's 7S framework (the Ss stand for strategy, structure, systems, staff, style, skills, and shared values) was that the organizational elements had to be connected together and support the strategy. We have drawn inspiration from Peters and Waterman's thoughts, but we have also placed a greater emphasis on leadership, work processes, owners, and external relations in keeping with newer insights in the field of innovation.

Above, we have discussed the need to balance between exploitation and exploration. Some organizations are put together in a manner that promotes efficiency. It is no coincidence that the U.S. government sought advice from a fast-food chain when it began rolling out vaccinations for residents in connection with the Covid-19 pandemic. The fast-food chains have production facilities fine-tuned for maximum flow and speed in deliveries. When an organization is locked onto efficiency, and all the cogs are moving in a direction that continuously makes the production system more efficient, then it may be challenging to clear space for more expansive innovation activities. The alternative may then be to separate out entities that can make room to work more innovatively, or to connect with other organizations with more innovation, such as start-up companies or ecosystems.

Before we get to that point and outline different organizational solutions for boosting innovation capacity, we must go a little deeper into the contents of each individual cog in Figure 2.1 and note some factors that will be important to aim the cogs in an innovative direction. Leadership and management are at the heart of the model as a completely central cog, which is decisive for getting the other cogs going. The owners are placed at something of a distance, since they are not directly involved in daily operations, while external relations are somewhat peripheral as potential opportunities.

Organizational structure

The design of the organizational structure cannot be viewed independently of the strategy the business has selected. If the goal is to renew and innovate, the organizational structure needs to support the development of innovation capacity. Relevant questions include: Is the collaboration across the organization fostering innovation or is it slowing down the innovation processes? Are there other, new structures that can speed up the decision-making processes?

The organizational structure is often displayed in the form of an organizational chart that shows how work tasks are divided and where the decision-making authority lies. Unlike small companies where everyone often does a little bit of everything, it is natural and necessary in larger companies for *work tasks to be divided* and employees to specialize in different tasks. We often distinguish between the functional, divisional, and matrix structure in addition to the project organization (see any introductory book on organization theory for a thorough description, or Anand & Daft, 2007). In this book, we also take a closer look at newer organizational structures in agile organizations where cross-disciplinary teams are organized into families or tribes.

Interestingly, Apple opted for a functional structure to facilitate innovation (Podolny & Hansen, 2020). One typically imagines that a divisional, market-based organization would be better for achieving innovation, since it brings the company closer to customers. However, after Steve Jobs returned to Apple in 1997 he changed the structure from a typical divisional, market-based structure to a functional structure. His view was that the divisional structure with its inherent emphasis on profitability within each division, as well as complicated internal pricing, resulted in suboptimality and short-sightedness, making it a liability for Apple's innovation. Jobs also believed that Apple shouldn't pay too much attention to the customers' needs. Apple's purpose was to create customer needs and meet needs that customers didn't even know they had. For this reason, Jobs changed the organizational structure to promote specialization and development of deep knowledge, attention to the smallest detail, and collaboration across the organization. The functional structure has survived for many years, despite Apple growing from 8000 to 137 000 employees between 1997 and 2019.

An important structural component is how much autonomy is to be delegated to different levels in the organization. On the one hand, wide-ranging autonomy is able to promote employee motivation and speed up innovation; on the other, extensive autonomy may also make management and overall prioritization difficult. This is a central dilemma for agile organizations in which extensive autonomy for cross-disciplinary teams has made it more challenging to manage resources and coordinate across the organization (Annosi et al., 2020).

Developing good *coordinating mechanisms* is an ever-recurring challenge for larger organizations. Excessive autonomy and independence may lead to a siloed way of thinking, particularly if it is reinforced with a strong emphasis on the results of each individual. Conversely, extensive collaboration may drive complexity, and make it difficult to know what is profitable and not. In the case study on Alibaba, which we will be returning to in Part 3 of this book, senior executive Jack Ma consciously chose not to facilitate much coordination across the organization. His assessment was that this could inhibit innovation processes and slow down the growth of the ecosystem.

During the Covid-19 pandemic it became much easier to gather employees from many areas of expertise and from different geographical locations in a single meeting. In our case study of the Norwegian compensation scheme, the virtual meeting places involving numerous people from different organizations were instrumental to the project being completed in only three weeks.

Skills

Knowledge doesn't last forever. The most important thing we learn is to learn. To keep up, we need to be in a constant loop of learning. Relevant questions related to skills include: Does the business have the skills needed to generate innovation? Are there skills that are no longer needed, skills that are technologically obsolete, or skills that should be developed and refined? Is the composition of skills sufficiently diverse to drive innovation?

To illustrate the importance of having the right skills, we draw on an example from the financial sector. Fifty years ago, 85% of bank employees served customers over the counter. Today, the share of employees who directly serve customers has dropped to below ten%, and the counters are largely gone. In the finance industry today, in 2021, there are about as many employees as there were fifty years ago, but they work on different things and in different ways. The composition of skills has changed dramatically. Some employees now work as design thinkers, some as robot trainers, and others help prevent money laundering. Still others protect the business against cyberattacks and phishing, a type of work that was previously unheard of. At the same time, productivity has risen. Paper checks have disappeared, and the bank branches (the few that remain) no longer handle cash, while the customers have become their own bank managers.

The expertise of co-workers constitutes an essential resource to achieve innovation. There are three possible approaches for assessing what kind of expertise is needed in the development of innovation capacity. One approach is to look at the fit between the strategic goals and competences in the organization. Another is to focus on what opportunities exist to replace people with new robotics and AI technology. Finally, it is important to assess to which extent there is a diverse composition of the workforce, a factor that has proven to promote innovative thinking.

Skills and innovation strategies

In the first approach, it is natural to start with an analysis of which skill requirements the strategic goals demand (Meyer & Norman, 2019). Given that we are focused on innovation in this book, this is a question of how the skills measure up to the company's innovation strategy. For DNB, this meant transforming the organization from a traditional bank to a more tech-oriented business (see the case study that follows this chapter), and thus changing the composition of skills to become far more technology-oriented. However, taking the organization in an innovative direction can also mean that the business primarily needs to become more sustainable, hiring experts on climate and environmentally friendly solutions like the architects of GXN did (this case is presented in Chapter 3).

The gap analysis assessing how the strategy fits the skills is only the first step. Once the necessary skills for the future have been assessed, the next step will be to assess how these resources can be acquired. This can be done by upgrading the skills of the organization's own employees or by recruiting employees in the market. Here, it is important to assess the extent to which the skills of one's own employees can be upgraded. Where there is a strong need to change the composition of skills, this may also trigger a need to phase out skills that are no longer needed. Such shifts in skills, where staff size is adjusted both upwards and downwards, may also fundamentally alter the culture of the organization.

In such a gap analysis, it is also important to consider that skills cannot be limited to single individuals, but that competences at the organizational level depend on the interaction between people. When entire teams are recruited to established companies from start-up companies, then this is a recognition that these teams possess innovation expertise. Recruiting a complete team whose members trust each other and are used to working together may allow a firm to get a head start on developing its innovation capacity. Similarly, skills cannot be viewed as being independent of other organizational elements. It doesn't help much to hire newly educated computer engineers if the organization lacks the technological platforms to exploit their fresh expertise. Their skills will not be put to much use if the job involves working on old systems that use COBOL as their programming language, or the use of Excel.

Robots and AI

The assessment of which skills are needed must also be measured against the technological opportunities that have emerged through robot technology and artificial intelligence. Many manual tasks can be replaced by robots, whether this means physical robots or robotic process automation (RPA). Agriculture is one of the industries that have come the furthest in their application of robot technology in a traditional sense. In 2020, nearly 50% of dairy cows (in Norway) were milked by robots, an increase of 500% in the past ten years. Predictions from Tractica indicate an annual growth rate of 30% and that agricultural robots will soon outnumber industrial robots. Agriculture has also come far in developing autonomous robots that move through greenhouses and fields. Robotic process automation can replace employees who perform manual and procedural work tasks, allowing organizations to reduce labor costs. As robots become smarter and begin learning, it may also be profitable to innovate and develop new services that were previously too expensive.

Robot technology may affect human skills in several ways (Brynjolfsson & McAfee, 2014). Both physical robots and robotic process automation may replace large amounts of labor force, and predictions are no longer limited to low-skilled labor alone, but also professions such as accounting and legal employees. The fact that robots do much of the "boring" work, such as running lookups and systematizing large volumes of precedent in a specific field of law, will simultaneously allow the labor force to be freed up to spend its time on other tasks. This may entail a need to re-educate the labor force to create value alongside their new robot colleagues.

Diversity in the labor force

Years of research in sociology, demographics, economics, and organizational theory show us that diversity drives innovation (Phillips et al., 2014). It may appear relatively obvious that groups with different educational background and experience are better at solving complex, non-routine tasks than homogeneous groups. However, groups with persons of different social backgrounds (ethnicity, gender, sexual orientation) also stimulate more innovative thought.

There are many reasons diversity drives innovation. The first and most obvious reason is that persons with different backgrounds bring a variety of perspectives and knowledge into the group. However, this changes the group dynamic too. By interacting, the group members are forced to come better prepared and to think through what alternative perspectives may emerge in the meeting. Not least, they must be prepared for longer meetings if the aim is to reach some kind of consensus.

To study the relationship between diversity and innovation, BCG 1700 studied companies of different sizes from different countries (Levine, 2020). It found that companies with above-average diversity had a larger share of revenue from innovation (45%) than companies with below-average diversity (26%). They measured innovation as the part of revenue that came from products and services launched in the past three years.

At the same time, one must not ignore the fact that diversity can bring challenges. It may be harder to build trust, personal contradictions may flare up, there might be more conflictual discussions, and people with different backgrounds may look down on each other. Hence, it may be far more comfortable and tempting to recruit people with similar backgrounds. This means that a strategy of diversity should ideally be anchored at the top. A study conducted by PWC (Levine, 2020) shows that over 80% of senior management felt they were doing too little to promote social diversity. At the same time, those who are leading the teams must be capable of creating psychological security (Edmondson, 1999) to get the team members to perform their best.

Work processes

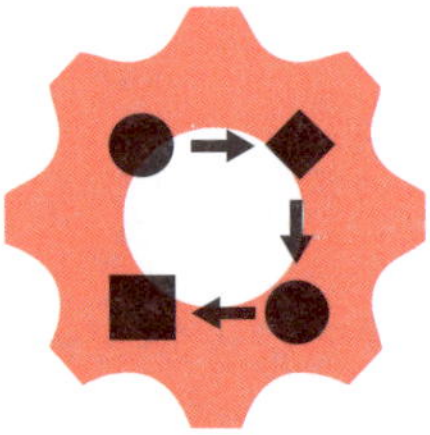

For a long time, the main focus was on developing work processes that could drive efficiency. Over the past decade, new working methods, which to a greater extent support innovative processes, have made a significant breakthrough in many industries. Relevant questions here include: What are the characteristics of innovative processes, and how do the work processes support the businesses' efforts to build innovation capacity?

The interest in work processes goes all the way back to the American engineer Frederick Winslow Taylor and his scientific approach to studying and structuring the execution of specific work tasks down to the smallest detail. Although one may debate Taylor's view of humanity and his assessment of workers as lazy people who only care about doing as little work as possible for as much money as possible, his ideas about how to best organize work remain with us to this day. Taylor believed that efficiency could be increased by dividing work into strongly specialized tasks where each person could develop their own specific expertise within a specific field. Taylor was sharply criticized, as his strict specialization led to monotonous and boring jobs, but we still see much of Taylorism in newer trends.

After Taylorism came Just-in-Time, Total Quality Management, Business Process Reengineering (BPR), Six Sigma, and Lean production, all with the common theme that work must be organized in a way that increases efficiency in production, with the attention in part being directed at removing unnecessary downtime in delivery chains. This kind of approach to work processes fits best when the goal is continuous (incremental) improvement, boosting efficiency, and automating. When the goal is to innovate at the customer interface or look for completely new business opportunities or business models, then such processes aimed at efficiency may be less suitable.

What newer innovation working processes such as agile ways working have in common with Taylorism and related work methodologies is that they are concerned with increasing the *pace* of the processes and in dividing work into manageable chunks.

At DNB in 2015, it took an average of 18 months to complete a standard IT development project using the waterfall methodology. In this methodology, activities are divided into sequential processes starting with the product owner developing detailed requirements that can then be sent to the supplier, who gives an estimate for expenses and time spent. After assessing the supplier's offer, and typically after making some adjustments back and forth, the supplier can develop the system/delivery, including design, implementation, testing, and validation. The same year, the bank launched the digital wallet Vipps. Vipps's transformation from a loose idea to a service in the market took just six months. Its development did not follow a typical project methodology but applied new agile ways of working, which we return to in Chapter 6. Vipps was taken out of the existing organization, and a cross-disciplinary, high-achieving team was delegated the responsibility and given extensive resources to complete the task. The goal was to launch the digital wallet into the market within a given deadline. The forms of work were highly flexible and adapted to the goal, while the board and management simultaneously gave the project the highest priority.

Where Taylorism deviates most from innovation methodology is perhaps its faith in *specialization*. New innovation methodologies, which to a great extent stem from IT and Design Thinking, distance themselves from strict specialization and support the notion of working in *cross-disciplinary teams*. The idea is that the teams can produce faster and more continuous innovations when they work on a cross-disciplinary basis rather than sending orders back and forth between different specialist functions.

Within IT, teams that work across boundaries have been termed DevOps (Development and Operations), or business DevOps, where things are taken one step further and the business side is brought in as well. DevOps was first used at a conference in Belgium in 2009 as a term for new methodologies that could accelerate agile processes. Since then, DevOps has become one of the more frequently discussed efficient working methodologies.

Central to new innovation methodology is also the idea that one should no longer work on concepts and services until they are completely perfect, but instead constantly test by making prototypes and preferably launching minimal viable versions followed by new improvements. This was the methodology that was followed for Vipps, but also for the compensation scheme, where the emphasis was on making schemes that would fit the needs for the majority of businesses, followed by the development of solutions for seasonal businesses and other businesses that needed special adaptations.

Last but not least, newer innovation methodologies are far more focused on customers, and this particularly applies to Design Thinking (Kolko, 2015; Capgemini Invent, 2019; Knight, et al., 2020). Design Thinking was primarily popularized through the design firm IDEO, a company founded by Stanford professor David Kelly in 1978. Aside from cross-disciplinary work, the core of Design Thinking is to start with the customer and to get into their perspective. Among other things, this approach has made concepts like the customer journey part of the vernacular of many established firms. Design Thinking is also known for using creative, visual tools to experiment and test ideas and concepts on customers, and the methodologies are increasingly being used in complex service fields such as healthcare.

Incentives

Incentives are powerful tools for steering behavior in new directions. However, incentives that promote efficiency are often fundamentally different from incentives that support innovation. Relevant questions here include: What kind of incentives should leaders adopt to drive innovation? Should leaders celebrate the mistakes employees make? To what extent can large corporations mimic the incentives in start-ups?

The strong effect of incentives often comes as a surprise. In the world of academia, many have been perplexed by how international publication has been assigned such immense weight relative to education and dissemination. However, when scrutinizing the incentives closely, it should come as no surprise to anyone. For years, international publication has been the most important qualification for becoming a professor and for being recruited to the best universities. A solid publication record in the top journals provides academics with a higher fixed salary and publication bonuses, and to top it all off, they receive a great deal of recognition from their peers.

Some will immediately imagine incentives to be material goods such as extra pay, bonuses, shares, or other fringe benefits. However, incentives may also be career-based, like the example from academia above. Furthermore, praise and recognition should not be ignored.

From work life research, we know that confirmation and good feedback work. This can come from the nearest supervisor or from colleagues in the same circle. Being seen can provide a boost to energy or make work more satisfying.

Part of what makes it difficult to shape incentives that support innovation is all the uncertainty (Manso, 2017). The best innovations may well be the result of considerable trial and error, and it may take a long time to realize benefits. It can be hard to strike a balance between not punishing trial and error while also rewarding those who succeed.

Not punishing those who fail may, however, also be too simple. It is undesirable to set up conditions for people to simply play around and fail repeatedly without learning anything from failure. Professor Gary Pisano (2019) therefore asserts that the will to let employees experiment must be followed by rigorous discipline and competence requirements. In that sense, any errors made are productive because lessons can be learned from them. "A willingness to experiment, though, does not mean working like some third-rate abstract painter who randomly throws paint at a canvas" (Pisano, 2019: p. 67). This not only places requirements on recruitment for the units that are to experiment, but also the will to remove employees from teams when they do not perform over time.

At start-up companies, there are often high risks of failure, but employees are often given a stake in the company through shares or assets, allowing success to provide great rewards. This way, the company's desire to succeed is closely linked to employee incentives. In major organizations it will often be challenging to give the employees the financial incentives that stimulate innovative behavior as in start-ups, since this may easily come into conflict with larger organizations' reward structures.

Consequently, other types of incentives will be necessary to stimulate innovation. These may include giving relatively loose reins to work in peace without the risk of being consumed by daily operations, i.e., allowing for some slack, or getting a team of resources to work alongside. We will be returning to this in the case study regarding TV 2 in Part 4, where this type of incentive was part of what enabled TV 2 to succeed in its innovations.

Culture

Culture shapes employee passion and engagement. It affects their creativity and capacity to coordinate and may be decisive for the company's attractiveness in the job market. What factors are decisive for the development of an innovation culture in a business? What is required from leadership to succeed in building a desired culture?

In the United States in 1950, Diners Club introduced the first credit card, which at the time was a novelty for the few. It would take no less than 28 years for the card to reach fifty million users. In 1967, the first ATM was launched by Barclays Bank in London. This roll-out went somewhat faster than the credit card, and Barclays reached fifty million users 18 years later. With the internet came online banking, and the speed of development increased exponentially. Facebook reached its fifty-millionth user in three years. In the summer of 2016, things exploded. While it had taken Diners Club, Barclays, and Facebook years, now we were suddenly talking about days. The Japanese company Niantic launched Pokémon Go in July 2016. In just 19 days, it had 50 million people outside on the street and in parks. They were out to catch virtual monsters. Fifty million in 19 days.

Diners Club, Barclays, Facebook, and Niantic were the first or were very early to launch their new and innovative services. They had created cultures allowing them to test out completely new products and ideas in the market. These were not just start-up companies with a young history. Barclays is one that has roots going back to moneylenders in the 1700s, although the bank we know today was first founded in 1896.

Culture is a term for the shared values, norms, and perceptions of reality that are developed when employees interact with each other and their surroundings

(Bang, 2013). Culture is easier to recognize than to define, and when making changes in organizations, one often encounters invisible barriers that are rooted in deeply anchored cultures.

Given that the goal of this book is to explore how organizations can build innovation capacity, we are most interested in identifying the cultural traits that support innovative thinking and behavior. Pisano (2019) claims there is a difference between what is often perceived as innovative culture and what actually creates innovative cultures. When asking what an innovative culture is, the words that typically come up are a tolerance for failure, the will to experiment, psychological security, collaboration, and autonomy. This all sounds well and good, but is that what creates an innovative culture?

Pisano claims that innovative cultures are full of paradoxes and that it is these paradoxes that drive innovation. Thus, each of the cultural traits has a counterpart.

- The tolerance to fail, but intolerance for incompetence
- The will to experiment, but structured processes
- Psychological security, but brutal honesty
- Collaboration-oriented, but with individual responsibility
- Extensive autonomy, but strong leadership

As mentioned above, during the discussion of incentives, it is important to have a tolerance for failure, but at the same time, there can be no tolerance for incompetence. You must know why you failed and actively step in to learn from your mistakes. It is also clear that you must be willing to test and experiment, but there must be discipline and a framework around the experiments so that ideas that don't take off can be put down quickly, while promising ideas aren't left in a quagmire. Having a team that feels secure with each other is also important, but this security must not come at the expensive of daring to be clear and brutally honest with other team members. Without clear feedback, it will be hard to learn from mistakes. Innovative ideas are often controversial and challenge existing knowledge. Collaboration in a team must therefore not tip over into everyone having to agree and the team having to reach a consensus. Last but not least, extensive autonomy does not mean management no longer needs to manage. On the contrary, in this book we will show that finding a balance between autonomy and direction may be one of the toughest issues to navigate in innovative cultures.

Technology platform

Most businesses do not sell IT, nevertheless IT systems and operations are increasingly central to supporting innovation processes. While an old, complex IT platform may create legacy problems for the business, likewise, transformation to a modern, modular, and open technology platform is no guarantee that innovations will succeed. Business leaders need to constantly ask themselves whether their technological platform is of sufficient quality and quantity to support their innovation strategy. Timing is also essential, and wrong timing and poor choice of technology can be detrimental to the future business.

The computers of the 1960s were massive in size and mutually incompatible into the bargain. During this time, IBM invested billions of dollars in development, and one technological revolution overtook the other. In the 1970s, microprocessors quickly made the leap from calculators to computers intended for personal use, and in the transition to the 1970s, personal computers made their way to companies. They reached the consumer market in the latter half of the 1970s, and companies like Commodore and the newly established Apple made breakthroughs with the PET 2001 and Apple II, respectively. However, there was still huge caveat to all this. Although PCs and software were relatively broadly available at the turn of the millennium, the costs of starting a new IT business were still rather substantial. In the year 2000, the estimated cost of establishing a new technology-based business was no less than US$ 5 000 000. However, the price of computing power and technology was falling exponentially. This development was undeniably going faster and faster. Soon, smartphones, wireless communication, tablets, and cloud solutions would provide available software at a much lower price.

By 2009, the cost of starting an IT business in the United States had dropped to US$ 50 000. Just a few years later, the cost dropped to a tenth of this figure – again. We're talking about a start-up cost of US$ 5000. It's not for nothing that one in every five newly established firms in Norway in 2020 was a technology company!

With the transition to cheap and accessible computing capacity, a clear foundation was laid for the private sector to alter its composition. With simple efforts a substantial number of businesses can compete against large, traditional businesses. The competition may take place within traditional industry boundaries, but it is just as often found within limited parts of the value chains. Innovation capacity will therefore become just as important for mature companies as it is for new ones. Moreover, it is not enough to innovate the end product itself. The entire value chain is exposed to unexpected competition.

Fintechs, regtechs, edutechs and SaaS businesses are examples of new companies that are popping up a range of technical offerings of products and services. Furthermore, the S that comes before aaS could be replaced with the initial of practically any industry. For this reason, established firms must at all times question the quality and capacity of their own *technological platform*. Is it suited to meet the new, more comprehensive competition? Can we offer our products efficiently enough through the existing technological platform? Can we change and develop it ourselves? Can we scale up activity to a large number of new users – even going beyond our own home market? Do we have software and digital surfaces that are competitive concerning our customers and users? Do we need to get rid of any technological baggage that is hindering our innovation? The technological platform has rarely been more important to innovation and the pace of change than it is today.

External relations

In large established firms, there seems to be a growing recognition that it is necessary to open the organization to stimuli and collaboration to speed up the ability to innovate. Bill Joy, one of the founders of Sun Microsystems, once said: "No matter who you are, most of the smartest people work for someone else." Relevant questions include: How can leaders relate to external actors to build their firms' innovation capacity? What does it take to make success of partnerships and what are the pitfalls?

One afternoon after the close of the stock exchange in January 2018, a new company launched. *Haven* would challenge the U.S. healthcare sector, which is the largest in the world. Three giants, Warren Buffett (Berkshire Hathaway), Jeff Bezos (Amazon), and Jamie Dimon (JPMorgan Chase), had joined forces to create a new challenger – a company that would turn the American healthcare industry on its head. Together, a partnership between an investment conglomerate, an IT and e-commerce conglomerate, and the biggest bank in the United States would rock the established healthcare providers. The day after launch, the Health Care Index also fell by more than five% for a short period. Many of the established firms were terrified, but without reason, fortunately.

Three years later, there was another stock exchange announcement. Haven was shutting down. The joint venture company never really managed to establish a competitive business model. Its employees were laid off and the company was dissolved in February 2021. The three conglomerates were unable to successfully make their ideas and ambitions concrete. Haven's services were absent from their platforms, and the company never really got the support it had expected from its founding company, Amazon. Together, it had more capital, expertise, and innovation experience than any of the players it had sought to challenge, but it all ended up a flop. Why? What is it that makes some types of collaboration between companies succeed so well, while others fail?

Partnerships can be an attractive opportunity to create innovation and growth, but these relationships can be difficult to handle. Efficient partnerships with external relations can be a key factor in strengthening the innovation muscle. The ability to partner with suppliers and other players can often create a win-win situation. This all comes down to a few simple factors. Have clear and common goals for the partnership been established? Has the organization been set up for partnerships? Has it been ensured that cultural differences won't give rise to difficult and unforeseen situations? Are profits generated through the partnership being shared in a sustainable manner?

It has become increasingly common for large and established companies to partner with smaller and newer players. In Norway, for example, Schibsted and Amedia partner with Kolonial.no to bring all kinds of goods from online purchases to front-door delivery. Other examples involve partnerships between established companies, and for many established firms, cooperating with the big tech companies is an attractive option. In order to improve the accuracy of online real estate ads, DNB Eiendom has cooperated with Facebook on algorithm development. Access to each other's customer or transaction data can generate added value for the customer as well.

We observe that the emphasis of innovation literature has shifted from companies prioritizing the development of skills within their own organizations, also known as closed innovation, to embracing open innovation to a greater degree (Chesbrough, 2001; Zobel, 2017).

Innovation rarely involves businesses inventing something that is completely new. They most often pick up ideas from other organizations or from their customers. It is no coincidence that many Norwegian businesses make a pilgrimage to Silicon Valley – but there can also be ideas acquired from suppliers, competitors, similar businesses in other countries, consultants, or from partnerships with universities.

Many organizations have also started working much closer with customers, activating them in the development of products and services, as well as actively encouraging feedback. The gaming industry is a frontrunner, where gamers not only play the role of customers, but often hop the fence to be co-producers.

For the purpose of innovation, opening the organization will be important to gain access to the smartest people who work for someone else, in order to sense what is happening in their surroundings, and to actively take a stance on what should be adopted, and just as importantly, what should *not* be adopted into one's own organization. However, opening the organization also provides an opportunity to learn from others, and to obtain impulses to change one's own culture to focus on innovation. Through collaboration with young companies, many established companies have picked up new ways of working, and many are attempting to adopt the working methods that characterize successful start-up companies. This means that openness to the outside world provides opportunities to both sense and seize opportunities to develop innovation capabilities in one's own organization.

More open borders also enable sharper strategic prioritizations with regard to resource allocation, and companies are increasingly thinking in terms of multilateral alliances and ecosystems (Doz, 2019; Jacobides et al., 2018). If there is a standard component or a standard product, then there is no reason to develop this internally. Similarly, if you are unable to develop products of equally high quality as other companies, the better option may be to purchase this product or service, or to enter into partnership. This can allow the meager funding for innovation to be used in areas where the company has an opportunity to set itself apart and build up a competitive advantage. In other words, open borders boost the chance of specializing and concentrating resources on the areas where the best conditions exist. In this book, we will go deeper into different ways organizations can open themselves to the outside world, whether this takes the form of collaboration with start-up companies, with more established companies, or in being part of an ecosystem.

Leadership and governance

Leadership and governance are about all of the above; how one attempts to develop each individual cog in a more innovative direction, how the cogs can be turned to get them going in a new, consistent, strategic direction. What is not covered in the cogs we have reviewed so far is how to set the strategic direction, create collective engagement, and lead the organization when forces are pulling in opposite directions.

As a leader, you are expected to create enthusiasm, create unity, support your colleagues, and lead the way. Leaders are expected to practice what they preach and step up as a good role model. If leaders fail to step up and show the desired behavior themselves, their ability to motivate evaporates. In an established business, tensions will often arise between exploration and exploitation, and leaders will have to handle paradoxes and contradictions.

Setting the strategic direction

One of the most important things a senior executive does is to *set the strategic direction for the business*. As we have examined in the first chapter, there may be significant uncertainty and it may be difficult to predict future customer needs, but without a clear direction and prioritization, the forces keeping us where we are right now will often end up the strongest.

Building innovation capacity is not something that can be done with a wave of the hand, it demands a constant effort to renew, rebuild, and especially set aside sufficient resources. The easiest part of the job is putting thoughts and ideas to paper, but this does not help much if you are not willing to prioritize – or as Pisano (2019) states: "Just tell me how resources are allocated and how you spend your time, and I can pretty much tell what your company's real strategy is.".

A good innovation strategy will clarify which innovation opportunities are prioritized and ensure that the different cogs are in harmony and support the strategic direction. Both Pisano (2019) and Nagji and Tuff (2012) recommend spreading the innovation portfolio between different types of innovations – some close to the core, some adjacent, and some initiatives that completely break with the existing business. Through our case studies, we will also stress the importance of taking time into account, regarding both the timing of investments and the launching of new innovations, but also to systematically build and sustain innovation capacity over time. There is little use in having a fantastic innovation strategy written on a piece of paper if management is unable to convey this to the entire organization. Management's ability to motivate employees and create both passion and engagement has received an increasing amount of attention in both theory and practice, and collective engagement is also one of the components that make up the building blocks of innovation capacity.

Purpose-driven leadership

Newer theory and practice from the field of leadership emphasizes purpose-driven (or mission-driven) leadership (Quinn & Thakor, 2018; Sandvik et al., 2019). The purpose expresses the company's unique mission, and the global trend is that organizations no longer simply chase profits but also have a prosocial purpose – with a mission to do something for others or for society more broadly. The thinking is that this will contribute to giving the company a direction, and that it will create energy and motivation among employees. Quinn and Thakor explains this as follows:

> A prosocial purpose is not about financial transactions. It reflects something that can inspire. It explains why people in organizations make a difference, why they experience their work as meaningful and why they offer their support. (Quinn & Thakor, 2018)

The quote above also signals that purpose-driven leadership more concerns the stakeholders than the shareholders, and that this direction is gaining more and more traction in the field of strategy (Barney, 2020; Kaplan, 2020; McGahan, 2020). Purpose-driven organizations are often viewed as attractive for employees who want to do good, whether that involves reducing carbon omissions, preventing social dumping, reducing poverty, or other purposes. This change of direction toward more sustainable goals has also given rise to a discussion of the extent to which purpose-driven leadership is compatible with the owners' profit goals (Birkinshaw et al., 2014).

The case study of Ørsted, which we will return to in Part 2, shows that it is possible to combine profits and prosocial purposes at the same time as getting owners onboard to support the transition from a black to a green corporation. Today, Ørsted is one of the greenest energy companies in the world.

The voluntary and public sectors are by nature more mission-driven. The director of the Norwegian National Library, Aslak Sira Myhre, is a typical example of a leader who is driven by social responsibility: his mission is to reach out to all Norwegians.

Another important leadership trait that is closely linked to innovation is the extent to which management delegates power and authority to its employees, empowering them to make their own decisions and their own assessments. This was touched on in our discussion concerning organizational structure, but what we discuss here is the leadership philosophy behind employee empowerment itself. In the Nordic countries there is a long tradition of empowering employees, though the increased focus on agile teams and agile organizations has challenged the degree of autonomy handed to the employees. One of the latest leadership trends promoting empowerment that is currently winning traction is servant leadership (Northouse, 2019).

In many ways, servant leadership appears to be something of a mystery. We are used to imagining that leaders lead the organization and employees follow, but here the leaders must act as servants to the employees. Although research on servant leadership has only picked up over the past few years, the leadership philosophy was proposed in an essay written by Robert K. Greenleaf in 1970. Servant leaders put their employees first, empower them, and help them develop their own skills and potential.

Although some would say that servant leadership is taking employee empowerment too far, nonetheless, it is useful to thoroughly consider how far one wishes to take employee empowerment and the room for management and managing in this school of thought. Organizations that have taken the route of agile organization have experienced this first-hand, and the example of the Norwegian advertising company FINN.no shows how important it is to be conscious of the leadership philosophy behind the delegation of the agile teams.

Paradoxical leadership

Another direction in leadership research that has gained increased attention over the past decade is paradoxical leadership (Smith, 2014; Miron-Spektor et al., 2018). This is a type of leadership that fits well with the approach in which established firms need to balance daily operations and innovation. Paradoxical leadership assumes that leaders are confronted with many competing demands – between stability and change, discipline and flexibility, planning, and self-organization, and particularly between exploitation and exploration.

Some leaders view these types of tensions as dilemmas that are in conflict and that must be resolved. They find it uncomfortable to live with uncertainty and competing demands. However, even though it is possible to find solutions to these dilemmas, it is likely that the underlying tensions will remain and resurface again and again. Other leaders have a different perspective and consider tensions natural and persistent. They embrace complexity and view tensions as something that gives them opportunities to learn and develop the organization in a world of volatility, uncertainty, complexity, and ambiguity (VUCA environment). The quote below is an illustration of these exact differences in their approach to leadership.

> The problem is not the problem; the problem is the way we think about the problem. (Watzlawick et al., 1974)

In this book, paradoxical leadership will be relevant for several of the different organizational solutions we will review. The paradoxes are perhaps at their most obvious when we review the ambidextrous solution in Chapter 3, in which the architect firm 3XN balanced between the established unit and the new, innovative unit focused on sustainability. However, paradoxical leadership is also relevant in situations where the cooperating partners both complement and compete. When Vipps was developed by DNB, the leadership of DNB faced a dilemma of whether they should invite their competitors to take part in their new adventure. When they chose to do so, it meant that both DNB and the Vipps leadership had to deal with companies that were both collaborators and competitors.

Ownership

There can be no doubt that ownership is of great importance to the development of innovation capacity. It may be difficult to unite owners that are impatient and demand quick results with a goal of radically renewing a company and developing completely new business areas.

So far, we have mainly been examining what managers can do to build innovation capacity. While it may be difficult for managers to choose their owners, this does not mean that managers are unable to influence them. In fact, in a situation where the company needs radical renewal, it may be particularly important to keep the board and owners close to ensure support for strategic choices. Innovating and radically renewing a business is associated with both higher risk and uncertainty, and according to Pisano (2019) senior leaders should be particularly alert that the board may put its foot down when resistance is encountered and results are still forthcoming.

One example of how changes in ownership may affect innovation capacity can be found in Autostore. For 25 years, Jakob Hatteland has been a part of building up the company Autostore on the southwest coast of Norway. In spring of 2021, the Japanese funding titan Softbank entered as a new owner with an ownership share of 40%. Autostore was valued at NOK 66 billion. Hatteland gives his former technical director much of the credit for developing the advanced robotics systems for storing different types of products. In addition, many patents and exciting products sprung from the blossoming technology community outside of Haugesund. Autostore got its first customer in 2004. Like many other technology businesses, product development took place in close collaboration with customers. Hatteland himself spent many hundreds of millions of Norwegian kroner to finance the development of the technology along the way. This was possible because past sales revenue from other successful start-ups were fed into the business. However, it's one thing to succeed with medium-sized customers in the Norwegian market. Taking the step up into the global world class is entering into a different league, and with Softbank as a new principal owner, Autostore was in a better position to take on the global market.

It began taking off in 2017. The previous year, EQT acquired 84% ownership. At that time, the price was set at approximately NOK four billion. EQT was introduced to Hatteland via his (then) ownership of the sports chain XXL. Through investments in new, automated storage solutions for the sports chain, it also became highly familiar with Autostore. It decided to invest there as well. What could the new financial owners offer Hatteland? EQT's specialty is to bring in people with heavy industry and market expertise to the boards of the businesses they own. They may be partners in EQT or called industrial advisors. These experts secure leading financial and commercial expertise for the business both inside and outside the boardroom. For Autostore, this enabled access to new and larger customers, particularly in Europe.

Just two years later, in 2019, EQT sold 90% of its ownership share to the American fund THL Partner. This time, the price was set at NOK 16 billion. While THL contributed extensive expertise and a broad network that could strengthen Autostore in the American market, the thought was that Softbank would do the same, considering the large and unexploited opportunities in Asia.

There is no doubt that these entrepreneurs in the southwest of Norway have been on an impressive journey. There can also be no doubting the contributions made by EQT and THL Partners. Owners can contribute financial muscle and commercial expertise. They can have networks that ensure market access and customer numbers. Specifically, new owners can spot opportunities and threats overlooked by others. We normally think that innovation capacity can be developed from within, but the case of Autostore also shows that it can also be strengthened from the outside.

In collaborating with the owners, there will be some factors that can be decisive for senior management's ability to lead innovation efforts. One obvious factor is that senior management must set aside resources to run systematic innovation efforts and not get locked into daily operations and short-term results. Furthermore, a long-term ownership perspective will be necessary, as it takes time to develop new business areas and to make them profitable. This is also tied to what parameters the board follows up on with management. Do they use historical accounting figures or more future-oriented indicators? The risks the owners are willing to tolerate may also be important.

At the same time, the board must not take too passive a role and be too patient and naive. On the contrary, research on innovation and ownership shows that it is important that the board is active, attentive, and asks the right questions (Wagner, 2018). Such ownership may be simpler when ownership is concentrated and someone is holding large ownership stakes, compared to a company that is more spread out. The former leadership of Schibsted claims, for instance, that Stiftelsen Tinius's ownership stake created space to operate innovation that radically renewed the group.

When the owner is a public body, there will often be other goals behind the ownership than pure profit maximization. For the owners of public agencies, it is important to clarify the purpose of the organization, something that may sound easier than it is in practice (Meyer & Norman, 2019). Many public organizations hold a particularly important role in developing infrastructure and common goods, and some of these, such as having a national grid for electricity and setting standards, serve as the basis for other private corporations' product and service innovation.

In some cases, the owners may also decide that they have no faith in the existing organization's ability to become sufficiently innovative and would rather invest in other businesses or assign their tasks to new or different companies. It is important that senior executives of established firms do not spread themselves too thin and overinvest in what will hopefully become a new business. Furthermore, owners will sometimes prefer to use their own funding to directly invest in new business. And if the owner is the government, then they may choose to split up and establish new government bodies and corporations to better cater to their needs and requirements. In Norway, the Ministry of Transport established Nye Veier (road construction) and Flytoget (air transport), giving a clear signal to the incumbent public corporations that they were not innovative enough to plan and build roads and acquaint themselves with new user needs.

Connection between cogs, organizational solutions, and innovation capacity

Different organizational solutions require leaders to assess and adjust different cogs. In Figure 2.2, we have illustrated the connection between the cogs, the different solutions, and innovation capacity.

This figure is intended to illustrate that each organizational solution represents a different configuration of the cogs. As such, the cog framework can be compared to a toolbox in which each of the organizational solutions represent a different set of cogs. In Parts 2, 3, and 4, we will show how the cogs can be configured in different ways, all depending on what organizational solution is being sought to be implemented. In the ambidextrous solution, a new set of cogs is established within the organizational boundaries, while other organizational solutions imply changes in only some of the cogs. In a partnership, connections to another organization's cogs are developed, but it is also likely that your organization's own cogs, such as expertise, will be affected.

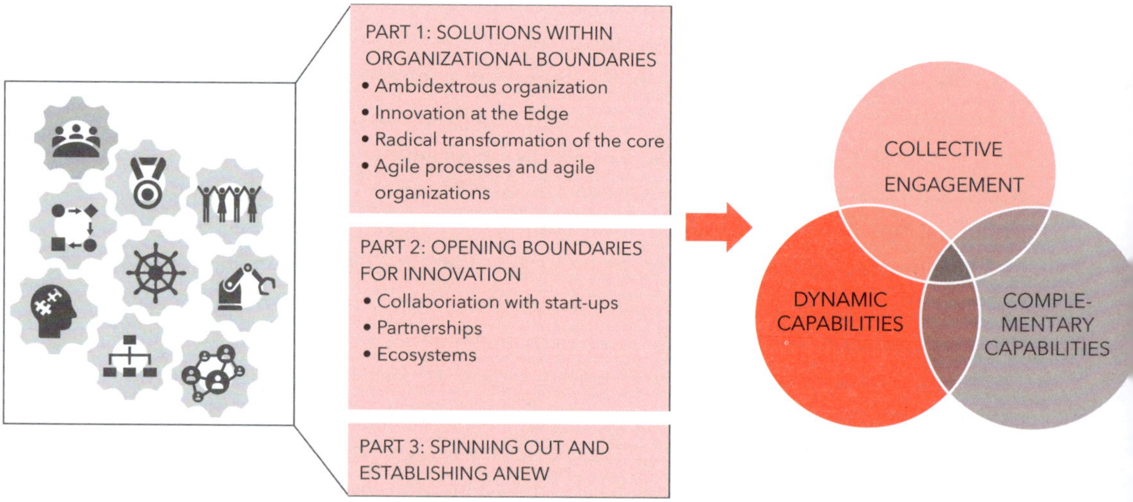

Figure 2.2 Connection between cogs, organizational solutions, and innovation capacity

CASE 2.1
DEVELOPMENT OF INNOVATION CAPACITY IN DNB

The aim of this chapter is to illustrate how the cogwheel framework in Chapter 2 can be applied to a case. We have chosen DNB, Norway's largest bank, as our case. During the time Rune Bjerke was its CEO, DNB underwent a radical journey of change where building innovation capacity was the goal. We start this case by giving an overall view of DNB's innovation journey, and then explore how the different cogs were set in motion to build innovation capacity.

DNB's innovation journey

DNB's transformation can be described through three different phases: restructuring and downsizing, technological awakening, and focusing; see Figure C2.1.1.

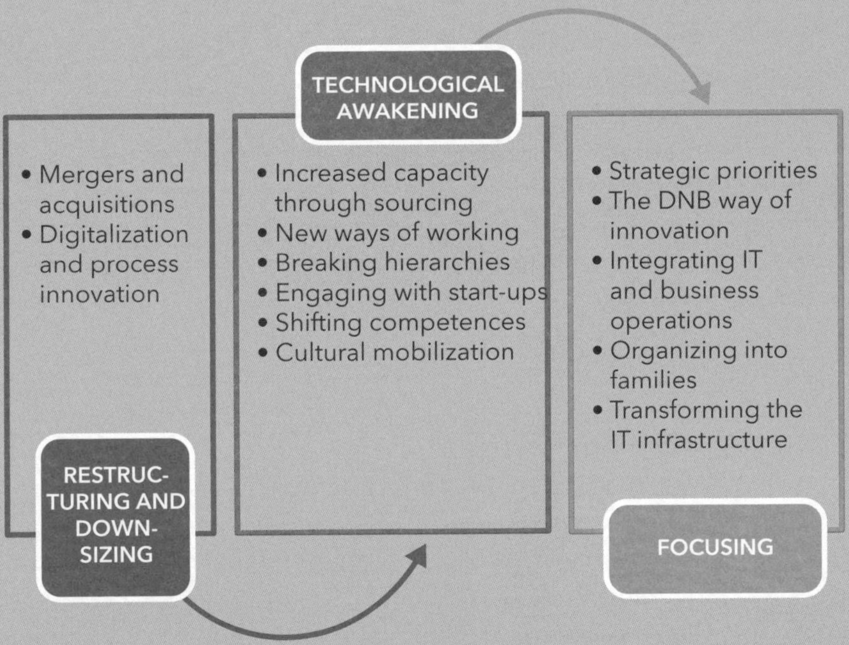

Figure C2.1.1 DNB's innovation journey

From the beginning of the 1990s, Norwegian banks have been at the forefront of digitalization. Simultaneously, significant consolidation has taken place through mergers and acquisitions on the one hand and downscaling the physical network of bank branches on the other. From the end of 1980 until 2015, the number of bank branches was halved from 2,000 to 1,000 (Finans Norge), and the process of converting the physical network to a digital one continued. In the twenty-year period from 1990 until 2011, the banks' operating costs as a percentage of operating income were significantly reduced, from 80 percent to 40 percent, and in 2020, Norwegian banks had the lowest cost ratio in Europe (Norges Bank).

From the deregulation of the banking sector at the end of the 1980s, DNB expanded its operations nationally and internationally through mergers and acquisitions to become Norway's largest bank. However, the number of employees did not increase in step with the mergers. Through the reduction of overlapping functions, digitalization and the closure of bank branches, DNB streamlined its operations to become more efficient. Hence, this first period primarily consisted of innovations that Christensen (2019) categorize as efficiency innovations, i.e., innovations that enable businesses to do more with fewer resources.

The phase of technological awakening started with Rune Bjerke's arrival as new CEO in 2007. However, the financial crisis put an end to the immediate innovation plans, and for the next three to four years, all management capacity was involved in handling the crisis. Therefore, it was not until 2011 that DNB could begin its radical transformation journey. One of the first major changes Bjerke initiated was to combine all the brands that originated from years of mergers and acquisitions into one overarching DNB brand. The aim was to simplify the structure to accelerate the innovation work and give the whole corporation a clear strategic direction.

> It was a financial holding company that had undergone major merger processes ... but at the same time it was a jumble of brands, systems and various units that were brought together....There was no organizational structure that allowed the utilization of expertise and resources throughout its units. (Former manager 3, DNB)

From 2011 onwards, several measures were implemented to build innovation capacity, and these measures involved the entire bank. Employees were invited to come up with new ideas and received training in new ways of working, the bank recruited many new employees with technological expertise, Vipps was developed in six months, and the bank started engaging with start-ups and fintech companies.

The ideas flourished and the enthusiasm for innovation accelerated, but it became more and more evident that there was a need for a more systematic and structured approach to succeed with innovation.

> It was Monty Python's 100-meter dash for those with no sense of direction. Everyone lines up on the starting line, the gun is fired and then everyone runs in different

directions. This is how we felt it was in DNB, so we needed more coordinated forces. (Manager 1, DNB)

The need for more structure marked the transition to a new phase where a more focused innovation strategy was developed. An innovation framework helped sort out the best ideas and weed out the others, and a clearer emphasis was made on upskilling and reskilling the bank's own employees rather than just recruiting new competence. At the same time, the development towards a more agile organization continued.

In the next sections, we describe the specific steps the management took to build up innovation capacity and highlight what changes were made in the various cogs, including management and governance, organizational structures and work processes, composition of expertise, culture and incentives, technological infrastructure and external relations and partnerships. We start with management and governance because it laid the foundations for other changes.

Management and governance

An important managerial task in major changes is to provide direction, especially when there is great uncertainty about the future. DNB's management assessed that the bank was at risk of losing both its competitive edge as well as significant income if it failed to act quickly. New EU regulations (PSD2) gave third parties the right to customer data, large technology companies with completely different business models such as Apple and Google took clear positions in payment processing, and new fintech companies were emerging like toadstools.

> The world outside was changing so rapidly, and digitization became a prerequisite for success with new innovations. And unless we chose a new direction with new products and new business areas, we would be in danger of becoming a dinosaur. (Former manager 2, DNB)

Innovation capacity was built up in stages, first by setting innovation as one of the strategic focus areas and setting aside significant resources to drive innovation. The goal of making the bank more innovative and technology-oriented was clearly communicated to the employees.

Gradually, management became clearer in its strategic ambition and set the goal of developing DNB from a traditional banking business into a far more technology-oriented financial group. In several talks by senior management, this was exemplified by labelling DNB a technology company with a banking license. At the same time, significant financial resources were allocated to innovation activities. The annual investments in IT infrastructure, systems and applications were increased from 1.2 to 2 billion NOK. The management wanted to show employees and investors that DNB was serious about its aim to become a more technology-driven organization.

In both internal and external communications, the top management of DNB portrayed the future as highly uncertain and said that jobs would be at risk if DNB failed to become more profitable and technology-driven. In a public talk in January 2017, Rune Bjerke said that he had no idea where DNB would be in 2025 and that DNB's 10,000 employees and union representatives would be lucky if there were more than 5,000 in ten years. If they were to maintain or increase the number of employees, a widespread transformation of the company would have to succeed. In any case, the product and service offering had to be radically restructured. The bank would no longer be just a bank.

> He told us that half of us would probably lose our jobs.... He didn't know, and he was the CEO. It was quite a special moment. (Former manager 1, DNB)

In a talk to the largest employee federation, LO, Bjerke repeated the need for continuous restructuring:

> There will be change, restructuring, and need for new competences as well as fewer employees. Many of our current tasks will be taken over by machines, robots or automatic processes. When someone asks where DNB is going, my honest answer is: I have no idea. But if we are not at the forefront of the change processes every single day, then jobs will be threatened. (Rune Bjerke in interview with Fri Fagbevegelse, 25 January 2017)

Naturally, mobilizing the employees to change was not enough; the will to innovate also had to permeate management philosophy. Rune Bjerke launched the concept of "let go management" where the aim was to relinquish control by delegating power and authority and allowing space for experts to make decisions. Group management and the board would no longer be a hurdle – the bank had make quick decisions in complex and rapidly changing environments.

Simultaneously with management letting go, there was also a stronger involvement of middle managers, new employees, and experts. The leadership meetings were expanded to include key resources and influential employees, and Bjerke established an advisory group with new employees with technological expertise.

DNB also changed the decision-making structures through the introduction of key teams in important strategic areas such as innovation, IT and payment processing. These teams were put together across hierarchical levels and professions. The aim was to gather decision-makers and experts in the same room, and to get the most urgent issues on the table. In this way, it was possible to allocate more time to each area and avoid decisions being sent up and down the hierarchy where important information was lost underway.

> A person at level four could typically be the one who knew the most in a niche area. He had to tell his boss what his boss should tell his boss again about how things should be presented to the top management.
>
> You would not make good decisions if you only had strategic perspectives without the professional expertise. But experts did not necessarily have the overall picture for the firm either. They could make a logical decision based on their perspective that turned out to be completely wrong for the business as a whole. Thus, combining the two became an important ingredient. (Manager 1, DNB)

The Board or CFO could choose to sit in these key teams, and in addition to the permanent members, experts in the various areas were brought in as needed.

Competence

An important restraint on innovation capacity was limited IT resources. As a first step to increase the capacity, DNB entered into contracts with three large IT suppliers in India. The Indian contracts substantially increased development capacity. However, the contracts generated limited renewal for DNB's organization, partly because the Indian consultants worked in traditional ways and partly because they were external parties.

> The innovation work changed character, suddenly we gained access to much greater capacity on the development side.... But sizable outsourcing agreements with a great deal of capacity are no guarantee that development will come faster.... And we learned that the work processes became much more cumbersome. (Former manager 3, DNB)

Therefore, to transform the organization and develop innovation capacity, a plan was initiated to recruit people who had IT and technology education and experience. Traditionally, the bank had recruited people with an economics and finance background; now the recruitment strategy changed completely. In 2014, fourteen percent of new hires had an IT and technology background; in 2019 the figure had increased to 50 percent. To be attractive to people with an IT and technology background, the transformation from a traditional bank to a technology company was important, and the managers of DNB actively sought out educational institutions and other recruitment arenas.

Scaling up the number of employees with an IT and technology background took place concurrently with the continued downsizing of several hundred positions in the branches. Normally, it would be demanding to increase and decrease staff at the same time, but this seems to have happened without much ado from the employees. A possible explanation could be that through years of restructuring and downsizing employees had gotten used to change. At the same time, it was clearly communicated that the new competence profiles were completely different from traditional banking competence. Although the shift in competencies was successful, one of the senior managers reflected on other ways this shift could have been made:

> In retrospect, we could have gotten more out of the resources if we had worked more systematically with reskilling and upskilling as well as more targeted in using work action packages.... On the other hand, there was a much stronger cultural shift as a result of what we did. (Former manager 1, DNB)

The new employees with a technological background had a profound impact on DNB's profile as a technology company. However, there was a much higher turnover rate amongst the new hires and as time went on, the management realized that this approach needed to be supplemented with the reskilling and upskilling of the non tech-employees.

Organizational structure and work processes

After combining the many different brands into a united DNB, the management put in place several structural measures to speed up innovation. A separate unit called New Business was established with a radical innovation mandate. This unit grew to become both a driver and facilitator of innovation. The IT-department was downscaled, and the developers were transferred to the business units to work side-by-side with the business experts. Vipps was set up as a separate project where new, agile working methods were also developed. The story about Vipps is further elaborated in case 8.2.

The purpose of New Business was to create a unit that would work with radical innovation and come up with new and innovative products and services. As expected in this type of ambidextrous organizational solution (see Chapter 3), several employees were opposed to the idea that all fun and innovative work should take place in New Business while other units should attend to "business as usual". They also argued for the need to be close to the customers to radically innovate.

> Many people opposed the idea of having a unit on the side that dealt with innovation while all the others run a normal business. However, you might need it during a transition period. We made an attempt with New Business which many then referred to as 'No Business'.
>
> Such a centralized unit is located too far away from customers to understand customer needs. It is the business areas together with the customer team who attract the brand new things. (Employee 1, DNB)

After some time, New Business changed its name to Payments & Innovation, and the roles and division between this unit and the business areas gradually became clearer. It retained its radical mandate in the development of new products and services and business models, particularly in the unit named New Tech Lab (see further description of New Tech Lab in case 4.2).

> The goal is, of course, that New Tech Lab becomes a unicorn. But if it doesn't, then we've learned a lot along the way, then.... We have to practice imagination ... set extreme reference points. In DNB, the three largest IT projects are mobile apps. But what if there are no mobile phones in the future? What are you going to do in banking service then? (Manager 3, DNB)

In addition to New Tech Lab the new unit (Payments and Innovation) consisted of Innovation Management and Practice, Open Banking, Corporate Venturing and Payments. The Innovation Management and Practice was more of a support unit which aided the business units in their innovation work, whereas the Payment unit was made responsible for coordinating the payment area across all business sections, an area that was designated as strategically important for the company and where it was important to make quick and well-founded decisions. For Open Banking and Corporate Venturing, the idea was to be at the forefront of important trends and develop adjacent products and services relevant for the banking operations.

Vipps was another disruptive entity that was set up as a project with the clear goal of developing a new payment app in six months aiming to win the mobile wallet market. The board's and management's evaluation were that it would take too long to put this into an ordinary development course (estimated to take 18 months) and that this would have to be established in a separate unit. Rune Bjerke used his authority to prioritize the necessary resources and to ensure that the best talents were recruited for the project. And although Vipps was met with some skepticism at the beginning, the successful innovation changed the hearts and minds of employees.

Vipps was also the first innovation project where the bank applied new and more agile working methods (see Chapter 6) and IT and business employees worked together in interdisciplinary teams.

The need to transform IT to work in new, innovative ways was not unique to DNB. The original idea in many large companies was that IT operations could be run like a factory with a traditional waterfall methodology.

> A few years ago, the mantra was that IT was a factory. Then it was like that when we started a new project, it had to be specified in detail exactly how it should look.... It took a long time from an idea to when you started

making something, and then what you made was often wrong, or poor quality. Those who sat and coded did not have any special ownership of what they created either, and typically there were dozens of handovers in a project. If you were to create similar functionality on another setup with a smarter way of working, you could do it for a fraction [of the cost]. (Manager 2, DNB)

The aim of the transformation was to get more out of IT resources and dramatically reduce the time it took to bring new products and services to market. In an appeal to the employees, the head of IT Transformation described how the work processes should be changed:

> Over the next few years, we will increase the output of the IT investments and significantly reduce the time to market for new products and services. We must become even better at creating minimum viable solutions which we can distribute to our customers and they can give us feedback that we can use in further development. This requires that we automate the testing, including all safety checks and controls, so that we can move faster into production. This is how the best technology companies work to develop good products for customers, and this is also how we should work. (Halvor Sannes Lande, DNB Nyheter, November 2018)

Vipps had also shown how effective it was to put IT and business together in interdisciplinary, agile teams, and consequentially more IT resources were transferred to the business operations. This created fertile ground for completely new development teams and for learning across the professions. In addition, it gave the business units control over scarce IT resources.

> Each of us received digital resources within our business area. I'm not particularly good at technology, but the result was that you gained much better insight and had better discussions, not as customers of IT, but through having control over our own resources. (Former manager 1, DNB)

Eventually, DNB organized the interdisciplinary teams into families taking a step further toward an agile organization (see Chapter 6). Due to dependencies and old legacy systems, a large part of the IT department was kept intact, but the organizing principles followed the agile approach.

Technological platform

One major obstacles to building up DNB's innovation capacity resided in the bank's legacy IT systems. DNB's technological platform was from the 1960s and 1970s, when COBOL programming was in vogue. This platform made product and service innovations more costly and demanding to implement.

> The bank has over 10,000 financial products. All of which are constructed in different ways, have different risk profiles, are reported in different ways.

> We have so much spaghetti here.... It's a bit like a heart transplant, then. Every time we do such things, we replace and buy off-the-shelf solutions and stuff like that, it sounds nice. But then we have to go in and tailor and fix all these interfaces. (Employee 2, DNB)

The legacy IT systems were not compatible with the need for continuous product and service innovations. When a team made alterations to its product, there were ripple effects on other teams' products due to multiple interdependencies. A further challenge was that the people with expertise on DNB's legacy systems were getting close to retirement age; as such, retaining the current technology platform was not a viable option.

> Today, much of our critical infrastructure runs on mainframes. In the mainframe section, around 60–70 people will leave in 10 years. And our strategic partners also have few who are adept at mainframes because people don't want to learn it anymore. The best [people] won't work with it. (Leader 4, DNB)

Although the need to replace the legacy systems became more and more evident, this was far from easy. Broadly speaking, DNB's management was faced with three solutions: perform a complete transformation of the core (like for example its competitor Nordea did), start a new bank on the side with modern technology, or choose a step-by-step approach.

DNB chose the latter approach, first through an attempt with the English fintech company 11FS, where the parties established the joint venture company Foundry. The aim was to build up a module-based structure which could be implemented in DNB, but which could also be sold to other companies. However, this collaboration was halted, partly because DNB deemed it too risky to bet on a such a young fintech company. However, the lessons learned from this collaboration were incorporated into a 10-year transformation race towards a new module-based solution.

Culture and incentives

Even though a small part of the bank's employees were directly involved in the innovation projects, the management wanted to get everyone on board to gain enthusiasm and endorsement for the innovative direction. In many ways, developing an innovative organization was at odds with traditional banking culture. Here, low risk, zero errors, predictability and regulatory management were the catchwords, while an innovative culture meant that risks had to be taken and employees had to be trusted. Mistakes were inevitable and desirable for learning in an innovative culture, and it was not possible to manage according to predictable and rule-governed frameworks.

The aim was to build an innovation culture and share tough lessons with everyone. You don't learn if you don't risk anything. It was a major change towards a culture where there was a willingness to fail.

> The idea was that whether you were in an operational role or in a new business area, you should understand what was happening outside DNB. I was in an operational role and for me this was a major change and I had to fundamentally change the way I managed my organization (Former manager 1, DNB)

In order to create engagement for the new direction, the management initiated a number of activities. They invited all employees to a brainstorming session where the aim was to generate new ideas and train the employees in new working methods. Around 5,000 ideas came up, and three of them were selected for further development and market testing. Furthermore, several gatherings were organized where the purpose was to share experiences about projects that had failed, which was unfamiliar territory to many employees, and required courage. A digital floor was established where agile working methodology was the norm, and DNB opened up to cooperation with start-ups and fintechs. In addition, there was a major culture shift through the recruitment of people with completely new areas of expertise.

The result of the massive mobilization was that there was no longer a lack of ideas, or as one manager phrased it: "It's like drinking water from a fire hose". However, DNB lacked a systematic approach for taking the ideas and converting them into innovations that potentially could succeed in the market. Employees experienced that the ideas were difficult to sell and for them to gain traction, and too many stakeholders needed to be involved.

> Before, you had to go around with your PowerPoint presentation to God knows how many management meetings, and then the new term that I've learned, HIPO (Highest Income Person with Opinion), became the decider. And that's gut feeling, not based on fact, because you haven't validated your idea. (Manager 5, DNB)

In addition, the capacity in IT development was very tight. There was no point in people in the business areas generated lots of ideas when the IT development budget remained strained. The need for more systematic selection of projects and clearer strategic prioritization was forced forward. Therefore, the management decided on pursuing a few strategic investment areas, and a separate innovation framework was developed to ensure progress and sufficient resources for the innovation projects.

> The innovations were too broad and too extensive.... It [the broad mobilization] served its purpose for a while, but focusing on fewer areas is the right decision. It is difficult because simultaneously, it means that you have to "kill your darlings" – in areas you also think are important. (Former manager 2, DNB)

It is relevant to ask whether DNB could have chosen a more direct path and gone straight to a more systematic approach to innovation. Given the major technological shift that was needed, and from the standpoint of a traditional banking culture, it is likely that it was wise to take this in two steps: first mobilize employees and create engagement, then pursue a more focused and systematic approach.

External relations and ownership

An important part of the cultural shift was increased openness to the outside world, not only through bringing in new employees with completely new skills, but also through entering partnerships with fintechs and collaborating with start-ups.

Interestingly, the engagement with the start-up companies did not begin with partnerships but through a strategic decision in the banking operations to provide credit to start-ups. The employees working in these operations experienced that taking on these businesses as clients meant they had to fundamentally change their ways of working.

> It's risky, and not really bank financing. You have to invest a lot of time in communication to advise them.... When we started this endeavor, I remember very well that traditional bankers said that it was not worth investing in this area, you should wait until they are bigger and then pick them up. (Former manager 3, DNB)

Working with start-ups required more frequent contacts with the businesses, and the new way of working had also positive ripple effects for the rest of the bank. DNB produced a book on how to start a business, and they went to entrepreneurship and start-up conferences around the country. This stimulated a further investment in start-up companies, and the development of a separate corporate venture arm, DNB Venture. The aim of this newcomer was to take the pulse of technology development and learn from young companies. It thus contributed to DNB's sensing capabilities.

Eventually, DNB also built up a more systematic focus on start-ups through collaboration with the startup community StartupLab (see also Chapter 7 for case on StartupLab). Together they developed DNB NXT, an accelerator program where start-ups are financed and given professional support from DNB and StartupLab in collaboration. Through the years of collaboration with StartupLab, DNB built up innovation capacity and developed greater maturity and experience in working with young companies.

> (In the beginning) they (DNB) supported us because we knew how to innovate, and this was new to them. But during the last three years, they have stepped up by employing many talented people of their own. Now we help them keep up with technological developments and new trends, in addition to being a neutral meeting place where they can meet younger companies. (Informant from StartupLab)

Alongside StartupLab, DNB has also harvested experience in collaboration with fintechs. The fintechs inspired DNB to pursue new, agile ways of working, but it has also been challenging to find good partnership models and give up decision-making power to other partners. Therefore, DNB increased its efforts to systematically build capabilities on how to enter into new partnerships, which aligns with our notion of complementary capabilities for innovation.

Summary

In the years since 2010, when DNB started its innovation journey, DNB has built significant innovation capacity. The bank's top management set a new strategic direction, supported by new management principles, new organizational and decision-making structures, more partnerships, and agile teams. All employees were invited to take part and learn new innovative ways of working. Some of the cogs are still work in process, such as the technological platform where the transition will take many years and the open innovation initiatives where the bank is still feeling its way forward in partnerships with young companies and fintechs.

In the DNB case we have touched on many of the organizational solutions that we will go into in depth in the next chapters of the book: the ambidextrous solution with the establishment of New Business and Vipps, innovation on the edge through the New Tech Lab, introduction of agile working methods, and cooperation with start-ups and larger firms.

The case of DNB illustrates how challenging and multifaceted but also rewarding it can be to build innovation capacity. And even if they have managed to build capacity, it will take substantial effort and resources to sustain that capacity over time. DNB's innovation journey shows how it has systematically built up its innovation capacity during the last ten years, but we suspect that it is far from over.

Part 2

Innovation within organizational boundaries

In this section, we present four different organizational solutions that contribute in diverse ways to building innovation capacity. Each involves various adjustments to the organizational elements we introduced in our cogwheel model in the previous chapter: culture, structure, competence, etc. Although the solutions primarily require changes within the organization's boundaries, this does not mean that external players are immaterial or absent; however the solutions we present in Part 3 of the book are completely dependent on external partnerships. The advantage of working within the organization's boundaries is a matter of greater control and a lesser degree of coordination compared to innovation that happens in collaboration with others. At the same time, it requires possession or acquisition of the necessary resources, skills, and technology.

There are various ways in which organizations can set themselves up for innovation by adjusting the elements in the cogwheel model. We present four organizational solutions: ambidextrous organization, innovation at the edge, agile organization and innovation at the core, which we call radical transformation. We describe each of these organizational solutions, discuss how they function, their inherent benefits and challenges, and the conditions under which each solution would be suitable. Each organizational solution is illustrated with specific cases from a variety of businesses. As will be seen, these are not either/or – each individual solution can be used in combination with others, and they each build innovation capacity in somewhat different ways that can complement each other.

Chapter 3

Ambidextrous organization

Established firms often strive to become as good at innovation and renewal as they are at streamlining and improving the existing business. In the research literature, the ability to balance efficiency (exploitation) with renewal (exploration) is referred to as being ambidextrous. There are different variants, but the best-known ambidextrous model is about making an organizational distinction between innovation and effective operation (O'Reilly & Tushman, 2016). This can be done by establishing a separate unit within the business that is given a mandate to innovate. The assumption is that it will be difficult to succeed with innovation within more established units; these other units must be allowed to focus on effective operation. There is a great deal of research that suggests that established firms develop structural and cultural inertia that makes them difficult to change. Any attempt at innovation and renewal within the existing firm risks being crowded out or killed by the existing culture.

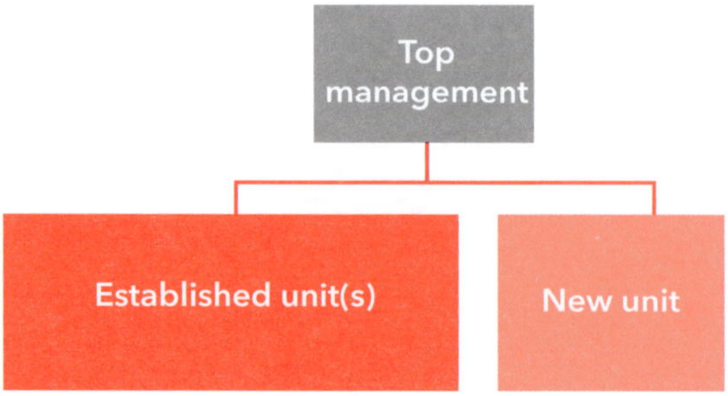

Figure 3.1 The ambidextrous solution

For established firms, it will primarily be the ability to *seize* new opportunities that is strengthened by the ambidextrous solution. The solution helps to ensure that sufficient time and resources are set aside for renewal. Also, *complementary capabilities* will be developed through the work in the new unit. Over time, the innovative culture and the complementary capabilities developed in the separate unit may also expand to the rest of the established firm.

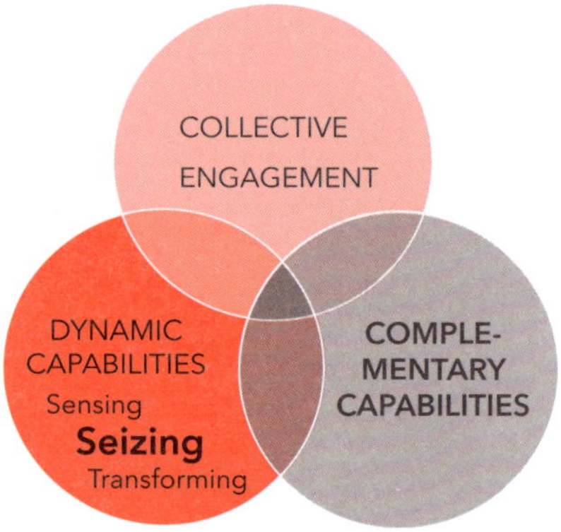

Figure 3.2 How the ambidextrous solution contributes to innovation capacity

Establishing a separate unit

By establishing a separate unit, space is created for renewal. The new unit is developed alongside the established unit(s); thus, the solution does not require that established units (or the people in these units) must change or adapt (at least initially).

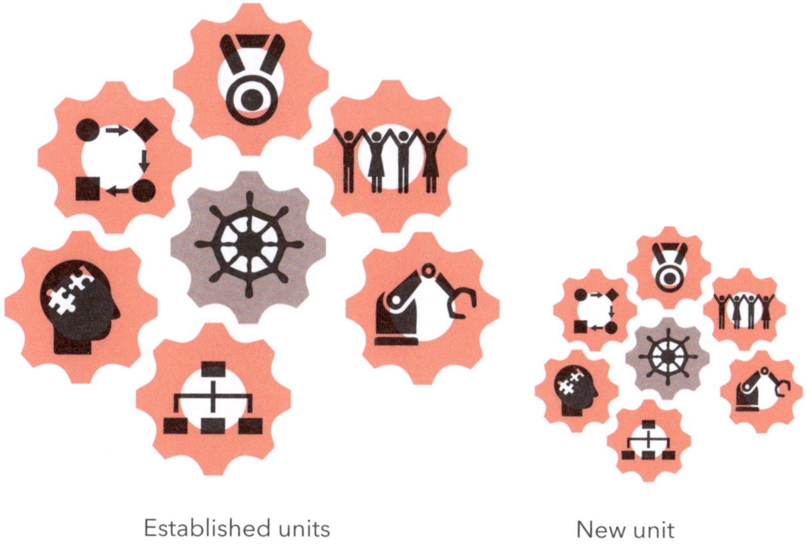

Figure 3.3 Two sets of cogs

The new unit has an explicit goal of innovation and is encouraged to develop a culture characterized by entrepreneurship, risk-taking, fast pace, and flexibility. Normally, the organizational structure in the new unit will be more adaptive and freer than in the established part of the business. Control and reward systems are linked to milestones and growth rather than margins, productivity and traditional KPIs. People are often recruited from outside to ensure that the unit is constructed to become something completely different from the established ones. The management of the new unit should be visionary and involved rather than controlling. In other words, this is about building up a parallel organization where the various elements (cogs) look completely different than those in the established firm in order to ensure innovation.

The new entity is constructed as a start-up; however, it will also have an important competitive advantage compared to the start-ups as it receives resources from the established firm and can draw on complementary capabilities in the established firm. Although there are obvious links between the established firm and the new unit, in an initial phase it is important to ensure sufficient separation – this is what provides space for innovation. Table 3.1 highlights some of the most important differences in the cogs between the established units in the firm and the innovative unit.

Table 3.1 Comparing the cogs in the established and innovative units

Dimensions in the cog model	The established business	The innovative unit
Structure	Hierarchy and formal structure	Adaptive and looser structure like a start-up
Leadership and Management	Hierarchical management with a focus on managing, controlling and further developing the operative enterprise	Focus on visionary and empowering leadership rather than controlling
Culture	Efficiency, low risk, quality, customers	Entrepreneurship, risk-taking, pace and flexibility. The unit develops a distinct culture and identity that differs from the established one
Work Processes	Standardized processes aimed at efficiency, quality, incremental improvements	The new unit develops distinctive processes, routines. Often makes use of agile work processes People are often recruited externally
Incentives, control, and reward	Margins, productivity. Target amounts linked to costs and profitability	Milestones and growth rather than margins, productivity and traditional KPIs

How and why the ambidextrous solution works

The solution we have outlined above is often referred to as structural ambidexterity. There are obviously some important structural aspects and these are perhaps the most visible feature, but the establishment of a new unit will rarely in itself ensure innovation. When taking a closer look at the solution, it is actually more a question of management.

Structural ambidexterity has been adopted by firms across industries and nations and there is a vast research literature documenting its effects (O'Reilly & Tushman, 2013; 2016). However, this does not mean that it is unproblematic or simple. We will come back to some of the most well-known challenges with this solution and the managerial implications, but we will first explain how and why it works.

By developing a new and innovative unit alongside the established business, an opportunity is created to start from scratch and recruit the new competence that is needed, together with building a culture that supports renewal. The new unit functions almost like a start-up and therefore avoids being hampered by structural and cultural inertia and any other "baggage" that lies in the established business. Legacy can of course also be valuable during change and innovation, but if the established firm is struggling to find space for renewal, then the ambidextrous solution can be helpful.

The solution also works through specialization. Separation allows for clearly divided tasks. The new unit will drive innovation and renewal, while established units will continue to run the existing business. Because the revenues come from the established business, so it will not be possible to focus solely on the new. However, specialization does not mean that all development and innovation ceases in the established units.

Established firm units should continuously improve and further development the existing business. This division means that employees who prefer developing the existing business can spend time and resources on it, and do not have to worry about radical innovation; the new unit takes care of that. Employees who want to develop something completely new and different can apply to the new unit. This division also makes it possible to create competing products and services in the new unit if this is seen as necessary. For many years, Schibsted has used the ambidextrous solution to ensure innovation, based on a philosophy that it is better to cannibalize oneself than leave this to the competitors.

As mentioned, the ambidextrous solution could be suitable if there is substantial resistance in the firm or if daily operations tend to consume all time and resources. This is because the ambidextrous organization creates space for innovation and renewal. The solution can also be suitable if there is a great deal of uncertainty surrounding innovation – for instance, what and how to innovate, or the right time for innovation. The ambidextrous solution allows experimentation on a small scale and without the established firm being changed, hampered or otherwise negatively affected. Trial and error are possible within the new unit.

The solution also provides flexibility if the time for renewal is unclear, since the new can co-exist alongside the established over a long period. For example, in the oil and energy industry, there obviously has to be a switch to more sustainable energy sources than oil, but the exact timing of when offshore wind or other alternative energy sources succeed is more uncertain, particularly as the geopolitical situation has created challenges in the supply of energy. The same applied to the newspaper industry when the Internet gained recognition and news began to be offered online for free. In many media houses, online newspapers were published alongside the established ones, and even today (25 years later) the traditional paper newspapers exist side-by-side with new ways of delivering news and other content. Therefore, the ambidextrous solution affords the flexibility to work with new innovative business ideas in conjunction with existing business over time. The ambidextrous solution does not require a radical change overnight, but it does involve some other challenges that can feel demanding for management. We discuss this in more detail below.

How to manage the ambidextrous solution

As mentioned before, the structural measures are perhaps the most visible and obvious, while the managerial issues are just as important and often more demanding. Consider what happens when you establish a new unit that gets a large degree of autonomy to create itself alongside the established business units and at the same time seizes both human and financial resources. Tensions can quickly arise between the established business units and the new one. Some ambidextrous firms have experienced that there emerges an A team and a B team, where the new one is given high status and lots of attention but in reality it is the established business units that are financing "the fun."

Senior management must therefore communicate a clear overarching strategic objective and vision that embraces both the new unit and the established one, emphasizing the need for a shared understanding. Senior management must illustrate what binds the various units together and show that there is a common ambition for the entire firm; if one part succeeds, the other will also benefit. Even if the new unit should develop a culture and way of working more in line with entrepreneurial activity, a common set of values and a common identity for the entire enterprise should be able to counteract tensions between the established unit and the new one. In addition, it is important that senior management shows unified support. Employees quickly observe disagreements or a lack of agreement among senior managers. Finally, the management must expect and accept that tensions may occur, and that they must be able to handle such conflicts. O'Reilly and Tushman (2016) summarized the role of senior management as follows:

- Clear overarching, strategic goals and visions that unite the entire firm
- Common set of values and identity
- Unified senior management support
- Research and innovation occur in own separate unit
- Senior management must tolerate and be able to handle tensions

Since structural ambidexterity clearly distinguishes between exploitation and exploration/innovation, allowing the units and the people within them to specialize, in reality it is the senior management who must be ambidextrous. Everyone else in the business is allowed to specialize. Thus, senior management has a central role in making the ambidextrous solution function in an effective way.

In addition to senior management, the head of the new unit plays an important role. In order for the ambidextrous solution to deliver on the mandate for innovation, the head of the new unit must protect the unit and the employees so that they can build something distinctive and avoid being overwhelmed by requirements from the established business. The head of the new unit must simultaneously build the unit's legitimacy within the company, and then it is usually important not to become too distinctive. If the innovative unit becomes altogether different and distinctive, it will quickly be pushed out by the rest of the firm. Especially as time passes, it will be important to build bridges to the established units. Managers of new, innovative units often also spend a lot of time on upward management, which is about ensuring continued support and resources from senior management. Stensaker (2018) summarized the role of head of the new unit as follows:

- Build something distinctive within the new unit by shielding the unit and employees
- Build the unit's legitimacy
- Gradually build bridges to the established units
- Work upwards to secure future support, resources and understanding

So far, the research literature has mainly concentrated on how the ambidextrous solution can be established. In the RaCE project at NHH, we have investigated how the ambidextrous solution develops over time, and it shows that as the new unit develops, new possibilities and challenges emerge.

In the early phase, which we know most about from research, separation and screening are important. The whole point of the solution is just to create the space to develop something completely new and different; therefore, the new unit must be as separate as possible and develop with a large degree of autonomy. In the beginning, this is largely about providing room to grow bigger and stronger in a different way. If the unit is unsuccessful, it will be important to evaluate whether and possibly when it should be shut down. If the new entity succeeds, it may become perceived as an even greater threat to the established units. A success will also entail the need to scale the innovation and the unit.

We mentioned earlier that the competitive advantage of the new entity versus start-ups is precisely its connection to the established unit. At the start, the unit receives resources from the established unit, but eventually it can also benefit from operational capacity and the ability to put new products and services into operation and scale this. In the even longer term, the new unit will be able to contribute to renewing the entire established business. Therefore, as a new unit succeeds in developing a new business, it will therefore become important to build bridges to the established units.

In the next section we take a closer look at a concrete case where the ambidextrous solution was used to facilitate innovation and renewal. It is important to specify that in practice there will be different versions of the solution.

CASE 3.1
GXN – THE GREEN THINK TANK IN THE ARCHITECTURE FIRM 3XN[2]

To illustrate the ambidextrous model, we will draw on a case from Denmark. It shows how an established firm can renew itself in a more sustainable direction with help of the ambidextrous solution. While the case contains some classic characteristics of the ambidextrous solution, it also has some peculiarities. For example, in this case there is never any discussion about the new unit having to compete with the established one; it should just support and complement it.

Background on 3XN

3XN is a Danish architecture firm in Copenhagen with satellite offices in New York, Stockholm, and London. 3XN has had success internationally, for instance as the designer of office buildings with zero emissions (net zero carbon) on Broadgate in central London, the north island at Rigshospitalet in Copenhagen, the fish market in Sydney and the Olympic House at the headquarters of the IOC.

The philosophy for 3XN is that architecture shapes behavior. Everything 3XN does is based on a vision of enriching people's lives by shaping the buildings in which they live and work, as well as their surroundings. The company was established in 1986 by three young architects, all with the last name of Nielsen – hence the name 3XN. The Scandinavian origins and the tradition of simple, aesthetic architecture and humanistic values in their working life continue as a strong foundation, even though today's working environment is internationally oriented and represents over twenty nationalities.

3XN establishes GXN as a sustainable, innovative unit

Like many other established firms, 3XN perceived it as demanding to find time for innovation at the same time as dealing with daily operations. There were few opportunities to develop and test innovative solutions within its current construction projects. There was rarely room for research, there was always a customer and a deliverable that had to be prioritized, and it was too risky both in terms of costs and time to experiment with ongoing projects.

Therefore in 2007, the management of 3XN established a separate unit – GXN – with the aim of longer-term and more sustainable innovation. G stands for "green" and thus indicates the sustainable and ecological design factor. From the beginning, GXN was organized as a separate legal entity within 3XN, with

2 This case is based on conversations and interviews with the manager of GXN together with a RaCE master's thesis written by Valentina Gonzalez Båkind and Marte Valleraunet Grønli during spring 2020. The case has been developed for the book.

its own business plan aiming to break even in just a few years' time, but soon after its establishment, the financial crisis occurred. While others downsized and shut down, 3XN stuck to its conviction of sustainable innovation, and its parent company gave the new entity support to survive through its early years.

Kasper Guldager Jensen was recruited as the leader of GXN. He was educated as an architect and had written his final project thesis on "New material and technologies," and he was a driving force in sustainability, the use of new materials, and new technology. Jensen describes his background as follows:

> I had spent my time on competitive architecture, which means constantly trying to design winning projects, but without having time to investigate if there were opportunities in other industries, in other materials, or in other business models.

GXN's mandate was to build a research department within 3XN. In accordance with the ambidextrous solution, the idea was to create space to develop something new; in this case, it was about innovative, sustainable solutions within architecture and the construction industry. As mentioned previously, the background was that there was not much acceptance for experimentation in ongoing projects, and this not only concerned 3XN, but the entire industry too. 3XN's challenge is described as follows:

> In the construction industry, you always try to get the best product and the best result. But it also binds you to specific phases where you are constantly under pressure in relation to the next incremental goal and constantly have to contend with a given budget, so in reality you end up designing architecture that is the best we have at a given time. There is not a great deal of time to try out something new that you do not have clue will work. This is not an industry where you are rewarded for experimentation ... preferably ideas should be proven and tested on other buildings. So GXN became a kind of "test chamber" where we could develop, document and test new solutions.

Thus, by establishing a separate unit, it created an opportunity to work with a longer-term view. Right from the start, GXN's work was characterized by an openness and ability to draw on knowledge from many different areas – not just architecture. In this unit, ideas were to be launched, tested, and allowed to mature, then implemented in practice later in 3XN.

> We have created a space to develop and draw out knowledge from others – a green think tank where ideas can mature, and possibilities and solutions could later be implemented in our [3XN] practice.

Profitability requirements and key performance indicators

A business plan was to be developed during the first year. Educated as an architect, Jensen had no experience in this, but he received good advice from more experienced managers in the parent company 3XN and spent the first year building up a network of business relations and surveying the market. In addition, he developed a mission, vision, and strategy for the unit. GXN closely connected its mission to its parent company. On GXN's website we can read, among other things:

> We provide knowledge about wellbeing in the interplay between physical environment, social interaction and increased engagement and effectiveness.

In the second year, GXN worked according to a criterion of success: that the outside world should know about GXN, and that the unit should become a reference point for sustainability within the industry. A number of partnerships were established, and the network around the unit grew.

In the third year, GXN was to be financially independent. This was roughly successful. During that year, Jensen was able not only able to pay his own salary, he also recruited his first employees. Sustainability meant not only green but also developing an economically sustainable GXN. The goal was not to secure the greatest possible return, it was that the unit should finance its own operations so that it did not drain the parent company of resources. At the same time, it should contribute to renewing and challenging the established methodologies within architecture and construction so that the entire 3XN would become more sustainable.

GXN's business areas are threefold:

1. Research on sustainable construction and architecture
2. Construction projects in collaboration with 3XN
3. Consultancy on sustainable construction and architecture

The research is applied and market-focused and with a stated objective that the activity should create value and that ideas should be able to be commercialized and scaled. All research is openly available ("open source"), which means that the knowledge generated can be used by all interested parties, including competitors. The research division is primarily financed through research project funds, which operates with a small deficit. The second part of the business, which cooperates with 3XN, does not aim for profits, thus it breaks even, and no overhead is calculated. The third part of the business – the consulting business – generates the lion's share of the income and produces a profit. Consulting services are sold externally, but not to competing architectural firms.

Autonomy and synergy

The GXN management has a large degree of autonomy and at the same time there are clear, important, and valuable links to 3XN. The clearest connection to 3XN is naturally the part that runs collaborative projects. Jensen describes these synergies as follows:

> When we conduct research, it must be applied. We can draw on the architectural firm's knowledge of the market. We can also draw on knowledge about the needs of architects. And if we work with more technical questions, we can draw on the exterior elevation specialists or interior design specialists in 3XN and invite them into our focus groups. Therefore, collaboration with 3XN is very valuable because it gives us a finger on the pulse; we gain insight into the demands and needs of the architectural firms.

The synergies between GXN and 3XN are made possible, among other things, by co-location; there are no geographical or physical differences separating the two units. Knowledge and experience flow across organizational boundaries. This appears to be in line with the philosophy that architecture shapes behavior. If one had created sharp physical divisions between the two environments, synergies, the sharing of knowledge, and collaboration would all suffer. At the same time, the organizational separation is described as important. We will elaborate on this further below.

The unit was established with a clearly defined purpose that would substantiate 3XN's purpose and strategy, and there do not seem to be any competing elements that trigger tensions or resistance in the established unit. The profitability requirement also means that there is limited risk of any tensions linked to the use of resources. Thus, geographical distance also becomes less important because known tensions between established units and the new unit do not seem to be particularly prominent here. What can create frustration in GXN is when new knowledge and insight are sidelined. It can be frustrating to those who work full time trying to evolve and renew existing knowledge when there is no time, opportunity, or will to make use of these new insights.

As mentioned, GXN is made up of many different professional areas of expertise. The whole culture appears open and curious. In addition to architects, the unit has recruited psychologists, anthropologists, biologists, and engineers. External relations also exemplify openness to a large degree. Breadth in competence is seen as inspiring and potentially relevant and useful.

> All our projects are set up with external partners. We see ourselves as a Swiss army knife where we can borrow and steal from other disciplines and create a synthesis, which we then test in practice.

Innovative solutions

There are primarily three services GXN delivers: behavioral design, digital design and circular design.

Behavioral design is based on knowledge of how architecture shapes behavior. In this area, GXN has established a research cluster with five Ph.Ds. An example is figuring out how a staircase can become a central meeting place. This was tested at an upper secondary school in Copenhagen, where meeting places were created on the stairs with the intention of stimulating learning. This insight was then further developed in a project for the Olympic Committee, where the architecture also included the Olympic rings in the staircase design. GXN is concerned with the value a building creates for the people who use the building and applies a multidimensional approach to costs. In addition to working with construction costs, GXN is concerned with lifetime costs and human costs:

> If we can link behavior to architecture, we can make a large difference; for example, if 30% of productivity can be connected to a good vs. a poor physical environment. We also visit "the crime scene" after we have finished the building. Most architects don't do that, but we like to take pictures of the buildings when there are people present, then to examine and analyze how the buildings are used.

The quote above illustrates the long-term thinking and understanding of value created through use. By systematically studying how buildings are used, new knowledge is developed about value creation, lifetime costs and human costs that can be included into the next building project.

Digital design is about how buildings are set up and operated. This includes how waste can be reduced. Among other things, GXN has developed a product – a small bird – that warns of poor indoor climate. It is sold to schools and private homes.

Circular design is linked to the footprint of the entire industry. Here one looks to nature and constructs as a basis an ecosystem approach similar to that in biology where everything is used and nothing goes to waste. The underlying philosophy here is based on circular thinking. A specific example here is a conference hotel with a green profile ("Green Solution House") where participants can learn about green alternatives, or just use the hotel as a conference arena. Another example is consultancy for nations (such as the Danish government) and regions/cities (like Amsterdam); such work takes place in partnership. A third concrete example is the publication of the book *Building a Circular Future*, which shows that even though recycling is big in Denmark, the value of its recycling is only 2% of the potential. Within circular design, work is also being done to make buildings less static and more dynamic so that they can be used in different ways: built up and taken down easily and quickly, inspired, among other things, by Lego bricks.

Results so far

After 12 years, GXN has grown from one employee (out of a total of 140 employees in 3XN) to 20. The unit is thereby larger and more significant within the parent company. As mentioned, GXN is also profitable and there are a number of new business opportunities in the pipeline. While in the initial phase they knocked on the doors of others to gain strategic collaborations, now the company is approached by others who want GXN as a strategic partner. GXN does something different that distinguishes the company from competing architectural firms, and as such, this unit also strengthens the overall brand value of 3XN.

GXN has also moved 3XN higher in the value chain by becoming a door opener to new customers who seek innovative and sustainable solutions. For instance, GXN was invited to pitch a project for Elon Musk. Moreover, the exposure they have puts them into contact with talented people they can recruit to the firm.

The path forward

Although GXN has had healthy growth and is now profitable, there are no plans to (re)integrate GXN into 3XN or to spin the unit off into a separate company. The five owners and partners in 3XN also own GXN, so they feel that they are in the same boat and have the same interests. By structurally separating 3XN, opportunities are created to capitalize on the synergies. The separate organization maintains the ability to explore and test new innovative solutions:

> In 3XN, people do what they do best. But in GXN we don't need to have the answers and know what is best. We have more questions than answers and we don't need to deliver … we can explore the market, the materials, collaborate, trial and error …, we must be able to drive the two different worlds forward, but then at the Christmas table we are all together. Mainly it is the structures, the routines and the pace that are different.

It seems obvious that 3XN has found a fruitful coexistence with GXN where the synergies and values are created through the close but distinctly different work done in the two units. The ambidextrous solution makes this possible by giving GXN the freedom to work with a completely different time perspective and without having to prioritize ongoing deliveries at all times.

CASE 3.2
VG, HIMLA AND VIPPS – DEVELOPMENT OF THE AMBIDEXTROUS ORGANIZATION OVER TIME[3]

In the case above, we saw that 3XN chose to keep the innovative unit GXN separate, even after twelve years, and there are no plans to integrate the two. However, this is not a given. The original theory of ambidexterity suggests that renewal takes place by first concentrating the innovation in the separate unit, but after a certain time – and especially if the innovative unit is successful – integrating it into the established parts of the business and thereby renewing the entire firm. We have seen this, among other things, in VG, which is part of the Schibsted group. The ambidextrous solution can also evolve along other trajectories, like Himla in Fana Sparebank, where a new brand was developed using the ambidextrous model. Below, we draw on three short cases to describe different ways in which innovation using the ambidextrous solution can develop over time.

VG and Schibsted – the ambidextrous solution set into system

The media industry has lived with the threat of disruption for a long time and has extensive experience with the ambidextrous solution. Some of the first research articles and teaching cases that were published on the ambidextrous solution were about the newspaper industry and the radical changes the newspapers faced in connection with the internet. Suddenly, most people could get free access to news. USA Today, Schibsted and a number of other newspapers established separate organizational units for online newspapers. Journalists and others who worked with traditional print media were skeptical; they believed, among other things, that online news would not be of the same quality and that in-depth journalism would suffer. The ambidextrous model helped to create a space for the online newspapers to develop in a slightly different direction from the print newspapers, with different expertise related to technology and how new technology can be used to develop and convey the news image. Gard Steiro, who in 2021 is editor of VG (which is one of several newspapers within the Schibsted group), has described how his way into the Schibsted group and the media industry was through the online newspaper Bergens Tidende (BT.no). He did not have the traditional journalist training, but because Schibsted wanted new and different thinkers, they recruited people

3 The information is taken from research within the RaCE project at NHH including from the doctoral work of Justin Harlan, conversations with managers at Fana Sparebank, and development of the teaching case Vipps at NHH Executive.

with different backgrounds to the online newspapers; therefore, an opportunity arose for Steiro and many others. The ambidextrous solution can be effective if there is great resistance in the established business. Steiro describes VG's thinking on innovation as follows:

> The culture inbuilt in the walls did not allow the new ideas to grow. But when it had become strong enough (in a separate unit), it was integrated into the parent company. This then became the new engine.

Just like the parent company Schibsted, VG has diligently used the ambidextrous solution. Time and again, VG has established a separate unit to drive innovation, whether it has been about online newspapers, mobile-based news, multimedia, or TV/video. The innovative unit has existed side-by-side with the established units for five to seven years. When the innovative unit succeeds, both in the market and financially, it is reintegrated with the established units and the expertise that has been developed "spills over" to the established units in the newspaper house. One of the interesting things about VG is that they do this time and time again. As the quote above describes, these new units are seen as "engines" for innovation, and the company has followed roughly the same "recipe" over and over again. They have implemented the ambidextrous model and built a muscle and capacity linked to exactly this way of driving innovation. This does not mean that this is the only way VG works with innovation, but it is a prominent, clear and in the end, a well-known model in the company.

Some of what the VG management itself believes is crucial for success is:

- The leader of the innovative unit must have a high degree of legitimacy. Torry Pedersen was chief of VG multimedia, and when he was given responsibility for the innovative unit, he was already a bright star. The department was located in an alcove under the stairs, but everyone wanted to be there – everyone wanted to work with Torry.
- If the innovation is driven by new technology, the new unit must ensure that it has the right skills and recruit employees who understand the technology and how it can be used in product/service development.
- The new entity must be financially secure so that it does not spend all its time hunting for funding.
- The new unit should have a clear and tangible mandate. In VG there has been relatively little uncertainty about what the innovative units are going to do because the units are only established once the management has developed a clear

picture of what is going to be worked on.
- The new units must be separate from the established ones.

Although the new units in VG are established as separate units, they are collocated with the rest of VG. All employees sit in the same locations, but in their work, they are 100% dedicated to either the new unit or established units. The culture that emerges in the new unit is also often completely different, and in some cases employees in the innovative unit have clearly marked the difference from the established ones through dress code or physical markers to clarify that "this is our space" and "we are different".

Just like in the 3XN/GXN case, VG's solution is based on structural separation while maintaining geographical proximity. This enables the sharing of knowledge. But unlike 3XN/GXN, VG (and Schibsted) allows competition and cannibalization. The new is built side-by-side with the established – not only to supplement and complement, but potentially to take over. The new unit has a mandate that explicitly allows internal competition with and cannibalization of other entities. The idea is that if the new thing "takes off", it is better that it happens within VG's walls than if it happens at a competitor.

If the new unit succeeds with its new development and moves into operational mode, it may be beneficial to bring it back into the established unit. In addition to VG, many media houses have done this with their online newspapers. After building up the online news alongside the print media using the ambidextrous solution, the need arose to deliver news across different channels (print, online, TV, etc.). It then made more sense to organize the news providers together to avoid the duplication of activities. In other words, when the new unit "takes off" and goes into operational mode, it can be reintegrated. The purpose is then that it should influence and further develop the established unit at the same time as the established unit provides power and resources to scale and operate the new business.

In VG's case, the time for reintegration has been after approximately five to seven years. In other words, the new unit has been allowed to operate under different frameworks and conditions for several years. There are three main criteria that are used as a basis for assessing if and when innovative units should be reintegrated into VG:

1. Is the unit viable? Has it established a clear position in the market?
2. Does the entity have legitimacy? Do the people and tasks in the unit have sufficient legitimacy for it to challenge the established unit rather than being swallowed by the culture in the established unit? If not, then reintegration could stifle the new unit.

3. Is the unit profitable? Profitability will contribute to legitimacy but is also an important criterion in itself for further investment.

As mentioned, VG and Schibsted have developed a systematic approach to the ambidextrous solution, yet reintegration does not always take place. FINN.no started as a separate unit that ran online classified ads within Schibsted, but when the unit eventually grew large and strong, it was spun off into a separate company. In other words, it is not a given that innovative units that succeed will be reintegrated. In large corporations such as Schibsted, we can find several different modes of innovation and renewal.

Vipps – the innovative unit is eventually spun off

Vipps is another example of an innovation that emerged within a large and established player. At the time, DNB used a combination of the ambidextrous solution and agile working methods. A few years after the mobile payment service Vipps took the Norwegian market by storm, it was separated from DNB and several new owners were brought on board. We describe the Vipps case in more detail later in this book (see Chapter 8). The point of introducing it here is to illustrate how new services that are developed by an established player through an ambidextrous solution can take different trajectories over time.

When DNB chose to invest in a mobile payment solution, the management considered various alternatives. An alternative was to continue a collaboration with Telenor, with whom they had over ten years of experience. Another option was to initiate a collaboration with Danske Bank, which already had a mobile payment solution (MobilePay) in the Danish market. A third alternative was to develop a separate solution for the Norwegian market. DNB chose to invest alone, and in order to succeed, a separate unit was established that worked according to agile principles. The time aspect was crucial since a mobile payment solution would have substantial first-mover advantage. The network effect of being first made it highly likely that the winner would take it all.

The time aspect and the competitive situation meant that few people knew about the work that was done to develop Vipps. Even if the very best resources were extracted from DNB to work with Vipps, it did not create significant friction, as an explicit focus on competing services (à la VG) would have done. However, some tensions emerged because the relocation of IT resources meant that other projects were downgraded and postponed.

Vipps took the market by storm and in a short time became Norway's number one mobile payment solution. After ten days, Vipps had 100 000 users; this figure grew to one million before six months had passed. During its first year it had two million downloads, but because the service was free, Vipps didn't make money.

Even though Vipps had taken the market for mobile payments in Norway, management explored potential partnerships to ensure future competitiveness.

> Vipps lacked BankAxept. Vipps lacked an immediate payment solution from account-to-account. Vipps lacked enthusiasm from the rest of the banks in Norway. And Vipps lacked a platform for further expansion abroad. In addition, the purchasing power vis-à-vis the person who processed the transactions, namely Nets, was weakened by standing alone. (Vipps teaching case, NHHE)

This was some of the background to Vipps being spun out and new owners (the savings banks) being invited in. The management and the board assessed the growth and development opportunities to be stronger outside of DNB. This shows how new innovative services can start their development within the boundaries of established firms and later be spun out and developed further outside – often with the established player as a central owner further on in the process.

Himla – the innovative entity develops into a separate brand that expands into new areas

Innovative services that are born through the ambidextrous model can also follow other trajectories. The new service can be developed into a separate brand. For example, Fana Sparebank did this when they developed a new low-cost concept in real estate – Himla – with the ambidextrous solution. The new and innovative unit was used as a springboard to further develop a new brand (Himla) which was then expanded to new geographic markets (from Bergen to Oslo) and new product markets (from real estate to banking).

The idea for Himla Eiendom came from Fana Sparebank's real estate brokerage department. One of the employees asked the question "Why should it be so expensive to buy/sell a house?". At this time, new players had entered the market offering real estate brokerage at a fixed low price. Fana Sparebank sensed the development in the industry and seized the opportunity by establishing a separate unit that would develop a fully digital brokerage service at a fixed low price of NOK 30 000. This was less than a third of the average brokerage price in the market in Bergen and would thus potentially not only compete with but also cannibalize Fana Sparebank's established property brokerage service. The new unit recruited technological expertise and built up the brokerage service based on existing technology, but with a completely different structure, more agile work processes and team-based incentive systems. Brokers would work in teams and not be profiled as individuals with their own portfolios. They received a fixed salary and joint bonus. Everything took place digitally, and the work was made more efficient. They did not carry out "free and non-binding valuations" – which took up valuable time in more traditional real estate work. The service was developed in two months. After six months, Himla Eiendomsmegling had taken a market share of 3%, which corresponded to half the market share of the traditional real estate department in the bank. The new service came as an addition to the established service and did not cannibalize the established unit's market share. So even though there was a threat of cannibalization, this didn't happen.

The work to develop a low-cost service did not go unnoticed. It created friction internally and among competitors in the market. Not everyone liked the idea of establishing a service with a fixed low price. Among other things, it was argued that it destroyed the market, but there were also other low-price offers in the market, so Fana Sparebank was not the first to offer this type of service.

Internally in Fana Sparebank, a win-win collaboration developed between Himla and the established property service. Customers were referred across the units, and technological solutions that had been developed for Himla helped to make the established unit more efficient. By offering both fixed low prices and full-service entities, the bank covered a larger part of the market. The year after the establishment of Himla Eiendom in Bergen, Fana Sparebank opened a branch in Oslo.

In addition, the development of Himla Eiendom has created an opportunity to expand the new all-digital, low-cost concept to other services. In 2019, Fana Sparebank decided to establish Himla Bank as a fully digital solution within the Himla brand. In 2020, Himla Bank was launched. In this sense, a new service developed through the ambidextrous model can allow the building of a new brand (based on a different structure, incentive systems and other work processes) which can be expanded to other geographical markets and other product and service areas.

Comparing the different trajectories

The cases above show how the ambidextrous solution can create various opportunities and challenges over time and how, over long-term, it can morph into other organizational solutions for innovation. It is not necessarily the case that the trajectory is planned from the start, but the cases above show how a given solution can allow different paths. Established firms that choose to innovate through the ambidextrous solution should reflect on the following questions:

- How much time should the new entity be given to experiment with innovation? If scarce resources are allocated to the new unit over a long period of time without it succeeding in innovation, should the innovative unit then be shut down?

- Does the innovative unit have good relations with the established business, so that the combination will constitute a competitive advantage?
- Should the innovative unit be reintegrated into the established business? If the competences, the culture and the work processes developed in the new unit will also contribute to renewing the established one, then this may be appropriate. The VG case provides some criteria that can contribute to the assessment of the right time for reintegration.
- Should the innovative unit be completely spun out of the established firm and potentially become a competitor? If the new entity will have better growth potential outside the established firm (possibly with several/other owners), then this may be appropriate.

Chapter 4

Innovation at the edge

In this chapter, we draw on insights from Deloitte and our own analyses to describe how innovation can take place at the edge of the established firm (Hagel et al., 2019; Hagel, 2019). In contrast to the ambidextrous solution, there is limited academic research that describes innovation at the edge, so here we draw on observations in practice and our analyses of these, as well as Deloitte's description of how innovation in established firms can occur at the edge. Therefore, this chapter contains fewer references than some of the other chapters. Since this solution is not well known, we also found fewer case examples. However, we introduce two interesting cases that illustrate the edge solution. Deloitte's Center for the Edge shows how the company applies this thinking not only to clients but also to its own organization. We also see a similar solution with DNB's entity, New Tech Lab.

What does it mean to innovate at the edge?

Innovation at the edge means that innovation is allowed to grow at the peripheries of the established firm. It can be in the form of a separate unit that we described earlier through the ambidextrous model, but it does not need to be so formalized. Innovation at the edge also has a number of other components that distinguish it from the ambidextrous model, and we will describe these below.

Sensing capabilities are developed through innovation at the edge. This happens primarily through interaction and connection between external and internal people. Innovation at the edge also fosters collective engagement, particularly among those who work at the edge.

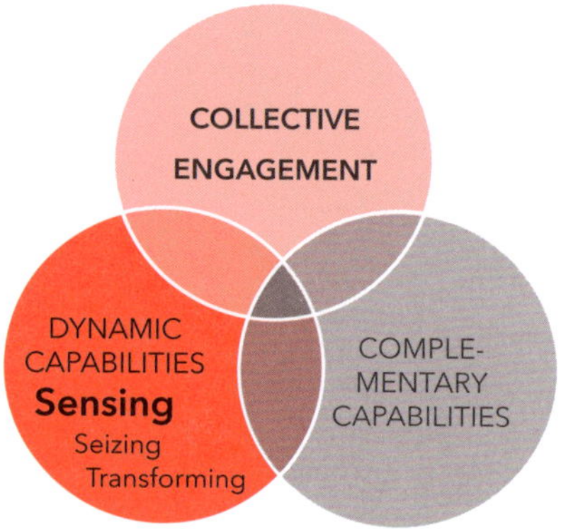

Figure 4.1 How innovation at the edge contributes to innovation capacity

To understand innovation at the edge, we distinguish between the core business and non-core. While the core refers to the most important activities within the existing business, non-core refers to supporting activities that tend to be more loosely connected to the existing business. The portfolio perspective that we introduced in Chapter 1 (see Figure 1.3) illustrates how innovation can happen near to the core or far away from the core. Innovation at the edge will typically include activities and business that are far away from the core. These can be radically different and do not need to be concrete (in terms of a specific product or service) or have a clear mandate.

Employees who operate at the edge typically orient themselves to the external environment to quickly pick up opportunities that arise due to radical changes in or around the industry. An advantage of operating at the edge is that it can be easier to initiate and invest in innovation here. Because the edge is not perceived as important and interesting as the core business, activities at the edge can avoid burdensome internal processes in the organization (Hagel et al., 2019).

Just as with the ambidextrous model, the idea behind innovating at the edge is about creating space for completely different ideas and business opportunities. However, in contrast to the ambidextrous model, innovation at the edge should avoid cannibalizing existing income streams to the greatest extent possible. In the long-term, the edge may be able to help transform the core. If and when that happens, it will be important that the edge can be scaled up so that the organization changes its entire practice and business activities – including its core activities. It is therefore important that edge activity does not pose a direct threat to the core.

There are also some interesting nuances in how the new products and services are expected to transform the established part of the business. The ambidextrous solution is about establishing a new unit that provides space for new and different thinking, but which will eventually be integrated into the established business. Conversely, the edge model assumes that the established core will be drawn towards (and integrated into) that which is developed at the edge.

Thus, transformation and innovation within the established parts of the firm take place as the core moves towards the edge. The established firm is drawn towards the new opportunities. The new is never imposed upon the established, but what happens at the edge is expected to create enough buzz and interest that the established model seeks out the new. The underlying idea is that transformation requires positive motivation. According to innovation at the edge, one rarely achieves transformation through coercion or fear (Hagel, 2019). According to Hagel, positive motivation comes when economic rationale and emotions meet.

It is only when new and innovative products and services create financial results that other parts of the business (the established parts) will want to learn more about the new business opportunities. In other words, there is perceived to be a positive force behind innovation at the edge rather than fear, cannibalization, and threats. According to Hagel, this form of innovation will contribute to sustained and successful innovation at the product, technology, and business model level. However, we do not yet have clear, researchable evidence for this. Perhaps this is because the solution has not been well known within academia, but has rather been viewed as a variant of the ambidextrous solution? However, we believe that there are some important and interesting differences, especially in the underlying thinking around how the established parts of the business are affected and renewed.

Innovation at the edge avoids triggering the immune system

There are a number of known factors which suggest that established firms will react negatively to change and innovation. Some refer to this as triggering the business's immune system (Hagel, 2019). The underlying factors that help to explain why radical innovation must take place at the edge rather than at the core include:

1. *Change and innovation at the core involves an uncertain outcome.* A company's core business has been developed and improved over a long time. Making significant changes to the core could be perceived as risky. If the project fails, it can have major consequences for the company's financial performance. Even if some key managers and change agents in the business have great faith in change and innovation, other managers will be able to create resistance that weakens or kills the initiative through their communication and behavior.
2. *Change and innovation at the core require a great deal of resources.* Changing the organization's core business requires resources and the will to accept risk during a transition period. Even if the business has sufficient resources to change the core, a reallocation of resources could be perceived as a threat to or downgrading of daily operations. It can also take a long time before the business achieves the values and sees the effects of the innovation.
3. *Change and innovation at the core demands a great deal of time.* A great amount of tensions in the organization can be distracting and time-consuming. If there is passive resistance, then an illusion of progress can be created, where the stakeholders appear to agree during meetings, but behave passively afterwards by neglecting to act, or more actively opposing the initiative behind the scenes.

These three factors can create unforeseen political and economic consequences in the organization, which in turn delay and derail change and innovation. By establishing an edge initiative, such known challenges can be minimized or even avoided because innovation will then affect the core to a lesser extent. The edge is far away from the core, marginal in size, and does not require notable resources or investment. In some cases, it flies completely under the radar.

In order to implement innovation at the edge, there are four important factors that must be considered: mobilization of resources, use of technology, and measurement of results together with renewal of the established business.

Mobilizing resources

To avoid triggering the immune system, the edge should not depend on reallocation of existing resources but instead bring in new ones. New additional resources and support can be obtained from external actors. In addition to increasing the overall set of resources, such collaboration with external actors will help to build a larger network in the development of initiatives. At the same time, those working at the edge can get rapid feedback and response from the environment so that learning can be reiterated and accelerated. Developing good collaborations with external entities will also contribute to increased legitimacy for edge activity. The development of long-term trust-based relationships is required rather than one-off transactions in order to be successful with external collaborations,

Recruitment of people to the edge should primarily be based on passion for solving challenges rather than seeking specific skills or the "best competence". Collective engagement and understanding of the uncertainty linked to innovative activity are central criteria in the mobilization of human resources. The assumption is that employees who are passionate about the initiatives at the edge are more likely to be excited about and succeed in tackling the unique challenges of innovation projects. Therefore, the edge should consist of individuals who seek new challenges and have a desire to learn. In addition to being skilled at exploration, the people at the edge need to be comfortable with trying, failing, and continuously learning from this. Initiatives at the edge often involve considerable uncertainty and are based on unknown or untapped potential. People who tackle risk, deal with ambiguity and are comfortable with trial and error will therefore be suitable at an edge.

In addition to the right team, it is important to have one or more sponsors at management level. The management must put its protective hand over the edge initiatives. The sponsor will act as a change agent who, in the long term, will contribute to transforming the established firm. The sponsor therefore needs both courage and persuasiveness so that the status quo can be challenged in a pragmatic rather than a conflict-seeking way. The edge is typically provided a minimum of resources. The idea is that this forces the edge to form external bonds and to be self-sufficient. Seen this way, the edge operates similarly to a venture capital firm, where investors make small, targeted investments and at the same time maintain high expectations for results. Limited financial resources will force the edge to utilize the cheapest resources, whether these are internal or external. This will also help to focus efforts on what provides the greatest value. The expectation is that the edge (just like a start-up) must show results before it comes back and asks for further funding.

Adoption of new technology

Innovation at the edge is often driven by opportunities and the exploitation of technological disruptions. But using the company's IT systems or joint services for technology creates dependencies to the core, something that can lead to the business becoming too involved in the edge and thus a hindrance to the independence the edge needs to succeed. To avoid this, the edge can utilize technologies outside of those offered by the core. In particular, it can be useful to rely on cloud computing, big data, and social media. There are several reasons why this can be beneficial. First, such technology is often inexpensive and easy to use. Secondly, such technology is accessible to many, which makes it easier to collaborate with external actors. Thirdly, new technology and digital solutions – especially social platforms or cloud computing – are powerful tools for quickly reaching out to many people and establishing contact with other players. Therefore, these often provide a wider reach than existing internal systems and enable broad collaboration on complex problems.

Measuring results

Measuring results is important for evaluating the edge's progress, but it is important that traditional target figures relating to income and costs do not govern the activity. Since the edge involves a completely different activity, traditional target figures will face a legitimacy challenge and the edge could find itself in a defensive position versus the core. The following parameters will be particularly relevant to assess edge initiatives:

1. Short-term milestones that measure the *activity* at the edge. These parameters should be easy to measure and adapt to the long-term goals of the edge initiative.
2. Measurement parameters that have a long-term time horizon. These will be linked to *growth* and should be seen in the context of developments in the market as a whole. Even though edge activity should avoid direct competition with the core, it is important to document – with the help of financial and/or operational targets – how the edge contributes to the whole. This will build the legitimacy of the edge.
3. It is also necessary to have a set of target figures for the edge's progress in terms of *collaboration with external actors*. These indicators will probably to be the key to predicting the long-term potential of the edge activity. Current measurement parameters can be the number of collaborations, the degree of trust-based and sustained relationships, as well as the degree

of complex problems that are solved through collaboration, and the extent to which all parties benefit from being part of a larger network.

4. A fourth important measurement parameter is the *degree of utilization of new technology*. This is important because this type of technology is expected to result in lower costs for the edge and make it easier to collaborate.

How the edge changes the established business

The solution that we have described here by innovating at the edge is largely about driving innovation disconnected from the core business. If we link this thinking to the cog model, we see that innovation at the edge, just like the ambidextrous solution, builds a separate set of cogs. But innovation at the edge is not as clearly defined in the form of a unit or a concrete mission, and it draws to a greater extent on the external environment and external partners. This approach to innovation will therefore in principle have little effect on the cogs in the established firm – at least initially. However, the ultimate goal is that when the edge succeeds, the established firm will want to learn from the edge and move in that direction. If we use the cog model, this means that the established environments that operate in the core business will eventually *desire* to change the way of working, structure, business model and the like. In this sense, the cogs of the core business will be affected and changed over the longer term in line with the edge.

Table 4.1 Edge solution versus the ambidextrous solution

Dimensions	The ambidextrous organization	Edge organization
Structure	Establish separate units that are given room to develop innovative products/services that eventually spill over and renew the core business.	Establish small innovation teams at the edges of the core that work on radically different products/services/business models driven by opportunities that new technology can represent. In the longer term, the edge can become the new core and/or contribute to transforming the core.
Management and governance	Senior management makes structural and leadership decisions tied to the establishment of an innovative unit. Senior management must secure resources, protect, and support the new unit.	The edge has an anchor in management which ensures a minimum of resources, protects and supports the unit. Ideas typically originate from others (zealots) rather than senior management.
Culture	The new unit develops its own identity and culture. This can challenge and threaten the established parts of the business.	The edge initiative is far from the core, and because it does not require a large amount of resources, it will often fly under the radar. It does not directly challenge the established firm nor its culture. In the long term, the edge can affect the established culture if the established moves towards the new.
Work processes	The new unit develops distinctive processes, routines and a distinct culture and identity. These are often more similar to a start-up than an established business. Agile work processes and teams are often used. During reintegration, new work processes will often be brought into the established units and "spill over".	The edge develops distinctive processes, routines and a distinct culture and identity. More like a start-up than an established business. Agile work processes are often used with frequent interactions with external partners and networks. The edge will not force its solutions and work processes on the core. Rather, the core may become curious and seek out the edge.
External partnership	External partnerships are not particularly prominent in the ambidextrous model, but the new unit can work closely with external partners if there is a need for this.	External partnerships are very important in the edge model. Here, it is not about only sporadic or occasional contact with external parties, but about building trust-based and long-term relationships that provide resources and expertise and enable idea creation, testing and iterations in the development of solutions.
Technology	Innovative unit can use other technological solutions.	New technology is used rather than the core systems of the established business. For example, cloud solutions, big data analytics and social platforms.
Incentives	Alternative incentive systems and KPIs are used in the innovative unit. It should absolutely not be measured on traditional KPIs.	Results are measured along four dimensions: (1) activity, (2) growth, (3) external relations and (4) use of new technology.

CASE 4.1
DELOITTE'S CENTER FOR THE EDGE[4]

In 2007, Deloitte established the *Center for the Edge* (C4E) in Silicon Valley, USA. The idea and vision to establish an internal research center as a think tank operating in the periphery of the established firm areas had matured for a long time. The goal was for C4E to produce insights, perspectives and reports on global and market changes and disruptions that would benefit Deloitte's clients and network. A particular area was how the rapid technological development would affect markets, industries, and the business models.

The ambition of C4E is to contribute to innovation in established firms by working at the edges of today's business and technology.

> ... our ambition is to help release the innovation potential in businesses. There's a lot of focus on start-ups ... but we think that if we can get established firms to become more resilient to disruptive changes and unlock the potential they have within them ... in a very smart or innovative way, then that's a lot more efficient than supporting two guys in a garage.

The C4E case illustrates the edge solution and how it can be used both in the work for Deloitte's clients, and internally in the company to drive innovation forward. Since the thinking behind the edge solution is taken from Deloitte, this case will show many similarities with the theory and highlight how it can be put into practice.

A key person in the establishment of C4E was John Hagel with his 40 years of experience from Silicon Valley as an entrepreneur and consultant. The idea of establishing C4E was born out of changes in the markets where key sponsors in the senior management of Deloitte saw a need to create something new. The idea quickly spread to other parts of the company as well. A few years after its establishment in San Francisco, separate C4E centers were established in Europe and afterward in Australia and Singapore. The various centers are relatively loosely connected to each other and have somewhat different focuses. While the United States (and partly also Australia) produces insight, the European units are more concerned with applying this insight in their work concerning the market.

C4E Europe has three main pillars in its work:

1. *Connecting* people and environments to accelerate innovation.

4 Information is assembled from interviews with key people in C4E and in Deloitte in connection with the research project RaCE. The case is developed for the book.

2. Producing new insights and new perspectives that lie at the edge of the established units.
3. *Influencing* by connecting the edge activity to the core activities in Deloitte and the work that is carried out for the clients.

The first pillar – connect: This is primarily about connecting external environments to business firms and connecting the internal to the external in new ways. All C4E centers are based on a philosophy that they must be independent of core activities – in other words, they are established at the edge, fully in line with the recommendations C4E conveys to its clients. C4E's services do not compete with the core but collaborate and support the core business in working with clients by producing insights, perspectives, and new methods. The idea is to connect Deloitte's managers, partners, and employees with an extensive network of external actors. This can involve think tanks like Singularity University, big techs, start-up communities or clients. Through open dialogue, experience and insight are shared, and this creates arenas for innovative thinking and the development of new ideas.

The second pillar – the edge: C4E is organized and operates at the edge of the core business in Deloitte so that each C4E is established as its own cost center and reports to the senior manager (CEO) in the region. Even if much of the staff's time in the centers is used to support and collaborate with the core business, the core is not charged directly for C4E's contributions.

> We're completely independent from our core business ... when someone asks about our budget, it would be like, "Hey, guys, we don't want to talk about that ... this is too important, that is just a small part of what we do ... And for this year, our budget is extremely low ... so don't go into it." So, we are protected by the CEO ... But in the beginning, we were also quite invisible to the majority of people at Deloitte ...

> The CEO is the only one who can keep us alive and protect us and help us grow.

This shows how important the internal support is, especially from senior management. Since C4E has no direct income linked to its activities, it is completely dependent on support from the CEO. Those who work in C4E feel that the biggest threat to its existence comes not from customers but from internal environments within Deloitte. Not all partners see the value in the center and the use of funds that go toward investing in the center, even if it is modest. C4E is based on a different business model than the established firm areas, which have revenue and cost responsibility. In contrast, C4E has a more long-term philosophy that is about helping to build relationships between the core business and the market, as well as inviting clients to become part of C4E's broad, innovative network. The purpose of establishing C4E is precisely to represent something other than the core business within professional services.

Therefore, C4E does not actively handle sales of its products and services – neither to clients nor internally within Deloitte. It works from the philosophy that change and innovation will only happen if people are motivated to do it. C4E therefore only wants to collaborate with people who actively request its insights and services.

> It might be a little tricky, but we made it explicit from the first moment onwards. If you don't want us, if you don't see the value in us – don't call us.

In line with the thinking about innovation from the edge, the management and target figures are different for C4E than for the core business.

> We have what we call a double-standard measurement ... our goals are completely different ... We are talking about ... gaining access to senior managers, gaining access to clients on various topics, changing the agenda of what preoccupies managers, and bringing in new points of view on technology.

Instead of traditional KPIs (like sales, income, invoicing rate) and target figures, value is assessed based on demand – both internally and with clients.

> I get questions every week from our colleagues: "Can you help me with a presentation about disruptive technologies, can you help me with new perspectives and design new solutions for our customer?" As long as this continues to happen, we create value and add value to Deloitte.

The third pillar – impact: Key people within C4E often talk about not pushing their services on others but want a "pull effect" (demand from the core of C4E). At the same time, this demand must be created. C4E, especially in Europe, sees its primary task as building relationships in the market.

> We are not there to sell today, we are there to build relationships in the market, and in the end, we believe that it will pay off in how Deloitte is perceived. The conversations we have and the information we get from the conversations with various senior managers about what concerns them – is information that contributes to being able to prepare services and offers that surpass what our competitors do.

There are several ways that C4E, especially in Europe, builds its legitimacy and creates demand. It never happens through direct promotion of its own services, but mainly through reputation, good experiences from various events, and word of mouth, especially from clients and senior managers.

> ... [demand is created] by talking – the clients talk about good events, senior managers talk about it, people began to talk about it and push for the next step and the next again.

While the US center was the original driving force and still accounts for the lion's share of insight production, the European office has grown and strengthened its position. One of the central people in Amsterdam describes how they work:

> First and foremost ... we are extremely good at responding and [we are] flexible. Second, we always link [our activities] to content and we are never transaction-based. I always try to make contact based on a common ambition where I bring in a challenging perspective that elicits a response like "Oh, I've never heard of that. It's really interesting!" And I think that in all discussions with senior managers, it's about bringing something else to the table ... That's where I get my energy! When leaders say, "Damn, I didn't know that!" and "Why didn't I know about this?"

In the next section, we describe how C4E works towards clients, which is, after all, the most important task Deloitte has as a global provider of professional services in auditing, consulting, and legal services.

How C4E contributes to innovation at Deloitte's clients

Deloitte's most important task is to create value for its clients, and here we will describe more specifically how C4E works and contributes value creation and innovation for Deloitte's clients.

The idea of the edge is to move far away from the core of the business. Senior management teams (i.e. Deloitte's clients) have visited C4E in Silicon Valley for outside inspiration. Among other things, they have participated in Singularity University and lectures by John Hagel and others in the C4E network. This can help senior management pick up and sense what is happening in the environment. In this way, senior management becomes inspired to rethink their purpose and business and gain common reference points and experiences.

The targeting of the senior management level is not accidental. According to the thinking around innovation at the edge, all transformation starts with senior management. This is precisely why senior management must be challenged in their thinking and given the opportunity and space to develop a common understanding around a long-term vision.

> If the CEO doesn't have courage and a conviction, then we have to give them courage by putting things on the agenda that should be there but aren't there yet. [We must] give them inspiration.

At the start, we were concerned with creating an "oh my god!" response through knowledge and inspiration from Singularity University and other innovative environments. Now we are at the point where we ask the question "so what?". What do you do with it and how? So, it's largely about addressing the future vision through inspiring, then moving it down to a structured process to address the steps on the way ... It's about creating energy, courage and conviction ... therefore positive energy.

Senior managers get inspiration from other environments with which they have not previously interacted.

So renewing ... it's also about making our knowledge available ... Some people create gigantic searchable databases, but it's really not about pumping out and archiving knowledge, it's about creating a network of people, where you can have the perspectives, you can then connect with those people, and be a part of those knowledge flows ... you draw in the external ones who also help to challenge, and also add new perspectives.

C4E also develops frameworks and methods that are used to challenge and assist senior management in how a future image and vision can be realized. A central framework developed by C4E is *zoom out/zoom in*, which is used to connect the long-term perspective to the more concrete actions that need to be done today.

... this "zoom out" horizon ... consequently, the understanding of how the market could be in 15 to 20 years and how your company should change to create value in that market – what can you do now, the next 6 to 12 months – as a result, very immediately is the contrast between [our approach and] the typical 3- to 5-year plans one has had [in the past].

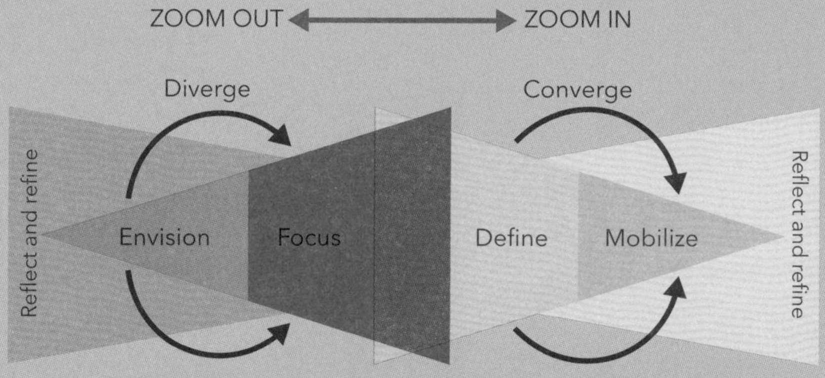

Figure C4.1.1 Deloitte's zoom out/zoom in framework

C4E thus contributes not only with insight, but also tools to be able to translate visions into action. Here, C4E collaborates closely with the consulting business at Deloitte, especially on discussions about how new technology changes society and markets and entails new opportunities for businesses. Since the establishment of C4E in Europe, there has been an increasing degree of collaboration between C4E and the core business directed to clients.

> We enter into the customer dialogue with the consulting business on strategy assignments where C4E contributes "out-of-the-box" thinking by providing insight and inspiration that helps all to see a vision that they would not otherwise have seen. This is important at the start of the process, otherwise you risk slipping into traditional thinking. And what we do is create experiences. Like for example through a zoom out/zoom in experience ...

When senior management has developed a common understanding of what is needed to realize their vision, the next step is to develop an edge initiative in the established business.

Avoid triggering the immune system by working at the edge

In the work to ensure innovation and renewal for clients, Deloitte's C4E adopts the mindset described in the edge solution. It conveys to the client that by establishing an innovative environment at the edge, it avoids triggering the immune system. People and environments who get triggered and inspired by change and innovation can seek out the edge, while those who are dedicated to the established methods can continue to use their energy there. John Hagel at C4E in San Francisco says that if senior management has to choose between the new and radical or the core, the core will always win. Therefore, the edge must be allowed to grow strong and become independent.

> I quote John Hagel. What he tends to say is ... if you stand in the middle of an organization and say, "Hey, now we're going to get change!", then you put a target on your back ... there are so many reasons why you're going to meet resistance. And it's not that people don't want to ... nobody wants to say out loud that they are against change, everyone loves change but after all, they are human beings and there are so many mechanisms through which we practically oppose radical changes ... and there may be logical reasons for that!

What is conveyed from C4E to Deloitte's clients highlights the link to psychology and the thinking that in order to bring about change and innovation, one must appeal to emotional aspects as well as rational ones. According to one of the managers at C4E Europe, it works best if a positive energy around change is achieved instead of a fear-based driving force.

> Because you won't be able to bring about this change with the immune system if you go in and do it directly, you will be ... almost screwed, one way or another. But if you manage to create a pull, through inspiring, then it has a completely different power. If you manage to show that the "edge" has value, then you are "beyond PowerPoints." So, then you don't need to stand up or defend it, because then you have created a success. And that creates a completely different momentum.

The C4E leaders describe how, in the longer term, the edge initiative will take over the core business, but until that happens the core must continue to develop.

> And John Hagel is far more radical, because – if you ask him – he says "No, the core business is going to die! In other words, it is the edge that is the future!" [ha-ha].
>
> So, we have two focuses: It's like "the edge" and developing it and "scale the edge", but also "optimize the core" ... In optimization, it's just as much about what to stop doing, and this is also a very difficult and brutal discussion. But there is also a lot ... a lot of very smart things you can do there too. So, if we think about both parts – "the core" and "the edge" and the fact that everything matures more over time, the power of innovation is triggered.

Deloitte's C4E has developed documentation that describes three steps that can contribute to establishing an edge with clients (Hagel et al., 2019). Here, the edge initiatives appear to be more concrete and to a greater degree similar to the ambidextrous solution. The three steps are as follows:

> *Step 1: Identify an edge initiative with great potential:* The first and most crucial step is to identify an edge initiative in the organization and give this initiative the right tools so that it can grow. An edge initiative can target a new customer segment, geographic market, or product. It should initially require minimal investment, while at the same time have the potential to create new values and income streams. The initiative should be built on long-term trends and radical (potentially disruptive) changes in the market. It should also have the potential to transform the established business.
>
> *Step 2: Get external resources to minimize the need for investment:* After the edge initiative is identified, it will need resources, capacity, and skills to commence and grow. The edge initiative should receive minimal investment from the business. It needs support from management but must obtain resources and support from external actors. The edge must not seize and take

away internal resources but instead bring in new ones from outside the business's boundaries. Overall, this will create more resources and at the same time help to build a larger external network. The edge also then receives faster feedback from the environment so that learning can be accelerated. To succeed in building valuable external relationships, the edge needs to build lasting trust-based relationships rather than one-off transactions.

Step 3: Accelerate to reduce lead times: Although edge initiatives can have a long (and uncertain) time horizon, it will be important to ensure frequent feedback from customers so that necessary course corrections are made. Companies' traditional approach to innovation relies on feedback from the market *after* considerable time and money have been spent in development. By testing a product earlier in the development cycle, the team can gather more detailed feedback at more frequent intervals that can be used to quickly delineate or change course as needed. Therefore, the key to scale a good idea into a successful edge initiative depends on the team's ability to quickly learn from iterations with the customers and use them for their own development and improvement. To do this, it is essential that the customer iterations are repeated in rapid (e.g., 6–12 month) cycles.

Is Deloitte taking its own medicine? C4E as an engine for renewal in own business

A relevant question is whether C4E, in addition to conveying insight and inspiration for renewal among Deloitte's clients, also renews itself – that is, Deloitte. Our research suggests that there are slightly different internal views in Deloitte on this. Few people actually see C4E as an engine for renewal at Deloitte. Some describe it as an important marketing move that makes it visible to clients that Deloitte is keeping up with the times and has something to contribute concerning innovation, renewal, and transformation. However, a few people see the C4E as Deloitte's own engine for renewal – that is to say, the center is Deloitte's own edge activity.

> … we have not said explicitly that we will be an innovation tool for Deloitte, because then we would have only "triggered" our own immune system. It takes time before you understand C4E's role and see its value … it takes time for it to sink in.

There are also several signs that the activities in C4E are developing the Deloitte partners' mindset and competence in transformation. Just as C4E moves senior managers from the clients into exciting dialogues with people they want in their network, they work in the same way internally at Deloitte.

> We have also tried to create our own seminars and courses with employees [at Deloitte] to talk about innovation

> at the edge, but I quickly noticed "Forget about it". In other words, people don't have time or people don't prioritize it. But if you invite them to a setting where they sit together with their client and perhaps even the senior manager at the client – then they participate. Then they don't just have to be there, then they have to prepare, then they understand the perspective on which the event is built.

Through its events, where more and more senior managers participate, C4E has created greater interest among Deloitte's partners.

> What has happened is that the [Deloitte] immune system, i.e., the [Deloitte] partners ... they have been invited and they see that their customers are coming. Thus, it has become "a pull" because the customers say yes! We have business managers at Level 1 and 2, and when you sit as a Deloitte partner and think "Shit, my customers come here and think it's super interesting". Then you actually have to participate.

It takes time to develop an understanding of the value of such events. While the partners are drilled in thinking about sales, such events are not directly linked to projects and sales, but primarily aim to create interesting meeting places. Some of the uncertainty and resistance to such events is about the immune system kicking in, but it is also about the fact that some may experience such events as outside their comfort and feel that their expertise and competence are being challenged. It requires both openness and courage to spend time on this form of long-term relationship building. The partners who actively use C4E describe these sessions as very engaging – both for the client and themselves – the least of which is expansiveness. These partners experience learning many new things and having a completely different contact with the client, as the quote below illustrates:

> ... the first thing I remember about exposure to the Center for the Edge was the networking they run ... they have events and research that touch on strategy work on innovation in large companies. By participating in the events, we gained insight into the major changes in society and perspectives on innovating at the edge, but to be completely honest, I didn't understand completely how I was supposed to translate it into something valuable in my own business. It took a little while, yes.

Both those at the C4E and partners in the core business who have collaborated with C4E argue that the C4E contributed to strengthening both their relevance and position in the market. The collaboration has been central to creating new arenas that bring different milieus together, both externally and internally. This has also led to new market opportunities in the core business. But time will tell whether or not C4E is going to take over and become the new core within Deloitte.

CASE 4.2
DNB'S NEW TECH LAB[5]

> It will be a bit like Columbus. We never know where we will end up. But at the same time as we allow ourselves to be led by the wind, then we measure the map along the way. There is no map that we can navigate by; no one has been there before. (Developer in New Tech Lab about the radical mandate)

> (The purpose is) to ensure that they have the opportunity to create the things that are a bit out there, that you don't immediately see the value of, perhaps not even in the next five years. But our belief is that it will have an impact on the bank's future if we explore and understand it better. (Manager in Payments & Innovation)

New Tech Lab is a small unit in DNB whose mandate is to engage in radical technological innovation. The unit has full autonomy and manages its own project portfolio, and the team works outwardly and innovatively. In this case, we will illustrate how New Tech Lab fulfills its role as DNB's innovator at the edge. The case has many of the characteristics described in the edge solution, which we will describe, but we will also illustrate some of the challenges involved in developing legitimacy for a unit with such a radical mandate.

A radical innovator at the edge

New Tech Lab has been assigned the most radical mandate for innovation in DNB. New Tech Lab has always had strong support from the senior managers at DNB, who also often emphasize the unit and its importance in both internal and external forums. Senior management uses New Tech Lab to build DNB's image of an innovative bank, for example when Yngvar Ugland, the head of New Tech Lab, and CEO Kjerstin Braathen, gave a joint performance at the Lerchendal conference talking about "How to make a dinosaur dance? Banking in the 21st century".

New Tech Lab is located in the Payments & Innovation division, a unit that started as a purely ambidextrous solution called New Business. The Payment and Innovation division has two distinct roles. The first is to facilitate many of the strategic ambitions for DNB, among other things by building infrastructure

5 This case is part of a mapping of DNB's innovation journey which was done by a part of the RaCE program. In this mapping, New Tech Lab came up as an interesting case. To gain more knowledge about New Tech Lab's role, Victor Bergerskogen wrote a master's thesis on how New Tech Lab has built legitimacy and been challenged in its role as radical innovator. Therefore, the case is based on interviews from the first and second study.

within payments, identity, and open banking. The second role is directed towards exploration and contains new technology (New Tech Lab), new business models, corporate venturing and strategic partnerships. The units in the Payments & Innovation division are illustrated in Figure C4.2.1.

Benjamin Golding heads Payments & Innovation and sits in DNB's senior management. He joined DNB in 2016 and has experience from McKinsey and several large Norwegian industrial companies. He has an important role as a bridge-builder between the business and technology side of New Tech Lab. He translates the radical ideas and innovations of the New Tech Lab and makes them relevant to the bank. At the same time, a manager in this role must also be able to assess when the ideas are perceived as too controversial and challenging.

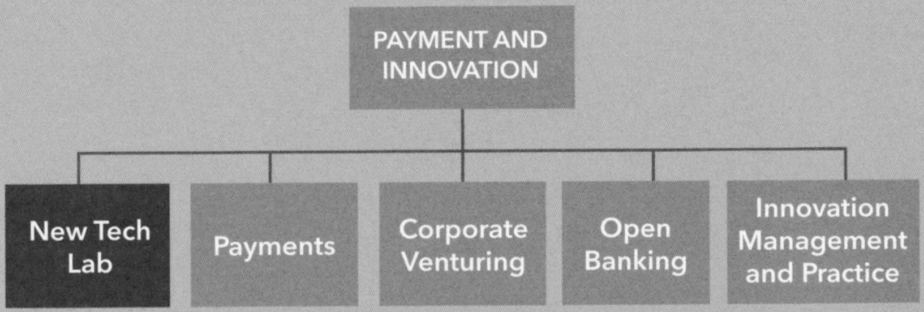

Figure C4.2.1 Organization chart for Payments & Innovation

New Tech Lab is the smallest unit in Payments & Innovation, with a team of just seven. All the employees, including the manager, can code, and in the lab, there is only one job title: developer. However, the team members are very different in their professional and cultural backgrounds; this radical diversity is important for us to come up with radical ideas. Nevertheless, the team is also aware that the members must not become too specialized.

> In a team as small as New Tech Lab, no one has explicit tasks – we must cover the entire range of architecture, cyber security, etc. That's the clue to interdisciplinary teams, and that's probably a bit of the success factor for New Tech Lab. (Developer in New Tech Lab).

The team has a great deal of autonomy and in comparison with other units in DNB, it gets away with less stakeholder management. The products and services are developed independently of DNB's core systems, and the team constantly uses new technology and methods, but is eclectic regarding what fits best in different projects. Moreover, although the team uses agile methods, it has discarded some agile tools because they are seen as too slow. The team aims to learn quickly from their mistakes and not be afraid to take a chance.

> We have a philosophy that we should fail very quickly in order to be able to quickly catch up and not dwell on things ... but more just like: "Can this be used?" Yes, keep; no, toss it. (Developer in New Tech Lab)

With only seven people and a limited budget for development, New Tech Lab does not take up a great deal of resources at DNB, nor are there any stated plans for the team to expand. On the contrary, it is important that the unit remains small and flies under the radar in resource allocation discussions. The limited resources also mean that the team must seek collaboration with other parties – internally or externally – as soon as it has created a prototype or developed an idea.

Even though the goal is to fly under the radar in terms of budget, New Tech Lab is also concerned with creating demand and legitimacy within DNB. The head of New Tech Lab, Yngvar Ugland, has taken the role as DNB's consumer technologist, and New Tech Lab has developed an innovation radar to be used by everyone and anyone in the bank. As part of this work, New Tech Lab also has an outpost in Silicon Valley – not to indulge themselves in innovation tourism, but because they need to be there and build trust with key players. In addition, New Tech Lab has taken on several projects that have contributed to creating social benefits beyond DNB.

> I think people appreciate that we have a radar where people can see what's happening, and can provide input, and be like "hey, have you looked at this?" ... When we do things that positively affect the bank as a whole, it also builds a certain amount of reputation within the bank. (Developer in New Tech Lab)

Internal tensions in the solution

Although New Tech Lab has a radical mandate, there are still tensions inherent in the solution, such as a balance between the long-term and the short-term, perceived relevance in the radical projects, and relation to the established IT departments.

> (There is a) balance between being exploratory about what is on the horizon, and ... taking the horizon perspective back to the concrete situation here today ... (Leader in Payments & Innovation)

As is natural for a unit that radically innovates at the edge, several of New Tech Lab's projects involve collaboration with external parties. It was one of these projects that developed the Compensation Scheme. 1.0, an innovation we will return to as a case in Part 3. This and similar collaborative projects that have solved important societal challenges have helped to give New Tech Lab recognition in DNB.

> The compensation scheme put DNB in a very good light. This was actually something we did for our nation; everyone else said that we can't do this. (Head of DNB)

Other projects at the edge that have not contributed in the same way to societal benefit were, for example, the development of a smart refrigerator – Smidge – which could order goods when the refrigerator was empty. This type of project was perceived by the organization to provide more media publicity than business value.

> If over time, over years, you only deliver solutions that get media attention, or that are exciting, but do not create direct value, then there will be a question whether there is a better use for these highly motivated people. (Leader in Payments & Innovation)

Recognition from both inside and outside can also create challenges in the relationship with the established departments because New Tech Lab is no longer perceived as something harmless that flies under the radar in the established firm.

> If you work with IT in Norway today ... then you are very proud of your job and you see yourself as an expert ... Some IT people in DNB will look at the New Tech Lab (and say that) "they are no better than me" ... So, when New Tech Lab engages in dialogue with regular DNB IT, some challenges may arise in terms of legitimacy ... "don't tell me what to do, we know best – we made it". New Tech Lab ... doesn't think in the traditional DNB way – it thinks outside the box. (Head of DNB)

Because of these tensions and the need to create legitimacy around the radical mandate, New Tech Lab has developed two distinct roles: on the one hand, to drive radical technological innovation; on the other, to participate in activities and projects that are perceived to be useful and valuable for DNB in the shorter term.

> It's a little twofold. One part is the innovation part, where the goal is for us to try to be very ahead technologically, to test out the most cutting-edge technology, which it can be since people barely talk about it ... The other half has become that we step in where needed, if there is somehow a crisis, that is "burning" some other place in the bank, it can be solved by sending in a development team that can work very efficiently and solve this in a very short time. (Developer in New Tech Lab)

Of course, the risk is that the unit becomes overwhelmed by daily operations and "putting out fires."

> The day they (New Tech Lab) only do firefighting … without it having an element of "outside-in" and applying this and having the long-term perspective on this, then we fail. (Leader in Payments & Innovation)

At the same time, the New Tech Lab team sets the boundaries around the radical mandate and makes sure that the radical projects, such as facial and voice recognition, will also be potentially relevant for the future banking enterprise.

> Many of the applications we found because we looked at technologies that we believe will be dominant in 5–10, 15–50 years, while we can use them for something today. Many are within the core business. It's either about creating a better customer experience, or making things more secure, faster, or simply just saving money. (Developer in New Tech Lab)

The team in the New Tech Lab is also conscious of using its abilities in new technology to find out what is relevant and what is *not* relevant for DNB, and this has proved valuable for the bank. An example of this is the team's testing of blockchain when many believed that this technology would radically change the bank's future competitiveness and position. The team concluded that they would not recommend this technology, and this helped to cancel the bank's large-scale, planned investment in blockchain.

Legitimacy building for entities that innovate at the edge

DNB's New Tech Lab is a good illustration of a unit that drives radical innovation at the edge, and the case clearly shows that this is a solution that is different from the ambidextrous solution. The mandate is obviously radical: the senior management supports the team and the radical mandate, the team collaborates with the external environments, and it works to create demand for its solutions.

At the same time, the case illustrates that, just as in the ambidextrous solution, there are some inherent tensions when innovating at the edge. In New Tech Lab, tensions involve tradeoffs between the short term and long term, being attentive towards the external environment and partners and what is closer to home, and the radical versus the immediately relevant. Fortunately, both the team in New Tech Lab and DNB's senior management have been conscious of these tensions and the need to create legitimacy within DNB.

Chapter 5

Radical transformation of the core

So far, the approaches to innovation that we have presented are all gradual adaptations that tend to begin in a small part of the established firm (often at the periphery). But it is also possible to innovate and renew an established firm more radically by transforming the core. This implies taking a critical look at the core business and rethinking "Who we are and what we do?" In this chapter, we draw on relevant parts of the extensive research literature on radical change and innovation. We present research-based insights and illustrate radical transformation through the case of Ørsted – the Danish oil and energy company (formerly DONG Energy) which within a relatively short timeframe transformed its core from oil and gas to renewable energy.

A radical transformation builds innovation capacity by enabling the firm to *seize* future opportunities more quickly. If the process is successful, it will also be able to build *dynamic capabilities* linked to transformation that can be valuable in future changes. It is also a solution that will involve rapid scaling of *complementary capabilities*.

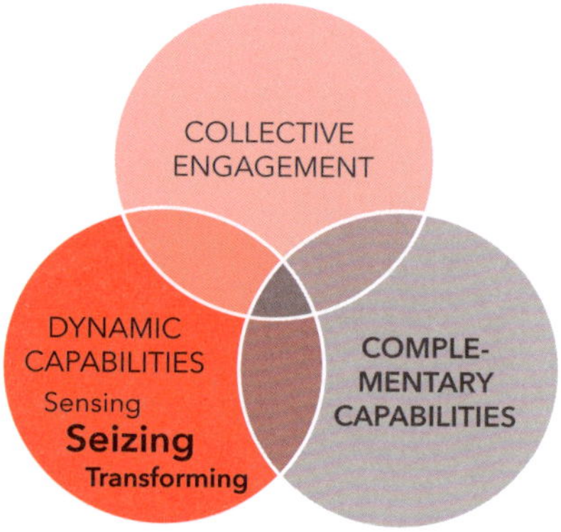

Figure 5.1 How radical transformation contributes to innovation capacity

Radically transforming an established firm

Within the organization change literature, it is common to distinguish between planned change and emergent change. All organizational changes include emergent and unplanned features, but if a decision has been made to change, for example through the company's strategy, resources will typically be allocated and activities aiming to implement the strategic decision will be initiated. In contrast, emergent changes do not start from an explicit decision. They can emerge from different parts and levels of the organization, and while they may result in major and important changes over time, the processes tend to look quite different. Emergent change processes require some advocates who seek support, for example, by trying to sell their ideas to others in the organization, while planned processes usually have a clearer top-down element. As mentioned, all planned changes also include emerging elements. In addition, for many organizations it is not either or, but rather a number of planned and emerging changes exist side-by-side (Meyer & Stensaker, 2011). Multiple changes can create momentum and collective engagement but they can also crowd each other out.

Planned changes can have a different scope – they can be radical or incremental. The latter (also called continuous improvements) involves minor adjustments within the existing paradigm, while radical changes are groundbreaking and often demand a completely different mindset. Radical changes challenge employees' understanding of "who we are as an organization" and "what we do", i.e., the organization's identity. Introducing a new system for travel accounting or an upgrade of IT systems will be an incremental change, while moving from stationary telephone systems to mobile telephones, as Telenor and other telecom companies did, is a radical change that will encompass the entire organization and require changes in all of the cogs in our cog model. However, this is subjective, as what most people will see as an incremental change can be experienced as quite radical enough for those it directly affects. And what some would call a radical transformation, others could experience it as more incremental. Nevertheless, the processes that are set up will often be different. Radical transformation will almost always involve changes in all of the cogs and therefore requires clear change management. However, this does not mean that everything must be changed at the same time.

Radical changes can be made gradually (evolutionary change processes) or quickly (revolutionary change processes). Although some "recipes" for change recommend rapid processes, empirical research shows that radical change takes time – usually a minimum of three to five years – and these may meet strong resistance, both internally and externally. This is especially true if the management is proactive and adopts radical changes when the business shows good performance and strictly speaking, the environment does not require such extensive changes. Reactive change, for example in response to a crisis, will normally not be faced with such a strong resistance because it is easier to understand that change is required.

Some might argue that it would be better to shut down existing business and let newcomers take over rather than transform, due to the demands on time and resources. The strategy specialist answer to that would be that if the established firm has resources, for example expertise, which can be used in the development of the new business opportunity and potentially create an advantage, then it may make sense to embark on a radical transformation, despite the challenges involved. But at the same time, it is important to specify that an established firm should not be artificially kept alive if other firms can do the job better. Then it would make more sense to downsize the established one, eventually shut it down, and preferably ally with or invest in the businesses that are best suited to create value within the new – for example in the case of the new establishments we write about in Chapter 10.

Implementing and leading a radical transformation

Radical transformation requires a good understanding of the context. What works well in one situation and context may not be as effective and successful in another. For various reasons, what may seem to be the most rational and efficient solution may not be possible to carry out. Diligent analyses of *why* change is necessary, *what* the change will concretely entail and *where* the change will be carried out, will provide important insights into how the transformation should be carried out and managed.

Some of the most well-known research-based recommendations include: (1) planning the process, (2) communicating the vision and coherent change narratives, (3) allocating resources, (4) establishing frameworks and structures, and (5) handling resistance and conflicting interests. We briefly discuss each of these five recommendations below.

Planning the process

In radical transformations, time is of the essence. Because such changes are time-consuming, it is important to construct a fairly realistic plan. Different challenges will emerge at different points in time. And no matter how well the process is planned, it will have to be adjusted along the way. Organizations are living organisms, and a lot of unforeseen things tend to arise during such processes (see Stensaker & Haueng, 2016, for a more thorough review of this). Planned changes can have substantial momentum and collective engagement at one point in time, but later fizzle out into nothing – sometimes due to factors outside management's control, but also due to how the process is planned and managed.

The vast majority of change researchers agree that in the initial phase it is important to create a shared understanding of what is to be changed and how this is to be done. We will go into more detail about the importance of a clear vision below, but an understanding of change can also come from concrete examples of other firms that have done the same, or examples from one's own firm. It often makes sense to plan some relatively simple changes initially that produce visible results. As these changes provide a better understanding of what one is trying to achieve, in addition, early results provide motivation to continue with the transformation.

Communicating the vision

A clear vision of the future that connects the present with the past can help to create a shared understanding of radical transformation. The early change research was concerned with the need to create an urgency and diagnosing problems. Discouraging facts and statistics were often presented to prove the need for change. This approach to change has been labelled "diagnostic" and today, change researchers have launched the dialogue approach where narratives and change stories have a greater place as an alternative (see for example Schein, 2015, or Bushe & Marshak, 2009). The assumption is that a shared understanding of transformation can be more effectively developed through dialogue that seeks to bring new insights and new mental models. Some researchers have further criticized traditional change literature for only focusing on problems and crises and believe that it is more effective to start from the strengths of the organization (through what is called *appreciate inquiry*, see for example Cooperrider et al., 2008). The underlying assumption is that this will trigger a different type of collective engagement among employees. There is also research that shows that stories about change create a different and deeper understanding than pure facts, because stories provide relatable context for employees.

In the Ørsted case, which we present below, the management tells how they tied themselves to the mast by describing the green shift in an opinion piece chronicle and by publicly expressing an overarching vision to reverse the relationship between black and green energy production from 85/15 to 15/85.

Resource allocation

Despite process plans and change visions, unless appropriate resources are allocated, the transformation will not happen (Pisano, 2019). The most visible proof that the management is serious about a strategic decision is that it allocates resources for change and makes visible investments. Resource allocation should support change initiatives and opportunities that arise in and around the organization that contribute to the overall direction. Emerging change initiatives in the organization can also find their place here. If ongoing activities are in line with the strategy, it would make sense for the management to support these; they will be able to create collective engagement among employees and help to pull the business in the direction of transformation.

Establishment of frameworks and structures

We have previously discussed how the establishment of new innovative business units can facilitate innovation (the ambidextrous solution). In connection with radical transformation of the core, projects (or programs including several projects) are often used. Projects are somewhat similar to the ambidextrous solution in that a new structure is set up with a mandate to transform, but projects are temporary and are set up alongside the hierarchy to specifically deal with restructuring (Stensaker & Haueng, 2016). They can create capacity by allocating the responsibility for change planned to others than those who are busy with operations. Because it is the core that is to be transformed, it can be challenging to assign the main responsibility for change to this same unit. When using projects, the responsibility is placed outside the operations line. As a rule, change projects are partly staffed by skilled employees who know the operation well yet are charged with change agency. Project members are dedicated time to radically transform the firm. This is one of the advantages of organizing radical transformation in the form of projects. There are also some familiar challenges. Power is shifted from the hierarchy to the project, and this can pose a threat to people in powerful positions. There are also some well-known challenges related to the transfer of responsibility from project to line – something that must happen at one time or another for the transformation to become a reality.

Dealing with opposition and different interests

Regardless of how good the job of trying to create a shared understanding and collective engagement to transformation is done, radical change will typically be met with resistance. It is only natural that people in organizations have different interests and opinions. A great deal has been written about resistance to change in the literature (for an overview, see Oreg et al., 2011, for example). Most researchers agree that reactions to change are multifaceted; in order to understand and deal with resistance, we must look at both individual and systemic factors, in addition to aspects having to do with the specific situation. There are different theoretical approaches to understanding and dealing with resistance to change. Stakeholder theory is about mapping interests and power relations (Freeman, 1984; Ackerman & Eden, 2011). Groups that have significant interest and power should be prioritized. Different interests can be handled through incentives, or by involving the parties and exploring if common interests can be found. Participatory processes can create greater understanding, motivation and collective engagement among employees. But bringing resistant employees close can also delay transformation and end up in eternal discussions and battles. Resistance to change can occur both within the organization and around it. Of course, powerful stakeholders in the environment can also contribute as supporters of transformation.

The above is by no means exhaustive, but hopefully provides a sufficient basis for comparing radical transformation with other organizational solutions for innovation. It also provides an analytical foundation for the Ørsted case, which illustrates how an established player can radically transform itself.

CASE 5.1
FROM BLACK TO GREEN ENERGY IN ØRSTED[6]

The company DONG Energy (formerly Dansk Olje og Naturgas) accounted for a third of the total CO_2 emissions in Denmark – *alone* – this was in 2008. Oil and gas were pumped from the North Sea. Coal was burned to distribute electricity to Danish companies and households, and the investment budgets included extensive coal power investments including the giant Greifswald project in Northern Germany. The following year, Denmark was to host the UN climate summit in Copenhagen. The alarm bells had long since started ringing for the company's senior management.

Today, the company is no longer called DONG. The new name became Ørsted, named after Hans Christian Ørsted – the father of electromagnetism. He laid the foundations for the modern production of electricity over two hundred years ago. Coal, oil and gas have almost completely disappeared from Ørsted's portfolio.

In 2021, well over 75% of power production in Ørsted was based on renewable energy. In 2023, its last two coal-fired power plants will close and green energy will make up 99% of the portfolio. Ørsted has become a global leader in offshore wind with close to a third of global production and has long since become a supplier of green energy on several continents – Europe, Asia, and the United States. The company has been named the most sustainable company in the world – three years in a row. Its market value has multiplied.

With this case, we want to illustrate the forces that laid behind the decision to fundamentally change the company's strategy, and which steps were taken to carry out the transformation. We provide an account of strategic shift, internal resistance and operational decisions that were made along the way. How can a firm transform from being one of the most coal-intensive companies in Europe to becoming completely carbon neutral? For Ørsted, the changes were so fundamental that we can definitely call this a radical transformation.

From oil and gas to coal-fired power plants

The oil crisis hit the Western world in 1973. It came as a result of OPEC (Organization of Petroleum Exporting Countries) implementing an oil boycott and

6 This case is based on information from various sources, including two Harvard cases, diverse magazine articles (Bower & Corsi, 2012; Reguly, 2019) and Ørsted's YouTube film about the transformation called "Our Green Transformation," together with the company's own reflections. In addition, we have conducted an interview with Jacob Bøss, the company's long-standing strategy and communications director. The case was written for this book, and the authors would like to thank Bøss for generously sharing his knowledge.

a sharp price increase as a punitive reaction to countries that supported Israel during the Yom Kippur War in 1973. This led to dramatic measures in the West. Rationing, driving restrictions at weekends and on weekdays and, not least, strong inflationary pressure in the Western economies. The fear was imminent that the automobiles would never get gasoline again and that interruptions in gas distribution to households and businesses would create enduring crises. At that time, security of supply was the goal for all countries that did not have their own production of hydrocarbons.

It is in this context that one must understand the establishment of Dansk Olje og Naturgas, as it was called at its beginning. The purpose of the state-owned company was to find oil and gas, at almost any price. It started with Denmark but was quickly extended to Norway and Great Britain as well. A couple of years later, the company was renamed DONG Energy.

At this time, Denmark's energy supply was almost completely based on oil – mainly imported from Saudi Arabia. When the availability of cheap oil disappeared almost overnight, its oil-fired power stations were replaced by cheaper but even dirtier coal. DONG was an upstream oil and gas company.

At the end of the 1990s, the EU's energy policy changed significantly. Liberalization of the energy markets was planned and the pricing of electricity became more market-based – both for companies and consumers. This led to a consolidation wave in most European countries, including Norway and Denmark. Market-based principles were decreed. The energy companies became fully integrated. Many also brought in private owners, and commercial principles were adopted.

In 2006, DONG merged with five other domestic energy companies. Two of them were producers while the other three were distributors. DONG produced oil and gas off the shelf and produced heat and electricity, which was also distributed and sold to households and businesses. Coal had overtaken oil's place in the power plants, and its coal identity was dominant. It was at this time that the investment plans in Greifswald (Northern Germany) were launched. And then within roughly a year, these were abandoned. What happened?

Opposition to coal grew in strength. Al Gore published *An Inconvenient Truth* as both a book and a documentary film. Lord Stern came up with his report in which he showed that it was cheaper to do something about the climate problem than do nothing. In 2007, the IPPC's (UN Climate Panel) fourth climate report was presented. The main conclusion was that the earth's climate is undergoing formidable change. Global warming, which is largely caused by human activity, can cause enormous damage. The report attracted considerable attention when it was published, and it was an important reason why the Climate Panel received the Nobel Peace Prize together with Al Gore. And two years later – in 2009

– Copenhagen hosted the UN climate summit. Taken together, these factors caused a change in attitudes in DONG's management and board. But attitudes are one thing, while actions are something else.

The moment of truth

In 2006, Jakob Bøss was executive vice president with responsibility for strategy and communications department at DONG. He recruited the first person for sustainability in the group ever. "We agreed that we should create a sustainability report, because it was so modern at the time. This had simply become a new buzzword in business", said Bøss in our conversation. The sustainability report was presented in 2007. It was the first time ever in the Danish energy sector that someone had depicted climate change as a problem that should be taken seriously by the industry.

Nevertheless, it was the planned IPO in 2008 that had the highest priority. A preparation process for a stock market listing requires enormous preliminary work, and the planning had taken more than a year. In the prospectus it was the fossil-based history of oil, coal and gas that aimed to attract private investors. The sales arguments were connected to a world-leading integrated energy company with special expertise in efficient coal-fired power plants. The financial crisis in 2008 led to the Danish finance minister, the board, and the management dropping the IPO.

"You can send a little friendly thanks to the financial crisis here. If it hadn't come then we would have committed to a different strategy direction," said Bøss. Lucky or unlucky. The average margin for European energy companies fell by 60% in the period 2008–2012. Oil and gas prices plummeted, and the strategic challenges increased for energy companies all over the world.

This opened the way for the quiet revolution in DONG. Based on attitudes, sustainability reports, revised faith in the future and a genuine concern for the lack of a viable business model, Anders Eldrup, then CEO together with his strategy director, Bøss, and the company's board, launched his 85/15 vision in 2009. At the time, only 15% of production was based on green, renewable energy. The rest was coal. The idea was to flip the mix to 85% green within one generation, i.e., in thirty years. It would turn out that the slow transformation would go faster. Much faster.

The actual launch of the new strategy was published in a newspaper opinion piece in September 2008. The vision of a transition from black to green energy was launched. The need for restructuring was global, but Denmark had to take a local lead. As the largest emitter of greenhouse gases – with a total of one-third of the country's total carbon emissions – DONG had to go out in front. According to Bøss, the article, which was also followed by a broad nationwide campaign, had the following main message: "We are part of the problem, now we also want to be part of the solution." Investments were to take a new direction.

A decade of fundamental change

Anders Eldrup was appointed CEO of DONG in 2001. In the coming years, he first transformed DONG into DONG Energy. DONG merged with five other Danish energy companies: Elsam, Energi E2, Nesa, Copenhagen Energy and Frederiksberg Forsyning. The company became an integrated Northern European giant that produced and traded in electricity, heat, oil and gas – in addition to distributing these products to companies and households. Following the mergers, the Danish state still owned 80% of the company. Ownership was controlled by the Department of Finance.

Eldrup had a background from the Department of Finance. He had worked here for nearly thirty years before eventually holding the post of Finance Councilor. His career in the department started around the same time as the oil crisis – in the early 1970s. Eldrup has described how this crisis showed him how dangerous it is to put all your eggs in one basket. Eldrup had an academic background from the Institute of Political Science at Aarhus University.

Jakob Bøss was brought in as a personal adviser to Eldrup in 2004. He had a background from McKinsey and was educated in Public Administration and Management from Harvard University. Bøss later held a number of management positions in the company and was also central in the integration team in connection with the mergers in 2006.

These two senior managers were key to the decision-making processes in both the restructuring and the change in strategy of DONG. It is interesting that none of them had typical profiles with experience from business and the capital market. When we asked Bøss if he thinks the background and expertise of Eldrup mattered, he replied, "Without a doubt. Undoubtedly. In some situations, a focus on traditional key figures such as ROE, EPS and P/E is insufficient. It helps to have the big picture. It helps to have the experience Eldrup had from the oil crisis and not least from regulatory change processes within the EU."

A new decade – the green wins over the black

In March 2012, Eldrup was dismissed as CEO by the board. According to the chairman of the board, Fritz Schur, Eldrup had exceeded his powers in connection with the salary and bonus of several executive directors. Others have claimed that it was actually a disagreement about strategy that triggered the shift of CEOs, but this has been denied by Schur and other key people in the company.

In August 2012, Henrik Poulsen was appointed as the new CEO. Poulsen was trained in business and had an impressive track record, but would not rest on his laurels, nor change the company's strategic direction, but rather accelerate the green transition at an impressive pace.

In 2016, Poulsen spearheaded Denmark's largest ever IPO, and DONG Energy went public. In 2017 the company sold its oil and gas division to Switzerland's Ineos for close to DKK 9 billion. Later that same year, a fundamental name change was made: DONG Energy was renamed Ørsted. Finally, the switch from black to green was realized. In 2018, investment plans for 200 billion in sustainable energy were announced. The company was now aiming to install 30 GW of sustainable energy capacity – globally.

The green wave hit its peak at the beginning of 2021. Global investors had jumped on green energy with full force. If green could also promise growth, it would be twice as attractive. In January, the market value of Ørsted reached almost NOK 800 billion. At the time, this was almost NOK 300 billion more than the valuation of Norway's Equinor. Green had won over black.

If one looks superficially at the events during the period when Poulsen was CEO, it may appear as if the strong acceleration towards green offshore wind was almost painless. That is not the case. The emergence of cheap shale gas in the United States, falling coal prices, and the economic fallout after the financial crisis created major financial challenges for DONG Energy. Costs had to be cut. Investments had to be prioritized very carefully and focus became a necessary mantra.

At that time there was low growth in the business, which was based on a historical business model that was creating little value. Being forced into a corner can be life-threatening for the business itself. "It was then that we saw that we needed a fundamental change," said Jakob Bøss. The company reviewed its technology platform. It mapped its qualifications and expertise and conducted thorough financial analyses. Risks stemming from the various options for action were carefully studied.

"We analyzed our business areas and saw that the only place where we had a competitive advantage and could create a business with great scaling potential was in offshore wind," said the CFO. There were many objections and substantial resistance within the company. Questions were raised about whether the pace of change in society was really that fast. Some argued that, technically speaking, the investment in offshore wind and the phasing out of coal could be pursued, but at huge cost.

The first commercial offshore wind farm in Denmark was not a great success either. In fact, it did not work at all as anticipated and hoped. The turbines had to be dismantled and brought back to land. They had to be rebuilt so that they could function out at sea, and then reassembled. Thus, the first project was both expensive and a challenging learning process.

Eventually, the company entered into an agreement with Siemens for the delivery of five hundred wind turbines. This was more than the total installed offshore at that time. The financial commitment was astronomical both for Ørsted and the suppliers. This came as a recognition that the only way to bring the price down was through a major upscaling.

The company conducted stakeholder analysis. It looked outside the company. It made careful evaluations of how to make use of partnerships without messing up its own core competencies and strengths. It worked in interaction with its surroundings and dealt with a large number of factors.

"We learned that when you have found a technology, a business or a product where you have a competitive advantage, and where there is great potential for growth, then you have to persevere. You really should put all your energy and capital into pursuing that opportunity," stated former CEO Henrik Poulsen.

In the industry, new targets were set for the price of electricity from offshore wind. The support and subsidies that were there from the authorities in the early phase would be reduced and eliminated over time. The costs of offshore wind had to be reduced so much that it could compete with other electricity sources – without subsidies. That is why Ørsted set a goal that at the time seemed completely unrealistic. A top-down management decision on costs was made that could not be backed up by any calculations: offshore wind should provide cheaper power than developing new coal or gas-fired power plants.

The vision that was adopted was for the company to become a global leader in green energy, primarily to make the world a better place to live. Poulsen explained Ørsted's visions in the transformation phase: "Many companies have a vision that revolves around what the businesses would like to achieve. What the company should be, not how the businesses can contribute to a better and more sustainable future for the world."

A handful of concrete goals were set up to make the vision itself tangible. The specific goals were further spread throughout the organization – right down to action points for each individual employee in the company. It was expected that these were the action points the employees would focus on in the coming year.

"If we aim for the right long-term vision and begin right now to do what is needed for us to move forward, then it will probably work," as the former senior manager explained his management philosophy to his employees.

When the company started its transformation journey, 7% of its profits came from renewable energy. Today, that figure is almost 100%.

The board and management of Ørsted have taken many calculated risks in the business, but a dynamic culture has developed that is ready to make major decisions using fast processes through which it assumes a significant risk. The company has developed self-confidence within its niche area. The company had experience of making decisions about gigantic investments from its time as an oil and gas operator. No one builds larger and more cost-effective offshore wind farms than Ørsted.

Therefore, the way it collaborates with external partners has also been refined along the way. Ørsted takes overall responsibility for the construction, management, and operation of the wind farms. Pension funds, investors and industrial players are admitted as financial partners and co-owners – within the collaborative model the company has evaluated as being the most efficient and frictionless.

The journey forward will also be about green growth; global infrastructure must be renewed and changed. Governments set aside enormous sums for investment and restructuring packages. New technologies must be developed, and huge investments must be financed.

In 2021, Ørsted hired a new senior manager, Mads Nipper. In a statement where the company presents itself on YouTube, he says the following: "We also have a duty not to stop and rest on our laurels. How can we contribute on a global level to expanding and speeding up the existing solutions? And how can we ensure that we constantly lead the way and create new solutions that make it easier to speed up the journey the world is bound to take? I believe that Ørsted's next change is about utilizing the strength, knowledge, and abilities we have, to ensure that we help countries over the whole world to accomplish an adjustment that works and accelerates the fight against climate change. Climate change's greatest danger is the perception that someone else will fix the problem. This is not just an opportunity; it is a commitment at the top."

What can other firms learn from Ørsted?

There are few established companies that can embark on such a radical and rapid transformation as Ørsted did. Nevertheless, there are several key learnings from this case.

Firstly, the management at Ørsted were very skilled at *sensing what was going on in their surroundings*, and discovered early on that the atmosphere in the environment was about to shift to more sustainable, green energy sources. Based on this understanding, they created a new and very ambitious vision to go from 15 to 85% green in thirty years.

But they did not stop there. They took active and courageous decisions to *seize the opportunities* that lay in new technology, not least by scrapping the plans for a giant coal-fired power station in Northern Germany.

Anders Eldrup's vision, which involved a radical transformation of the company, was apparently not perceived as very dangerous among the employees. The transition was planned to take thirty years. When the transformation itself only took ten years, this was not due to a conscious choice by the new leader who succeeded Eldrup but to the financial crisis during which the prices of oil and gas plummeted. Instead of trying to save the remains, the new CEO Henrik Poulsen invested heavily in switching the company to green energy sources in line with the vision for the company and sold off the black assets at a rapid pace.

But it was no simple operation to go from being a black to a green energy company. The general sentiment at the time was that offshore wind was far too immature; then the first attempt also went completely wrong, and Ørsted lost significant sums of money. This experience showed that costs had to be sharply reduced and production reorganized. Again, the management took forceful action by deciding where the cost level should be in the future without a clear business case. The shift from production of large individual projects in which they had expertise, to industrial production of sea turbines, required *complementary expertise* in industrial production, which was secured by linking up with partners in areas they did not define as their core business.

The key to Ørsted's transformation from black to green lies in a combination of looking far ahead and at the same time being able to make bold decisions that rapidly moved the company in the desired direction. And although many would say that the company was greatly helped by the financial crisis, it was not given that the company would respond by taking on even greater risks and moving into an immature business area with a high level of cost.

Chapter 6

Agile work processes and agile organizations

One of the hottest organizational trends these days concerns agility. The idea behind agility is to ensure faster development of new and innovative products and services, so pace is clearly an important factor. But even though many companies are working to become more agile, there is no unified understanding of what that means. Several different perceptions exist side-by-side both in practice and in research. In practice, the term is used to describe how work is carried out, and also how the entire firm is organized. In research, we find a number of different definitions at different levels – some are linked to specific IT projects, others to working methods more generally, while there is also research on agile teams, organizations, managers, and strategies.

In this chapter, we examine the origins of agility and present our preferred definition. We describe agile working methods first and then take the ideas a notch further and move up to the organizational level to discuss what an agile organization entails and how this can be implemented and managed in an effective way that fosters innovation capacity. Afterward, we present two cases that illustrate agile work processes and the agile organization in practice: Fana Sparebank and FINN.no.

The agile solution contributes to innovation capacity by strengthening the ability to *seize* new opportunities. It also creates collective engagement among employees, partly due to the autonomy the teams have to solve a task and focus on this, rather than doing many parallel jobs. The solution can also help to increase *sensing* capabilities if the responsibility for this is delegated to the teams.

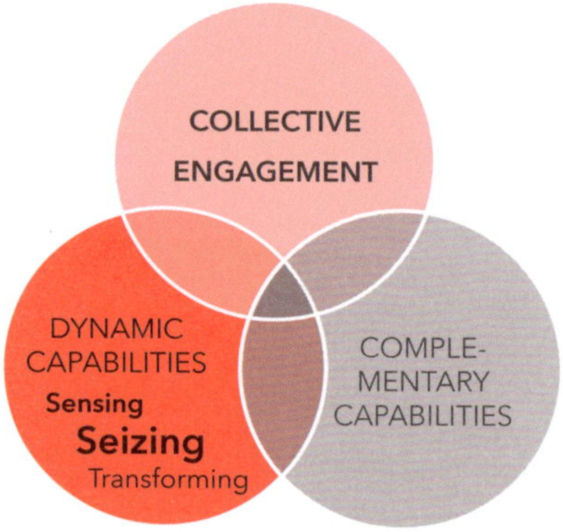

Figure 6.1 How an agile organization contributes to innovation capacity

Agile working methods

Organizations have always been concerned with adaptation and change; trends such as total quality management (TQM), business process re-engineering, and lean all aim to ensure further development, change and improvement in the established firm. In Chapter 2, we described some of the historical development of work processes, and as we see it, agile work processes are currently one of the clearest trends.

The ideas about agility come from the software industry. In 2001, a group of software developers developed a manifesto (The Agile Manifesto) to describe alternative development processes within IT (Rigby et al., 2016). With their detailed documentation, existing development processes were perceived as too complicated, which made the processes slow. Traditional development processes often followed what is called the waterfall method, which is a linear, step-by-step approach that often takes a long time – easily up to several years.

Agile working methods were launched as a contrast to the waterfall method. With the waterfall method, the risk was that the technology and innovation would be obsolete when it finally hit the market. In addition, adjustments were expensive and demanding. There was a need for faster development processes and an opportunity to test and adjust new products and services along the way.

However, the agile manifesto was more of a philosophy than concrete working methods. The manifesto consists of four values that emphasize people and interaction between people (Beck et al., 2001; LeMay, 2018).

The values in the agile manifesto are:

1. Individuals and interaction over processes and tools
2. Working software over comprehensive documentation
3. Customer collaboration over contract negotiations
4. Responding to change over following a plan

Within the IT and software industry, agility is over twenty years old, but the thinking has spread far beyond these environments.

Agility spreads from software to other parts of the organization

One of the reasons why agility has become so popular could be that technology is playing an increasingly important role in innovation. In order to develop new attractive products and services, software and IT developers often have to be involved. However, many different milieus – even those not directly connected with IT and software – have since been inspired by agile ideas.

Agility is about the organization's ability to quickly adapt and respond to changes in such a way that it creates value for customers. The agile organization can seamlessly redirect its most valuable resources (Teece et al., 2016).

While IT developers compare agile to the waterfall methodology, others outside these settings use the metaphor that turning a ship is frightfully difficult. The large established firm is often described as a ship that moves steadily in one direction but may have difficulty changing course. Agile organizing implies converting the ship into an armada of sailboats that can be sent out to explore unknown waters. Sailboats can quickly and flexibly turn with the wind and change course if they find they are heading in the wrong direction. Variations of this metaphor have been passed around for over thirty years. In the 1990s, the chairman of the board of the pharmaceutical company Glaxo Wellcome stated: "We need to transform from a big (aircraft carrier) to flotillas of small, fast ships."

Inertia within large, established firms is by no means new. While size can bring advantages of scale, it also comes with a number of well-known disadvantages, such as the inability to turn around quickly. The total number of large organizations has increased through waves of mergers and acquisitions, so we can assume that today there is increased need for agility and flexibility. TietoEVRY is an organization that has recently merged across the Nordic countries and is actively working to become agile despite its large size.

Another image that is often drawn as a contrast to agile is about silo thinking. Because large established firms are organized into different functions and divisions – which is necessary for large organizations – cross-functional coordination can suffer, and this can create delays in product development and innovation.

The illustration in figure 6.2 shows how the agile approach breaks down the hierarchy and makes interdisciplinary collaboration possible (illustrated by the color contrasts) in teams to ensure a focus on tempo and customer orientation and thus contributing to adaptation, innovation, and tempo. According to Aghina et al., 2017, the traditional hierarchy focuses more on control and consensus across levels, which ensures implementation and control. In the field of organization theory interdisciplinary teams and projects is nothing new, but by combining the team structure with new and agile ways of working, something different is introduced.

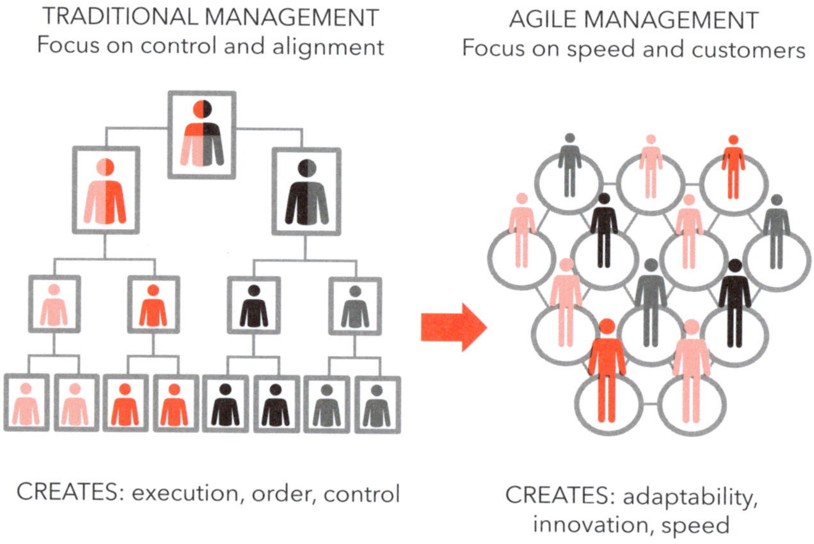

Figure 6.2 The contrast between the traditional and agile organization (Aghina et al., 2017)

Both of the organizational problems (ship and silo) that agility is supposed to solve are well known. These challenges often persist in large-scale organizations – they can rarely be solved with a few simple actions. Organizing work in a different way may solve some issues, yet it tends to bring new challenges. We will take a closer look at some concrete examples to investigate potential benefits of agility, but first we will describe the agile working methodology in more detail and then move on to the agile organization.

Key characteristics of agile working methods

A number of master's students at NHH have investigated what agility means in practice and if and how it contributes to the capacity for change. They have explored companies across industries to better understand what agile looks like in Norwegian businesses (Førland & Klemp, 2021; Glesne & Pedersen, 2020; Kamath, 2020; Løvik, 2020). Characteristics that are repeated across companies in the finance, media, and consulting industries are: Interdisciplinary teams that work according to a clear mandate, but with a large degree of autonomy to set their own goals and decide for themselves how and when those goals should be reached. The teams are usually (but not necessarily) co-located. Agile teams work in close dialogue with the customer. Often, complex tasks are broken into smaller modules and worked on in intensive periods, called *sprints*, where a specific task is solved. A sprint can last two weeks, after which a new task must be delivered and/or tested by the customer. A new language is often introduced: in addition to sprints (short deadlines), *tribes* or families (composed of several teams), *scrum* (a framework that describes the work process), *kanban* (white boards that show the workflow), and product owners (the person responsible for the product/service the team must deliver). Some of the mindset and language overlaps with other organizational trends such as *lean*.

In other words, some characteristics of agile working methods are:

- Multidisciplinary teams with a clear mandate/task
- Autonomy to set own goals and organize the process
- Work is divided into sprints (for example two weeks)
- The teamwork is customer-oriented and interacts frequently with the customer. Teams often develop a prototype (minimum viable product), which is tested along the way and adjusted accordingly.
- A new conceptual apparatus is introduced, e.g., tribes (possibly families), scrum master, product owners, user of visual aids, process overview and flow charts. The methodology is often combined with other forms of work such as lean, scrum and kanban.
- Frequent (preferably daily) stand-up meetings

The research on agile working methods is fragmented and does not provide clear answers to the *effects* of this way of working. Some researchers question what is really new about this way of working (Puranam & Clement, 2020). Trends that come and go without necessarily representing anything new within organizations is a well-known phenomenon (Abrahamson, 1991; Røvik, 2007). Many of the elements we have listed above have existed long before the term agile was launched. Multidisciplinary teams have been recommended for over twenty years. It is well known that autonomy is motivating and contributes to job satisfaction, and that frequent deadlines create the work pace. Customer-oriented work where prototypes are tested underway has long been recommended in the research literature on innovation processes. In other words, the individual elements that characterize agile working methods are well known, and research can show documented effects here.

So, what's really new? Employees with experience of the working methodology seem to be very enthusiastic, which suggests that the collective engagement increases, and this part of the innovation muscle is strengthened. Employees report that having direct responsibility for the work themselves and not being disturbed by other tasks, makes their work more motivating. The very way these elements are combined appears to increase employee motivation.

In the master's theses we referred to above, the students found that agile working methods also create innovation capacity in the form of flexibility and pace for product/service development. Indeed, the examples of innovation were typically related to product/service innovation, new apps and the like, while there were few immediate signs of more radical innovations.

In the international research we find that agile working methods do not solely produce positive effects. There are also some signs of negative effects of agile working methods, such as new silos being developed, that employees feel alienated and stressed instead of experiencing autonomy, and that innovation is inhibited rather than enhanced by this way of working (Annosi et al., 2020).

It is relevant to ask whether agile working methods, which were developed within IT and software, are more suitable in certain firms and for certain types of jobs. For instance, some studies indicate that agile working methods are effective for tasks that can be done in parallel and that can be broken down into sequences, as well as those that can be developed into prototypes (Rigby et al., 2016). Software/IT, product development, new design and product characteristics are good examples of this. However, the methodology is less suitable for finance, accounting, and risk management (Rigby et al., 2016; Puranam & Clement, 2020). Managers who want to speed up innovation should therefore think carefully about the types of tasks to organize in an agile way.

From agile working methods to agile organizations

The agile organization is not just about new working methods but also about how the entire organization is set up to ensure faster adaptation to changes in the market.

> An agile organization has organizational structures and administrative processes that are fast and seamless and create value for the customer. (Gunasekaran, 2001)

Figure 6.3 below illustrates different levels of agility. On the left is a typical first step on the journey: establishment of project-based interdisciplinary teams that have a given task to solve and/or that are positioned to experiment, for example in the form of an innovation hub. This is in line with the previous description of agile working methods. In the next step, development continues with the gradual establishment of several interdisciplinary teams which are supported by operational functions in the organization. Finally, the entire firm is organized in the form of autonomous, customer-focused teams. There are few organizations that have today reached the extreme point on the far right of the figure, but the Dutch bank ING is often cited as an example. It is more common among established firms to be located in the middle, where they have a structure that consists of both flexible and stable elements. Then, flexibility and adaptability can be balanced against the need for stability, which may be necessary particularly in operational and support functions.

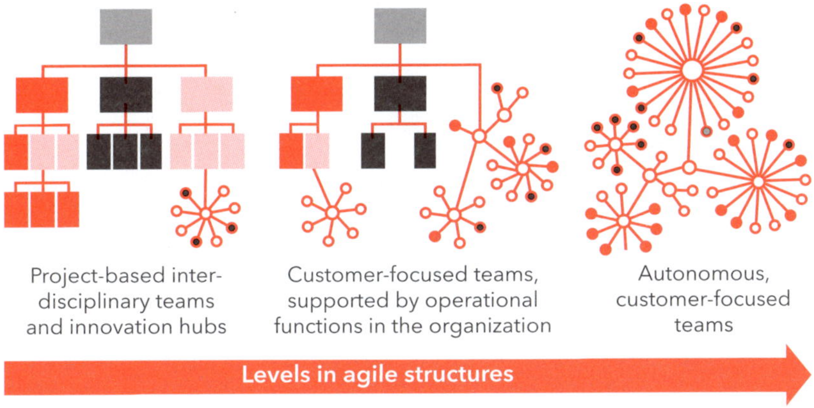

Figure 6.3 Different levels of agility (from Deloitte's Adaptable Organization, 2018)

The project-based team structure is a common way to organize work, whether the team is temporarily established to solve a specific mandate, or is of a more permanent nature. Important questions to consider include whether the team is placed at the right level in the organization, and possibilities to interact with the rest of the organization, and whether the team has sufficient legitimacy for the results and solutions developed by the team to be used in the organization.

A fully agile organization, as we see on the right in Figure 6.3, shows a network of autonomous and customer-focused teams. Their work can be coordinated based on clear mandates and task, but also through informal processes. Such informal processes and networks in the organization can be powerful; especially if they consist of employees who come together across horizontal boundaries to solve customer needs that cannot be solved alone in one department, or to develop completely new solutions and services that require collaboration across disciplines and expertise.

Moving towards a completely agile organization is a tremendous change which may call for a step-by-step and incremental process where one can experiment and learn underway. The Dutch bank ING required eight to nine months to introduce agile organization (see Figure 6.4); however, ING had moved in this direction for many years (Aghina et al., 2017).

Figure 6.4 ING's agile organization (Aghina et al., 2017)

Key characteristics of the agile organization

To describe the agile organization, we will use the cogwheel model we presented in Chapter 2. There are five cogs that are central to the development of an adaptable and agile organization:

- Work processes
- Organizational structure
- Management and governance
- Competence
- External relations

Work processes

We described the work processes in the first part of this chapter when we referred to how the teams themselves plan who does what when and working in sprints, often with the help of kanban boards, stand-up meetings and the like.

Organizational structure

The agile organization consists of networks of teams. While the teams have extensive autonomy, they should not be "blindly trusted" to meet the organization's needs. Coordination mechanisms can secure this.

The Spotify case illustrates the challenge of lack of coordination between teams. As Spotify grew, it needed to introduce a system and structure between the autonomous teams. To succeed as a company, it became essential that the teams viewed themselves not only as autonomous entities but as part of a holistic organization that worked together across boundaries. The management's role was to connect the teams by establishing a common direction and structure so that it became possible to interact across functions (tribes), teams (squads) and specialist/professional groups (chapters).

An example of a firm that successfully organized itself through interdisciplinary teams is the Norwegian Petroleum Directorate (OD). It introduced interdisciplinary teams (called levels) with team leaders. This structure worked well for OD over a long period, and it became a model of flat structure with team organization. An important premise in making this organization function was instruction and management training for the team leaders in the new roles. Over time a lack of interaction across teams became more and more apparent, and as a consequence, a middle management level was introduced.

If several teams work in an agile way, dependencies will emerge between the various teams and the rest of the organization. Processes can become delayed because one team depends on deliverables from another team, which in turn can cause pressure and stressful situations for one team, while other teams may have spare time. The need for coordination was particularly evident at DNB when it introduced the agile organization in its IT division. Its tightly interwoven core technological systems involved strong dependencies between the teams.

The agile structure must further balance customer adaptation against scalability and efficient operations. Tensions between efficiency and flexibility may lead to a perception that one must choose, but in well-functioning agile organizations, the key is to balance both aspects. On the one hand there is the need for flexibility by quickly being able to change and adapt to new needs, and on the other hand, the need to develop systems and standardized solutions that support efficient production and deliveries. Organizations in regulated industries, especially, will need to maintain stability and predictability in internal support functions.

To accomplish a good balance between efficiency and flexibility, customer-centric interdisciplinary teams (squads) are often combined with more traditional departments that are stable over time. Such a solution ensures efficiency and economies of scale across the organization. What becomes important in such a hybrid solution is to ensure that the agile teams interact well with the traditional units. It is not only agile teams that work in new ways; the traditional units also have to work differently in order to support the teams.

The total number of teams in the agile organization will depend on the requirement for different deliveries. As changes occur in the market and the organization, the number of teams often changes. Some teams have responsibility for end-to-end deliveries, while other teams are responsible for specific tasks and then hand over the job to another team or department. FINN.no distinguishes between vertical teams, solution teams, and platform teams, as these have different tasks and expertise. We describe this in more detail in the case that follows, but books have also been written that introduce team typologies (see for example Skelton & Pais, 2019).

Management and governance

To ensure well-coordinated teams, it is important that the team's goals and mandate are seen in the context of the more general vision and objectives for the entire organization. In other words, each team has its own mandate and requirements for deliveries, which is clearly connected and aligned with the broader firm objective.

Since agile organization involves autonomous teams, the role of the manager has been the subject of debate. Some have asked about whether one needs managers in an agile organization; in particular the middle manager has been a "victim" in this debate. A leading researcher in the field of strategy, Gary Hamel, has published a bestselling book (Hamel & Zanini, 2020) which refers to management groups as 'wormholes' and a 'bureaucracy that few defend, but that is everywhere. However, in our experience as researchers and practitioners, getting rid of the middle manager has never been a recipe for success when aiming for increased innovation capacity – not even among agile organizations.

A flat organizational structure is not synonymous with fewer managers, but rather a different type of management. In a model that puts the team at the center, it is tempting to view leadership as servant leadership, as we discussed in Chapter 2 (Northouse, 2019).

The management's role in the agile organization is to facilitate and ensure collaboration across organizational boundaries, connect silos, and trigger possible synergies to cultivate and strengthen networks of teams. The agile solution assumes that it is unrealistic and inaccurate to expect that a handful of people at the top of an organization will always have the best answers and ideas. Therefore, managers are encouraged to delegate responsibility and relinquish control in order to utilize the collective capabilities of the entire organization. Encouraging and supporting the employees and the multidisciplinary teams to experiment, continuously learn and to fail quickly is seen as important. The management's most important job in the agile organization is to facilitate that teams can do their work.

Competence

Changing from a traditional structure based on functions and professions to interdisciplinary teams can be challenging for the individual employees. Questions that arise are: what happens to my own professional development? Who can I learn from? Do I have sufficient competence to represent "my" field in the team so that the team succeeds? Interdisciplinary teams can come at the expense of cutting-edge expertise and specialized professional fields. New team members risk feeling alone with their expertise in a team where everyone else has completely different expertise.

The consequences of underestimating the need to support and train employees in new ways of working can be detrimental. Moving from a more traditional organizational structure with known career opportunities to an agile structure will also change the systems and structures for employee development and learning. Career development may shift from an emphasis on moving up in the hierarchy towards horizontal transfers which allows for the acquisition of new knowledge and skills that support the company's mission.

Employees will also need to develop collaboration skills. One of the pitfalls Spotify experienced (Lee, 2020) was that it was taken for granted that collaboration was an innate competence. But efficient collaboration requires trust and psychological safety within the team. In the agile organization, it is therefore important to ensure that employees are trained in collaboration.

External relations

Agile organizing can also have implications for customers, suppliers, and other external relations. Accelerating innovation may require that customers or suppliers also organize themselves in an agile way. Partnerships with start-ups, for example, can be a way for established firms to learn from younger and more agile organizations. We will come back to partnerships with other organizations in Part 3 of this book.

One type of external relationship that can provide momentum to innovation is outside groups that contribute in one way or another through crowdsourcing. External crowds can test or respond to a product or service before it is launched. They can thus contribute to sensing and needs in the market.

Mobilizing external relations presents some obligations. To successfully involve external parties in agility, the firm must invest time in getting to know the external partner and considering whether formal agreements need to be made.

A critical view on agility

As mentioned, a company that is often cited as a good example of an agile organization is Spotify. However, a former employee of Spotify, Jeremiah Lee, has warned against uncritical use of agility and says that "Spotify does not use the 'Spotify model' and neither should you!" (Lee, 2020).

Lee described how the company tripled in size to three thousand people in 18 months. What companies call squads (teams) and tribes (a department consisting of several squads/teams) was really just an ambitious idea that was never fully implemented. According to Lee, the agile organization created chaos, and the company's managers were gradually "forced" into more traditional management structures that ensured management and collaboration across tribes and squads.

> Even though we wrote it, we didn't do it. It was part ambition, part approach. People have really struggled to copy something that didn't really exist. (Joakim Sundén, agile coach in Spotify 2011–2017)

In Norway the "Spotify model" has been an inspiration for a number of established companies that have made the pilgrimage to Sweden to study the agile organization. New trends and ideas such as the agile organization can create power and energy for renewal and innovation. But an uncritical approach to agile organizing can also become an expensive and energy-consuming process.

Changing the organizational structure in established and mature businesses is in itself a very demanding process for both managers and employees. Introducing a new tribal language at the same time as an agile organization risks that too much energy is used on understanding the methodology and concepts themselves, rather than what agility attempts to achieve. As mentioned, the purpose of the agile organization is to increase the firm's pace of adaptation to customer needs and external changes. Large complex change processes require capacity for change (Meyer & Stensaker, 2011; Stensaker & Haueng, 2016), and new "language" can create unnecessary misunderstandings and uncertainty among employees.

In the research literature, we also find studies indicating innovation in some cases is hampered by agile organization (Annosi et al., 2020). Therefore, following the latest fashion uncritically can in itself become an obstacle to increased innovation capacity.

How agility changes the established firm

Clearly, developing an agile organization is not something that happens overnight. It requires a long-term focus with systematic work along several cogs to gradually change the established firm's DNA. Often this will involve several minor changes over time. The agile organization places the customer at the center and gives employees considerable scope to explore, develop and innovate. These are some central and important prerequisites for increasing the innovation capacity in the organization.

To illustrate the agile organization, we will now present two cases: Fana Sparebank and FINN.no Both companies have been on a journey towards agility. Furthermore, both companies started by experimenting with agile working methods in individual teams, and thereafter the ideas have spread. Eventually, the entire organizations have become more agile, with structures and decision-making processes changing accordingly. Whether beginning to experiment with a few teams or approaching the work more radically, a key feature will include external orientation and rapid adaption to what changes in the environment.

CASE 6.1
FANA SPAREBANK – FROM FIVE-YEAR STRATEGIES TO SEMI-ANNUAL SPRINTS[7]

Fana Sparebank introduced agile working methods in 2018. This method was used in the development of Himla Eiendom (a new and innovative business model for real estate brokerage), which we described in Chapter 3 under the ambidextrous solution. Today, the bank has a hybrid model where a good part of the work is carried out through agile teams, while support functions are organized in a traditional hierarchy.

Fana Sparebank is an independent savings bank based in Bergen. The group consists of Fana Sparebank, Fana Sparebank Eiendom, and Fana Sparebank Boligkreditt. The company has approximately 135 employees. In 2020, Fana Sparebank was voted Norway's third best workplace by Great Place to Work Norway.

A new director for innovation and digital channels was recruited some years ago, and she initiated a number of changes. The long-term strategic plans were not actively used in the organization, and the management saw a need to think anew. Five-year strategies were replaced by semi-annual sprints, and new agile ways of working were introduced in parts of the bank.

Director for innovation and digital channels, Marianne Wik Sætre, described it as follows:

> ... the bank has moved away from the traditional banking organization and the old customer segment approach, where the categories of private customers, corporate customers and the capital market were typically the basis of the structure. Today, the bank is more geared towards the individual customer's needs, and tries to find the proper channel to reach them – regardless of which customer group they belonged to previously. (Magma, 2018)

Prior to introducing the semi-annual sprints, a clean-up process on the IT side was set in motion in which the bank's digital resources were reassessed in an overall perspective. According to Sætre, this initial process was absolutely necessary, but generated no new income or services. However, it paved the way for the agile way of working with quick sprints.

The comprehensive strategy document was replaced with a short and action-oriented memorandum that is updated twice a year. This memorandum

7 This case is based on research in the RaCE program and in particular a master's thesis at NHH written by Samyuktha Kamath, 2020.

forms the basis for the selection of projects to be organized in sprints. The very first time the agile working method was introduced, the bank ran a workshop where all employees could propose innovative projects. This resulted in several hundred proposals for innovative projects. In this way, the entire organization has participated in the innovation work. The management prioritized the proposals and several years later, they continue to look back at these original ideas to assess whether there is anything here that should be implemented in a sprint. Also subsequent innovation ideas normally come from employees, and the entire process of the half-yearly sprints has been put into a system.

Interdisciplinary self-organizing teams

For each sprint project, an interdisciplinary team is set up comprising three to five members. Of course, the largest projects include more people, but typically large projects are broken down into sub-projects to keep the team size at a reasonable level. In 2020, about 20% of Fana Sparebank's employees were involved in sprint projects. Developers work together with experts from the business and marketing side. One of the team members describes it like this:

> You work across silos, across departments. You get access to resources you don't normally have and working together on a project is very valuable. You don't have to sit on your own and then check with other people ... it's more efficient and it creates more momentum to work together.

Examples of projects that have been worked on in an agile way range from new business models (such as the totally digital, low-cost concept Himla Eiendom) to new ways of providing advice and digitizing loan applications. Here are some descriptions of what the agile teams have been working on and how they proceeded:

> We investigated how the loan advisors in the bank worked because all of them said they did not have time for the customers ... So we set about investigating what the underlying problem was. We interviewed people and asked questions about why it was so busy and what the advisers spent their time on ... We ended up changing the way they grant loans because the existing system was not efficient ... We developed a CRM system that made it easier for the advisers to have control over their portfolio. This was one of our larger projects within support systems.

> Previously, we entered in all the data from the customer in connection with loan processes. The customer gave us the information and we manually entered this into the documents. But then we implemented a digital process for loan

applications ... so now the customer can apply online, and we can automatically check pay slips and tax settlements etc. from Altinn (Norwegian tax authority). Then, all we had to do was collect all the pieces and create an application that made everything much easier for the customer. And it is much faster for us to process the applications. If we have all the data, we can respond to the customer within one day.

To solve the tasks described above, different types of competencies are required. The team needs developers with IT and programming skills, but also insight into how the advisers or those who process loan applications work, as well as insight into the customer's perspective. In particular, the IT and business side often describe how they have worked far too separately and specialized in the past.

Self-organization means that the team can follow the entire process from problem definition to fully implemented solution. This is important and valuable because it provides a different understanding of the entire process and enables rapid feedback from the recipient of the solution (whether these are internal deliveries or new services to the customer) as well as the opportunity to quickly correct any errors or challenges during use.

The management does not engage in details. They are concerned with the results. This gives us a large degree of freedom in the way we run the projects.

In other words, the team decides for itself how the task is to be solved. The project manager has overall responsibility. The experience so far indicates that the projects require different approaches, so there is no standard solution.

Common to all projects is that they are run in sprints, normally of six months, but they can be shorter and can also run over several periods. There are several benefits reported by experienced project members in Fana Sparebank. Tight deadlines assign a very clear priority. All other tasks must wait, and potential new tasks must be considered for the next six-month period. The project members can spend all their time and attention on the task in question with a clear conscience. Short deadlines provide greater flexibility in that unforeseen things can be considered.

When we have these short sprints, it's easier to say okay, now we prioritize this for three more months. And if it doesn't materialize, then we can change direction at the next sprint. Instead of collecting data for over a year and then finding out that it is no longer relevant, we can be more flexible.

Stand-up meetings and whiteboards

In addition to working in sprints with relatively short deadlines, another common denominator for all projects is that they begin with a start-up meeting where objectives are defined and an overall plan is developed. Goals and plans are drawn up. Extensive use is made of visual aids, both in planning and communication. To communicate status and progress quickly and clearly, visual tools such as kanban boards and lean boards are used. These boards provide a good overview of the flow and workflow and also show if the work comes to a stop.

> We set up the mandate, deadlines, tasks, who is responsible for what, timelines. In every meeting, we set up the board and show: OK, we've done this, this is the status. And we ask for input on facts and status.

The visualization is experienced as creating clarity and transparency because you can convey a lot in a compact format. It is also a flexible way of communicating goals and progress because the illustrations can be quickly changed and updated. Since the illustrations hang on the walls in the common areas, they attract attention and make the sprint work transparent.

A key aspect for making agile teams function well is the stand-up meetings every 14 days. These are described as "game-changers" in the way information is shared and progress is reported. These meetings are open to all employees throughout Fana Sparebank and take place in common areas.

In just under thirty minutes, all project teams report on their progress and status. The visual illustrations together with verbal debriefing have replaced written reports and make quick checking off possible. Hand-drawn illustrations are updated weekly so that everyone in the bank can follow the progress.

The stand-up meetings are experienced as an effective information channel. Because they make progress so clearly visible, they become a driving force that motivates, but they also create demands and expectations:

> We have a much more hectic workday and we have high demands on what should be possible to produce within a given timeframe. We often see that employees in other parts of the bank think that we are really efficient because we speak aloud about what can be done in a short time.

> We become like a small family that cares for each other. We are more open to new ideas and very dedicated to the job. We work 24/7.

> It is rather embarrassing to have to report that within 14 days we have not managed what we were supposed to. We must also report whether we have control or not.

In addition to the regular stand-up meetings every 14 days, the projects have internal meetings where the visual tools also play an important role. Some projects arrange meetings every day, while others have weekly meetings. Therefore, the white boards are used both in communication internally in the teams and externally with the rest of the bank's employees.

> I can summarize a meeting on the kanban board instead of sending emails with detailed information to those who have not attended the meeting ... then everyone will be able to see what happened in the meeting ... it is much better for sharing information. Everyone gets an overview of the process, and you don't have to help others see the big picture ... The board visualizes what is important and what is less important ...

By organizing the work in semi-annual sprints, the selected projects receive resources and capacity. The projects can be run without being constantly disturbed by other tasks. If new tasks and projects arise, they have to wait until the next six months and be assessed against alternative projects. While such a focus is described as important and valuable, both managers and employees believe that they have become more open and receptive to what is happening throughout the bank.

A self-managed team does not mean leaderless

The agile working method with self-management and autonomy can be perceived as making management superfluous. However, this is not the case in Fana Sparebank. Management has a clear role in the agile working method, although somewhat different from what we might think of as traditional management. In order to make the agile teams work effectively, management has the following role: selecting projects, ensuring a good start to the sprint, removing obstacles and ensuring the right expertise and sufficient resources throughout the project's duration. The management also safeguards that other urgent projects do not steal attention and ensures good collaboration with the rest of the organization that does not consist of agile teams.

Selection of projects takes place as follows. Twice a year, the innovation director collects all proposals for projects and evaluates them against the strategy and current challenges. The projects are ranked and presented to the rest of senior management. Everyone in the bank can propose projects, and there are still a number of good suggestions from the first major workshop. Once projects are selected, resources are allocated. Employees can signal interest, but management is involved in putting together optimal teams with the right mix of skills. This means that the teams are staffed based on competence needs. There are consequently no fixed teams; instead, the composition changes from project-to-project. Some members work on several projects or switch between projects and lines so that there is not necessarily a 100% allocation of time to the sprint projects.

The innovation director organizes the kick-off for the projects to ensure a good start to the sprint. These gatherings usually take place outside the bank. In the beginning, the kick-off centered on increasing understanding and knowledge of the agile way of working, but as this working method was implemented, the kick-off was more about how the teams can develop trust, psychological safety, and motivation, and about how to get the social and psychological aspects to function well. In other words, the kick-off is no longer linked to practical questions and planning of the work itself but goes deeper into what is needed to achieve effective interaction within the team and towards the rest of the organization.

In order to clear away obstacles and secure resources, the innovation director schedules an hour every morning for drop-in. Then project members can stop by without an appointment to discuss challenges or make quick clarifications, get agreements signed, etc. Usually four to five people come by to get clarification on issues that enable the work to proceed quickly and efficiently. The director feels that this has also become a possibility for informal updates on how the work is going and how the people are thriving. As mentioned earlier, it is also an important task for management to ensure that other urgent tasks do not steal attention and resources. The projects cannot undertake other work without management's approval. The projects must have full support in prioritizing the task in the sprint.

The majority of employees – 80 per cent of the organization – are organized along traditional lines. The interaction between the agile teams working in sprint projects and the line organization is important. The management is concerned with involving the line organization in projects where this may be relevant, but also to let the line take part in the projects by being open and transparent about what is being done. The stand-up meetings are an important arena for giving out information to anyone who may be interested, and many have taken advantage of this opportunity.

Results from agile working methods

Employees and managers in Fana Sparebank experience that the agile way of working has made them more capable of change; they have greater faith in the organization's ability to innovate, and more people in the organization scan and sense what is happening in their surroundings. According to the innovation director, the agile working method has contributed to a situation where "one can move focus and resources around in the organization to where they are needed at any time, without the processes becoming too demanding" (Lem, 2018).

Employees describe how in the beginning, they were stressed by the new way of working, but gradually became more confident that they could cope with it. The pace and frequent visible deliveries are perceived as motivating and give faith that the bank can succeed with innovation and has developed an ability to do this.

> We see that the sprints are successful, and we have become used to this way of working. We are definitely better at change now than we were three years ago.

The agile way of working also seems to have resulted in employees – also those at the operational level – picking up what is going on in their surroundings and linking this to innovation in the bank. Agility can thus help build the first dynamic capability: sensing.

> When we work on smaller projects, we become very aware of what others are doing, how we can do something different from our competitors. So, we use the knowledge of the market ... we are more out in the market.

> We must be skilled at picking up signals from the external environment. I don't think we'll ever be the first to launch something completely new, but we have to be ready to throw ourselves into it. If we do not follow what is happening outside the bank, we will not survive. We must be curious about what is happening around us.

As the quote above shows that agile working methods will not necessarily ensure that we are first-movers, or come up with the most radical innovations, but it gives us impetus and belief that we can quickly catch on to new trends and work with product innovation.

> This way of working makes us more innovative. We are more open to change and to changing the way we work. The pace is fast, and we can take in new things. We are more open to listening to others. We have meetings with external parties. We look at the world in a way that we didn't before.

A pitfall might be that all employees expect to be able to act based on what they pick up in their surroundings, it can become chaotic and uncoordinated. The fast pace risks that employees run very quickly, but in completely different directions. However, the structured selection process mitigates this risk and all projects that are put into sprints are clearly linked to the strategy.

Last but not least, time is allocated between sprint projects to reflect and learn. Instead of running onto the next project, systematic learning loops are set up after a sprint has been completed. Employees who work in sprint projects in Fana Sparebank express great enthusiasm. Perhaps the agile way of working has also contributed to the award from Great Place to Work?

CASE 6.2
FINN.NO - GROWTH AND SCALING THROUGH AGILE ORGANIZING[8]

FINN.no embraced agile working methods early and began experimenting with these methods in 2006. To combat slow and inflexible development work, the company began testing scrum, which focuses on transparency, visibility, and collaboration between different teams. This increased the job satisfaction of the IT developers and management, and projects that used this new methodology delivered higher quality and better progress than other projects.

In 2007, it was decided to roll out the scrum methodology throughout the company, and since then FINN.no has continued on its agile journey. Today, the company consists of about thirty cross-functional teams that all use agile working methodology, such as scrum, kanban and what they call *radical focus*, which is about measuring what really counts.

About FINN.NO

Norway's largest marketplace, FINN.no AS, was established in March 2000 and specializes in digital advertisements and services for buying and selling between private individuals, as well as small and established firms. FINN.no is today the largest Norwegian online service gaged by the number of page views. The company is part of Schibsted ASA and forms part of Schibsted Nordic Marketplaces, which organizes the classified business of the group. At FINN.no, users can search for almost anything. It has sections for

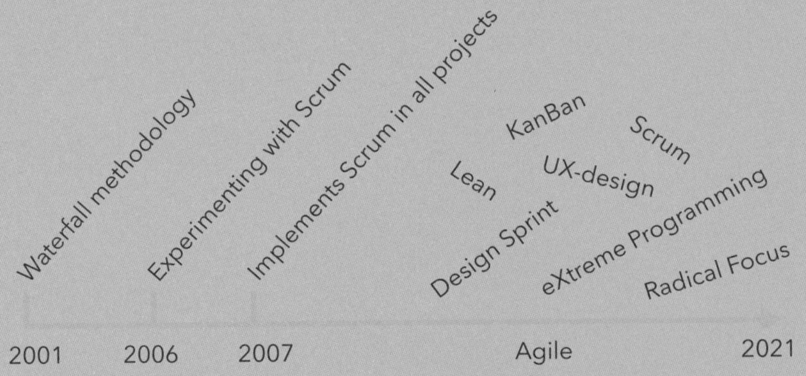

Figure 6.2.1 FINN's agile journey (Hestad & Solheim, 2021)

8 This case is based on conversations with key persons in FINN.no and a master's thesis at NHH written by Sondre Hestad and Lise Solheim. The case has been developed for the book.

property, jobs, automobiles, the marketplace, travel, and services within personal finance. Everything from holiday homes in the ski resort, bowling balls, cars, flights, and real estate, to jobs and much, much more. People from all over the country sell products and services on FINN.no.

FINN.no has existed since people began actively using the internet. It was established on the basis of the position Schibsted had in the newspaper classified market. At the time, there were other players in this field such as Stepstone and Eiendomsnett. Today, there are several million users every week on the FINN.no marketplace. The company has experienced rapid and impressive development and growth since its beginning. Its turnover exceeded NOK 2 billion in 2019, while for 2012 it was just over NOK 1.2 billion. FINN.no has a leading market position in most segments of the digital advertising market and is one of the companies in Norway that scores best in reputation surveys. According to FINN.no, continuous innovation and experimentation are key factors in its success.

Although FINN.no has a strong market position, the company is constantly being challenged by increasing competition from global actors such as Facebook, Google, and Amazon, as well as from niche companies with new business models and value propositions. Increased competition especially threatens the younger target group (Gen Z). An example of this is the Norwegian recycling app Tise, which has a strong position among young people between the ages of 18 and 35 for the sale and purchase of clothing and interior items.

In addition to a changing competition, FINN.no experiences that fast technological solutions change user habits and customer expectations. On digital marketplaces this implies more seamless solutions. Technological developments and changing user habits create a steadily increasing pressure on the development of new services and the further development of existing ones.

Increased pace through agile working methods and autonomous teams

Agile methods were introduced as a solution to a number of challenges associated with more traditional working methods (such as waterfall methodology). The traditional methods gave FINN.no an illusion of control, but when the company started experimenting with scrum, it observed that the project teams were able to deliver faster and with higher quality.

In traditional development methodology, changes to software took place step-by-step, and typically changes to the software were put into production four times a year. By using agile working methods, FINN.no achieved a completely different speed in production settings of solutions and went from planning how many production settings it ought to have, to "we have to do this all the time". From four rollouts a year in 2006, the status in 2021 was five hundred updates to the software **per day**. FINN's journey to a more agile organization is illustrated in the figure below.

With agile working methods and the establishment of autonomous and cross-functional teams, FINN.no has gained both speed and flow in development and production, and this has increased its ability to react quickly to changes in the environment.

FINN.no has prepared some central overarching ideologies for its agile working method; development must be *user-centric*, *target-driven*, and *iterative*. In addition, its teams have great freedom to experiment and possibly test approaches within these three principles. If someone has an idea, it is up to the team to consider what to do with it. There is a broad scope for idea implementation and it is up to each individual team to solve this in the most efficient way possible. Team leaders have decision-making authority and do not need to confer with the management of the organization. This decision-making authority means that the teams can make faster decisions without having to go through several layers in the organization. The teams will therefore be able to respond more quickly to changes that occur in the market.

FINN.no has worked systematically to cultivate a culture for agile development. Among other things, it developed a common understanding of the concepts and the implementation of the new working methods. This has been important so as to avoid misunderstandings and have the different teams develop in different directions.

In order to succeed with autonomous teams, management is central to FINN.no. Autonomy is not equivalent to lack of control. Through an overarching strategy, clear goals, and clear priorities, management gives direction and maintains control while it safeguards the teams' degrees of freedom and self-determination. The organization has developed a management platform with two main elements: being clear, and caring. Being clear means setting clear goals and guidelines for

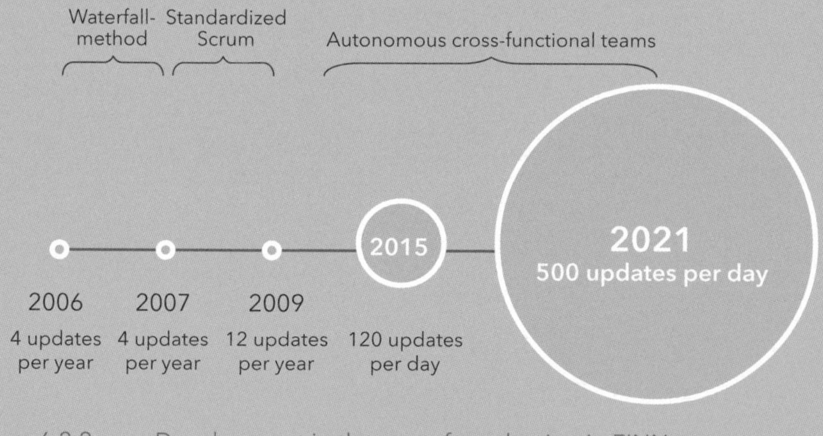

Figure 6.2.2 Development in the rate of production in FINN.no

what the organization should achieve, as well as clearly giving feedback. Caring means being relationship-oriented, as well as looking after and motivating the employees. FINN.no is very concerned that managers must master the balancing act between these two central management principles in order to succeed with agile organization.

From agile working methods to agile organization

Currently, FINN.no has approximately thirty teams, and there has been a great deal of focus on getting the individual teams to function as well as possible. In 2015, the management saw a need for a reorganization of the teams. They needed to strengthen the flow of tasks and activities both within and between the teams, together with increasing flexibility in the staffing of the teams. They therefore created departments called *spaces* consisting of developers, product managers and team leaders. The team leaders were given the responsibility to organize the teams within the spaces. The changes also included the introduction of some new ways of working in the teams and new requirements for the teams. Among other things, the introduction of whiteboards was an important tool to get a better overview of the work and production in the teams. The teams could choose how they wanted to work, but they had to communicate to the other teams what they were working on – "everyone must work together in a way" – and the whiteboards were used for this.

In theory it should be easy to change the teams as priorities changed, but this turned out to be challenging in practice. The teams had become more stable and autonomous than one had imagined, and some teams "stiffened" a little in composition. The dialogue between the teams was not optimal either. One challenge was that some of those teams were too loosely connected to the other teams. This was experienced as demanding both for coworkers and the management, since central dependencies and interfaces between the teams were sometimes inadequately supported.

The planned structure, which was supposed to facilitate a large degree of flexibility, was thus not fully implemented. Employees liked working in fixed teams better and building relationships within the team. In addition, permanent teams made it easier for the rest of the organization to have an overview of who worked on what. An important experience and realization with the establishment of flexible teams in FINN.no was that to a greater extent, they should have a clearer process for when a team is created or terminated, and not simply split up teams that work well.

Further development of the agile organization to accelerate the strategy

Although FINN.no had come a long way in working with agile working methods and the organization of autonomous and interdisciplinary teams, there was a need to take the agile organization a few steps further. In 2019, FINN.no decided to adapt the organization to their strategic investment, which was to create "next generation marketplace".

In order to succeed with an agile organization, it was especially important that marketing, product development and technology development would work more closely together. FINN.no started a process of exploring further improvements and adaptations of its structure.

Challenges and fundamental guidelines for organizational development

Some of the challenges that had emerged over time in the organization were:

- *Distance between the business and purely technological teams,* which among other things led to different priorities for the teams and across the organization.
- Some of the teams experienced *limited ownership and insight into the customers' needs and market* developments. This applied to the more technological teams who were responsible for solution components without necessarily being responsible for the "entire" solution. This was also a challenge in marketing and an acknowledgment of a need for closer collaboration across the board.
- *Insufficient coordination between the teams* could delay the launch. The fact that a solution requires deliveries from several teams puts pressure on coordination to be as optimal as possible to avoid the pace being reduced.

Based on a thorough analysis and assessment of the organization in relation to the strategic objectives, the management defined a set of governing principles for organizational development. These principles should address both the challenges of today's organization and provide direction and support the strategic goals. Even though the principles were defined based on FINN's needs, at the same time they are characteristics of what embodies an agile organization. The principal guidelines were:

- The customer is in focus at all "stages"
- Flexibility, but also stability to pursue economies of scale
- Clearly allocated roles and responsibility for results make teams accountable through clear mandates
- Facilitate learning and experimentation

In addition to this, management in both the product and technology departments added guidelines for the new organization. The next step was to explore different organizational approaches and solutions. Until then, the process had been led by a joint management group with a large degree of involvement of all unit managers in the respective departments, in addition to a large proportion of the employees having the opportunity to share experiences and views through an interview process.

Exploration of different organizational structures

To move even further towards an agile organization, FINN.no looked to other companies for inspiration. To an increasing degree, organizations are delivering digital services and products, and especially within banking/finance and the telecom industry, the growth in digital services has led to the testing and exploration of new working methods as well as new organizational models. It also drew inspiration from the books *Inspired* (Cagan, 2017) and *Team Topology* (Skelton & Pais, 2019).

Some of the central findings from this insight were summarized in two distinct types of teams where the different teams were composed and established for different purposes:

> *Vertical outcome teams* have the responsibility to experiment and develop new products and solutions within one segment/business area. The composition of this team is interdisciplinary so that it has both marketing and technological expertise and insight.
>
> *Outcome teams* are responsible for developing solutions for the vertical outcome teams. These teams are stable over a specific period of time (3–12-month duration) and have a mandate directly linked to strategic objectives through optimizing production and ensuring growth. Outcome teams can also be highly stable, such as a team that was set to process large amounts of data.
>
> *Platform teams* are responsible for maintaining and building capabilities within infrastructure and systems that are necessary to ensure economies of scale and support the solution teams. These teams are stable over time.

A creative and contributing process

FINN.no set up a highly participatory process of exploring and coming up with different proposed solutions for new organization. The strategic goals of FINN.no constituted an important foundation the principal guidelines for the organizational structure. All managers and employees were invited to participate in workshops where they gained insight into the analyses and assessments of both the strengths and challenges of how they were organized, as well as how other businesses had approached agile organizing.

The process of exploring alternative solutions started with a full-day workshop where all employees were invited to participate. It was set up as a creative process where employees were gathered in teams made up of different skills and subjects to come up with concrete actions. The teams then had to assess and evaluate their own proposals against the guiding principles, which then became the object of discussions in the assembly. There was a wide range in the proposed solutions, but also a number of similarities. The number of alternatives were then narrowed down so that a few solutions could be further developed. Another important result from this process was that it became clear that no one wanted to maintain the status quo, which obviously could also be an alternative. With this engaging and participatory process, a good platform was formed for the further organizational design process.

Moving step-by-step towards the agile organization

Therefore, FINN.no explored different options for an agile organization. The various types of teams, as described above, were an important platform in this process. Important considerations in this process involved assessing which teams they should establish, the composition of the teams, interfaces between the teams, as well as the purpose and mandate of the individual teams. Furthermore, the process involved evaluating flexibility, such as how stable the teams should be over time and within which areas of the organization permanent, stable teams should be established.

Customer-centricity is key in agile organizations, and for FINN.no it was important to decide on the trade-offs for the competences and resources that would make up the outcome teams. Should there be a small number of people who primarily had product and marketing responsibility, or should the team also increasingly include solution architects and system developers? These discussions resulted in the development of distinct types of teams as presented previously.

A step-by-step process was selected instead of a "big bang" (implement all changes at once) implementation process. It was considered inappropriate to change the organization too quickly; it would also entail too great a risk for the organization's ability to simultaneously take care of day-to-day operations. FINN.no therefore chose an approach where they tested out structural changes within some selected areas of the organization in the form of pilot projects.

FINN's journey towards an agile organization illustrates how such a change can take place through gradual steps. In this process, it became clear that a new structure alone would not produce the desired effect. Further work thus involved identifying measures in areas such as management, measurement and measurement indicators, incentives, competence development and culture. These areas correspond to several of our cogs. FINN.no pursued these changes in parallel with continued experimentation with a new structure.

Part 3

Opening boundaries for innovation

A clear trend in the recent decades is the recognition amongst established firms that they need to open up their boundaries to keep up with the increasing pace of innovation and develop sustainable solutions. (Chesbrough, 2003; Chesbrough & Bogers, 2014). Being introvert and holding on to one's own insights and resources has become a less viable option for businesses which want to stay in the game. Some businesses are also experiencing impatient owners giving them less financial and time room to innovate. Thus they become more dependent on reaching out to actors in their external environment (Borgers et al., 2019). Successful collaboration, however, is about more than just jumping on board. Businesses need to build up capabilities to interact with external actors, and these capabilities are fundamentally different from managing internal innovation processes (Dushnitsky & Lenox, 2005).

Having reviewed various organizational solutions to develop innovation capacity within the organization's boundaries, we will now explore different solutions to build innovation capacity by opening the boundaries. We want to direct the attention towards newer forms of collaboration and interaction with the clear aim of developing innovation capacity in the established firms. Collaboration or interaction means that one relates to one or more sets of cogs outside the business, and how it affects one's own organization will depend on what the purpose is, the size and number of the partners, and how closely and broadly the partners are integrated into the established business.

There are two general ways in which businesses can engage in open innovation (Bogers et al., 2018). The first, from the *outside in*, is about obtaining impulses and knowledge from the world outside the business. In order to obtain knowledge and resources externally businesses need to be able to codify this knowledge and also be relevant to external partners. In the second approach, from the *inside out*, the thinking that every idea or innovation should remain inside the walls of the business is challenged, and we will go into this in more detail in Part 4 of the book. However, the section on open innovation that follows in the introduction to Part 3 covers both approaches.

The outside-in approach encompasses a broad arsenal of opportunities, including collaboration and interaction with complementors and competitors, tech communities, users, and customers. Three well-known solutions are acquisitions, alliances, and clusters. The focus in Part 3 will be to describe and explore the newest approaches that emerge from the well-known solutions:[9]

1. *Interaction with start-up companies*, both individual businesses and start-up communities (Chapter 7)
2. Different forms of *partnership* that involve competitors, more than two parties and/or which go across sectors (Chapter 8)
3. *Ecosystems* that resemble clusters but are geographically disconnected (Chapter 9)

Before we go into the different solutions, we will first describe what has driven the established firms to open up to the outside world and systematically build

9 We draw on the RaCE research program at NHH in order to demonstrate some of the challenges in these co-operations. Together with master's students, we studied how established firms collaborate with start-ups and how they build their readiness and competences to deal with partnerships (for master's theses, see Mutoloki, 2020; Rahause, 2020).

competence by sensing and seizing knowledge. An overarching theoretical mindset that provides insight into this is open innovation, and we shall briefly reiterate the most central insights that are relevant for building innovation capacity.

Open innovation

Professor Henry Chesbrough's book on open innovation in 2003 hit a nerve and put words to the flood of innovation initiatives that occurred when firms opened up their organizational boundaries to search for new knowledge. Open innovation means that knowledge development takes place in an interaction between actors across organizational boundaries rather than internally in one business. However, openness in itself is no guarantee that knowledge will flow. For open innovation to work for an established business, the innovation processes must underpin the innovation strategy (Bercovitz & Chesbrough, 2020).

The idea behind open innovation is that the knowledge that comes out of these innovation processes has value beyond what a business can create. As mentioned above, there are two approaches to open innovation processes – one approach where the actors gain access to and can utilize knowledge generated in external environments (from *outside in*), and the other approach where the business's own knowledge and resources are made available for others (from *inside out*) through mechanisms such as licensing and selling all or parts of companies. From the inside out will often be based on ideas and technologies that the companies themselves cannot exploit or take full advantage on their own.

Open innovation can take many forms, anything ranging from informal collaboration to alliances, to ecosystems; different groups may be involved, for example customers/user communities, start-ups, competitors, universities, public bodies, and others. Open innovation is not limited to innovation processes that aim to develop new products and services; it also includes the more demanding processes around scaling.

Although it is easy to embrace the philosophy behind open innovation, open innovation processes can also be challenging (Felin & Zenger, 2020). First, open innovation does not provide any guidelines as to what companies should be open to. Moreover, there is a failure to recognize and acknowledge that much of what lies outside the firm carries a price tag. Given that open innovation takes place in interaction with other actors, open forms of innovation are often notoriously difficult to control and manage.

In order for open innovation to provide value, it is important that the business has some underlying strategic priorities and that the search for knowledge is relevant. If one has no idea what to look for, it is easy to aimlessly search and waste resources. It is also likely that the business will have to make investments in its own organization in order to be able to codify the knowledge and be attractive to potential partners. If the knowledge is potentially valuable, this can attract a lot of interest and the price will be correspondingly high.

It is therefore important that businesses are conscious of what they should do internally and what they ought to do in collaboration and interaction with others. Equally important they need to be aware of the timing of the various strategic choices. If a business has chosen to enter into partnerships, reversing the decision can both be difficult and expensive.

In addition to challenges around access to relevant knowledge and management, there are also risks associated with the ownership and distribution of the financial returns. Opening up may on the one hand increase the value creation potential and lead to more people being able to benefit from the innovations. On the other hand, there is always the risk that other actors will run away with the lion's share of the profit. Typically, profit distribution models are based on educated guesses on the success of the innovations, and most likely these guesses will be proven wrong. The dilemma between openness in development and the desire to develop proprietary rights in commercialization can also be illustrated by a comparison of the mobile operating systems of Google and Apple. In 2018, Android had a market share of 77% compared to 19% for iOS. At the same time, the gross profit of the iOS App Store was almost double that of Google Play (Schmeiss et al., 2019).

Innovators fear – often rightly so – that their ideas will be stolen when they pitch their projects and work with collaborators. More robust legislation protecting proprietary knowledge in this area can make it easier and safer to collaborate, though sometimes, and particularly in the earlier phases, it may be hard to protect or keep the ideas and solutions secret.

The question of how to handle intellectual property rights is therefore an important strategic issue for a business (Borgers et al., 2019). An example of a company that has chosen a non-proprietary approach in its *inside out* innovation strategy is Tesla. Elon Musk stated in Tesla's own blog in 2014 that "All our patents belong to you." Tesla's choice not to actively protect its patents is rooted in a belief that it had more to gain from openness than protecting its intellectual property rights, and Tesla's phenomenal turnover has not been driven by the software it puts into its cars. Tesla stands in contrast to the mobile technology company Qualcomm, which has licensed its technological solutions to complementary players, who in turn have designed and developed services and products based on Qualcomm's underlying technological solutions.

In practice, businesses will often choose both methods. Companies that develop game platforms are experts in balancing between opening up and providing access to code and protecting proprietary rights. They typically share *kits* with gamers so that they can develop their own versions of the games, while at the same time keeping some of the code strictly secret to secure revenue streams and sustainable customer relationships.

One of the most demanding aspects of open innovation is management and governance, particularly when open innovation involves a need to coordinate internal and multiple external forces. Other governance mechanisms than hierarchical control must be adopted both to navigate and structure such collaborations. Building up competence to meet such a reality will be absolutely central if one chooses to pursue the open innovation track.

Chapter 7

Collaborating with start-ups

In order to build up an innovation muscle, many established firms establish corporate ventures (CVs, see Dushnitsky & Lenox, 2005; Weiblen & Chesbrough, 2015) where the purpose is to invest in and collaborate with start-ups. The established firm provides funding to the start-ups; in addition, access to complementary resources such as production facilities and customer base can make them more attractive to start-ups compared to pure venture capitalists (VCs).

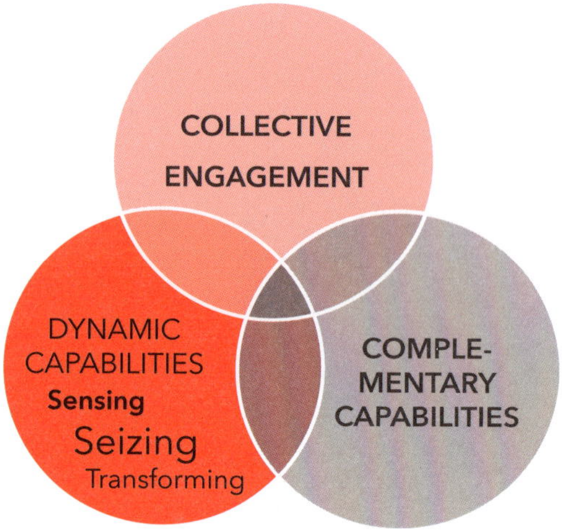

Figure 7.1 How collaboration with start-ups can contribute to innovation capacity

For established firms, the ability to *sense* what is happening in the external environment is strengthened through their collaborations with start-ups. Such collaborations can also allow the established firm to *seize* new opportunities, but this capability will normally be weaker compared to partnerships with larger and more mature firms. Many established companies also experience collaboration with start-ups as a small vitamin boost that brings in a new and more innovative culture, and which can potentially spill over and create collective engagement in the established firm.

From the outside it may seem that established firms and start-ups are a perfect match. The established firm has financial resources, customers and an organizational apparatus to scale production and distribution, which are resources that start-ups lack (Eisenmann, 2021). On the other hand, start-ups are overflowing with new ideas, the founders have their mind on their ventures around the clock, and they are not afraid to take on big risks. These are attractive qualities for established firms that crave becoming more innovative. Yet research shows that the gains from these matches are difficult to realize in practice (Weiblen & Chesbrough, 2015; Sopra Steria, 2021).

In this chapter, we will discuss what makes it so hard for established firms to collaborate with start-ups and describe how established companies have tried to mitigate such challenges through acquisitions and collaboration with start-up communities. We will also describe how the interaction with start-ups affects the various cogs in the established firms and illustrate the key concepts through two cases involving start-up communities. The first case shows how

StartupLab as a start-up community has been instrumental in building up innovation capacity in both the University of Oslo (UiO) and in established companies. The second case illustrates how a shipping corporation, Wilhelmsen, collaborates with a start-up community in Singapore in order to boost its innovation muscle.

Collaboration with start-ups

For start-ups it is often resources other than funding that attracts them to collaborate with established corporations. Today, access to data has become a vital and attractive resource for many start-ups, but other resources such as production facilities and marketing knowledge can also play an important role to develop and scale a young company. Moreover, collaboration with an established company might bring in the start-up´s first, large customer. Such a customer will ensure demand for the company's products or services and be important in attracting more customers. The collaboration between the start-up company Strise and Danske Bank is an example of this. It started with a small pilot project at the end of 2019 and resulted in a commercial agreement where Strise's tools were applied to combat money laundering in the corporate marked of Danske Bank.

Collaboration with start-ups is relatively new but increasingly popular in Norway. In a survey carried out by Sopra Steria (2021) in collaboration with NHH and UiO in which 31 established firms and 122 start-ups participated, 85% of the large companies stated that they had experience from collaboration with start-ups. However, both parties experienced the collaborations as challenging. The start-ups and the established companies often had completely different expectations for the collaboration and there was insufficient planning as well as too little respect for each other's differences and cultures.

Leading researchers in the field of strategy and innovation have described the established companies' collaboration with start-ups as swimming with sharks (Diestre & Rajagopalan, 2012; Katila et al., 2008; Hallen et al., 2014). The dilemma for the start-ups is that the sharks are often the most attractive partners because they control valuable resources, but they also have incentives to misappropriate ideas and intellectual property developed by the start-ups.

One entrepreneur who claims he was subjected to sharks has written a book about "start-up hell" (Prydz, 2020). Prydz and his start-up company Hipdriver sued the Norwegian telecom company Telenor for having misused confidential information and for breaching the Marketing Act, but did not win in court. Other start-ups have also attempted legal action to prevail against established companies, but these are often demanding cases, and it remains difficult to prove potential misappropriation.

There are several ways for start-ups to try to protect themselves against misappropriation. The simplest and perhaps most obvious is to avoid collaboration and instead seek collaboration with pure venture capitalists. Collaboration with these types of companies will provide funding and often also strategic expertise, but it will not give access to resources such as customer relations, data, and production facilities (Cox et al., 2014). At the same time, the incentives of the venture capitalists will be more aligned with the start-ups; both aim to create companies with strong growth potential and profitability. Start-ups can also protect themselves by applying for a patent, copyright, or trademark.

For established firms, collaboration with start-ups can be a means to sense what is happening in the environment and gain access to new, potentially disruptive innovations that may be difficult to develop internally. By investing in and/or collaborating with many start-ups, established firms can develop a broad sensory apparatus and bet on different technology options that may become future winners (Weiblen & Chesbrough, 2015). Although research indicates that established companies increase their innovation capacity through collaboration with start-ups, successful collaboration requires that the established company has developed the capabilities to utilize this collaboration.

Two entrepreneurs have made this into a business idea and developed a young company that can step in and take responsibility for driving innovation in established firms. Through several successful entrepreneurial ideas, Maths Mathisen and Vinoth Vinaya have gained a lot of experience in collaborating with established firms. On this basis, they are now focused on developing *venture squads,* which set up and operate an innovative unit within the established firm (see for example Hauge, 2021).

Paradoxically, some of the characteristics that make start-ups attractive to established companies also create challenges for collaboration. The willingness to take big risks and achieve a high tempo are important qualities in the competition for disruptive innovations, but for an established firm the assessment of risk may look different, and they often need more time to anchor the ideas internally.

For the established actor, there can be a high risk associated with scaling up a new, slightly unknown product or service for its own customers. If a mistake is made, it can damage the whole company and the brand.

> If you are going to do that with X's brand, you need to know that you have the quality and capacity to distribute (the product or service) … You need to have customer

service in place, and you need to know that the technology is sufficiently robust to serve the customers in the manner they expect from us ... (Manager in a large established firm about collaboration with start-ups).

It is also important to understand that the time horizon in an established company is often fundamentally different to a start-up company. For a start-up, a few weeks is a long time, especially if financing the company is a struggle and a lot is at stake. However, for an established company, a few weeks may be far too little time to anchor a decision.

> You learn a lot how to cooperate when you have what I call "The elephant and the mosquito". A mosquito has completely different needs from the elephant, which is slow, big, not very fast-moving ... The fact that we spend time on our process very often became difficult for the startups. (Manager in a large established firm regarding collaboration with start-ups).

On top of this comes the fact that there is a considerable imbalance in the power relationship, not only because one is the mosquito and the other is the elephant, but because for one party it may be a question of survival, whereas for the other established firm, meeting the start-ups is very inspirational and improves their sensing.

Even if the established companies are seemingly the powerful party in the collaboration with the start-ups, acting as the dominant part in the collaboration could make the whole collaboration unravel. If a business gains a reputation for stealing ideas or shutting down start-ups, it could lead to it struggling to connect with young, innovative companies further down the line. In addition, the established companies also need to build up expertise in what it is like to collaborate with a start-up. The start-up company may have completely different expectations for the collaboration and it may be quite immature in the early phase of its development.

From collaboration to acquisition

One way to deal with the challenges in collaboration between an established actor and a small start-up is to leap forward and acquire the small company (Weiblen & Chesbrough, 2015). Many large companies also have active corporate venturing units through which they take positions in or acquire young companies. The advantage of acquisition over collaboration is that the large companies can gain more control over the smaller companies and also secure their rights. Acquisitions also provide the opportunity for the large companies to eradicate the smaller companies, thus avoiding them being sold to a competitor (Katila et al., 2008). However, when established companies buy start-ups in order to shut them down, the motive is not to increase the established company's own innovation capacity. If the aim of the acquisition is to become more innovative, the owners need to tread more carefully.

An example of an established player who bought several small security companies to become more innovative (among other things) is the Norwegian energy utility corporation Hafslund's purchase of the alarm company Varslingssystemer og Vaktservice in 2001. The aim was to gain more momentum in Hafslund's core business and make the company more innovative and market-oriented. The alarm companies were not only technologically innovative but also very sales-oriented. They had advanced equipment for access controls and security locks, and walked the streets and knocked on doors to sell alarms. This was unfamiliar territory to a business that sold electricity. The first acquisition was supplemented by several other acquisitions within the security area. After having a positive effect on Hafslund's innovation capacity, the entire home alarm portfolio was sold at a profit to Securitas Direct in 2008.

The question of whether to acquire smaller stakes of a company or take over the whole business depends on the purpose and the necessity of having motivated entrepreneurs. The advantages of allowing the founders ownership is that it provides incentives for them to stay and work for the company, but it can also be challenging if the upscaling requires substantial capital investments.

> We really needed to speed up and build capacity and scale. In order to do that, it would mean more capital and more resources from X. They didn't want to expand their capital base because they didn't want to be diluted. (Manager in a large established firm regarding collaboration with start-ups.)

Allowing the entrepreneurs some ownership may also be difficult to implement because it would go against the established corporation's remuneration policy. Nevertheless, the incentives need to mirror the strategic goal, and when the goal is to build new innovative solutions, incentives need to be adapted to risky and innovative projects.

Another dilemma established companies face is how closely the start-ups should be integrated into their operations (Jemison & Haspeslagh, 1991). When the goal is to learn from the young company and sense ideas, the company should remain independent and not be integrated into the established firm in order to preserve its uniqueness and autonomy. When the value of what is being acquired is easy to codify and/or lies in patents, the company can be fully integrated into the established firm without the risk of losing its valuable assets. The biggest challenge is ending up somewhere in between. On the one hand there is a need to integrate the operations in order to realize gains, for example by putting the start-up company's developers together with the firm's own IT people. On the other hand, there might be a need to preserve autonomy to retain and not alienate key people in the start-up, and this calls for a lower degree of integration.

From single start-ups to communities of start-ups

Another way for established firms to work with start-ups is to collaborate with communities of start-ups. Gathering together several start-ups is in line with recent trends where established companies see a need to interact with several start-ups simultaneously. A number of larger and more global start-up communities exist today (Weiblen & Chesbrough, 2015).

Since the 2000s there has been significant growth in start-up communities, and several of these run their own accelerator programs. These are time-limited programs where the start-ups must apply to be given access and often pay an entrance fee. In the programs, the entrepreneurs get help to build the companies as well as access to large networks of experienced advisers. In Norway today, there are several tech accelerator programs for start-ups, including Antler, StartupLab, 6AM, Katapult and The Factory.

Table 7.1 Start-up communities in Norway

Companies	ANTLER	STARTUPLAB	6AM	KATAPULT	THE FACTORY
Description of companies	Antler is a venture capital investor and start-up generator that was founded in Singapore in 2017. In Norway, the program is primarily aimed at the areas of energy, property, and mobility.	StartupLab is a tech incubator started in Oslo in 2012 and is aimed at technology companies with global ambitions.	6AM Accelerator is an incubator established in Trondheim in 2019.	Katapult Accelerator is an accelerator started in Oslo in 2016 with the aim of creating tech solutions to global problems in the environment and society.	The Factory is an accelerator/incubator started in Oslo in 2017 which started in Fintech, but has gradually spread to research, real estate and retail.
Description of programs	Through the 11-week program, participants get the opportunity to find co-founders and build a company. Participants gain access to an international network of over 500 partners and advisers who help validate ideas.	The companies in the program are in StartupLab for an average of 12 to 18 months. Two dedicated members of the StartupLab team follow the companies closely, and affiliated partners from large companies and the investor side assist with knowledge and guidance.	The program spans six months, where a large network of mentors has the opportunity to connect the companies to the industry in Trøndelag, in addition to also connecting them to other international programs.	Katapult admits companies from all over the world and offers a three-month learning program to scale the companies' businesses. Participants gain access to Katapult's global network of investors and experts within various industries and technologies.	Startup Academy is The Factory's accelerator program and has a duration of 3 months. The program consists of lectures, workshops and meetings with The Factory's mentors and corporate partners. Startup Academy is a similar program for growth companies.
Ownership and financing	Antler usually takes a share of between 10 and 12%.	StartupLab takes an ownership share of between 5 and 15%.	The accelerator does not take equity.	All participants receive an investment in which the Katapult fund takes an 8% share.	The Factory has individual negotiations with each company, and the companies they invest in have an average ownership share of 7%.

Source: Shifter (30 September 2020).

For large established firms, it may be easier to deal with start-up communities. Instead of trying to find the individual start-ups themselves like needles in a haystack, they can use the incubators to screen candidates and recommend which companies are suitable. Because the start-ups are taken up through the programs, their ideas will also often mature and develop, which in turn means that the ideas are better tested and more realistic when they reach the established companies. The start-up communities can also be used as a sensing mechanism to discover trends and developments that are relevant for the established companies. For start-ups, being part of a community may be a safe haven offering them protection from sharks. Start-up communities can also help young companies to draft contracts with established firms that better protect their intellectual property.

One feature we have not yet discussed and where there is new research (Seran and Bez, 2020) is how to connect the front- and back-ends of the established firms. Typically, the front end consists of people with great enthusiasm for external collaborations, but they also need to connect the back-end (consisting of other operative units in the established firms that do not have direct contact with the start-ups) to the collaboration get the right expertise on board and to scale the innovations. Mobilizing the back-end may be a strenuous task, but a singular focus on the front-end may end in failure. As such, the front-end people should have a dual focus connecting the back-end to the start-ups. The importance of connecting the front- and back-end is something we will return to in the Wilhelmsen case.

Start-ups and the cogs

In collaboration with start-ups, it will primarily be the cogs consisting of external relationships and ownership that are affected. But the collaboration can also affect the competence, management and governance, culture, and incentives in the established company.

Collaboration with companies outside one's own organization means dealing with one or more new sets of cogs. If the purpose of the established firm is primarily to sense, the cogs of the established firm will not be significantly affected, with the exception of an increase in *external relations* and *ownership*. If the purpose is to seize the opportunities and scale ideas and innovations from the start-ups, it will have a greater impact on the cogs of the established firm.

Collaboration with start-ups will often be associated with taking ownership positions, either in the form of participating in the funding of the start-ups, or acquiring them. Central to building innovation capacity is that the investments are not purely financial, but that they are strategically motivated. In order to be attractive to start-ups, it will also be important to have orderly contracts that protect the start-ups' ideas or proprietary knowledge. Given the challenges in collaboration between small and established firms, the established firms need to build up competence to handle external relations. This includes, for example, a stable, established apparatus that the entrepreneurs can deal with to make quick decisions.

If these investments are to have any effect on the established firms beyond sensing, *systematic skills development and management attention* is required in the established companies. As we will show in the case of Wilhelmsen below, an important prerequisite for a successful collaboration was being able to anchor the collaboration internally and thereby mobilize complementary expertise. The established companies can also learn from collaboration with the start-ups and be exposed to an *entrepreneurial culture* with agile working methods and new technological solutions. If one acquires a start-up, it will be a question of how closely the start-up company's cogs should be meshed with the established company. The biggest danger with such acquisitions is that the large company becomes too strong and tone-deaf, therefore killing the values it sought from the start-ups. If one goes down the acquisition track, *incentives* will be necessary to ensure that the founders stay sufficiently long in the company's early phase.

CASE 7.1
STARTUPLAB – AN ECOSYSTEM FOR FOUNDERS[10]

In this case, we illustrate how a start-up community – StartupLab – functions and how it has contributed to building up innovation capacity not only in the established companies, but also how the established research environment at UiO has become more market-oriented and innovative. In this sense, StartupLab has assumed the role of an intermediary between the university environment and the established companies.

From research to incubator

In 1984, Innovasjonssenteret A/S was founded in Oslo. This was the start of Norway's first science park. The science park was launched as "a tool to strengthen cooperation between industry and research." The original owners were the University of Oslo, Oslo municipality, the research institutes in Oslo and eleven large industrial companies. In 1998, SIVA (a Norwegian state enterprise aimed at building an innovation infrastructure) became an owner.

Svenning Torp was managing director until 2010, but he then handed over the baton to Karl-Christian Agerup, who developed the park further over the next ten years. Agerup renamed the Science Park to Oslotech AS, which is behind and operates the Science Park, and it has initiated and owns in whole or in part the various initiatives StartupLab, Aleap, ShareLab and several initiatives for growth. In 2021, 250 companies and 2500 people work here on a daily basis.

Agerup built his first company, Hugin, from an office along the lower part of the Aker river, Mølla, in Oslo. He worked together with Alexander Woxen, who would later become the entrepreneur behind StartupLab. The Norwegian business paper Finansavisen refers to Agerup as the godfather of the Norwegian venture industry and the actual founder of Northzone (the venture fund that became immortal after making billions on Spotify). Not long after Agerup began as head of the Science Park, he recruited Alexander Woxen. From this point on, things moved fast. StartupLab was established just over a year later with Woxen as founder. Agerup took on the role of chairman and actively used the new community to secure a broad expansion of the park.

At the start, the new university surroundings were somewhat unfamiliar for the founders. They had been used to meeting at Mølla. That was where First Tuesday had started, and this had been an important meeting point for countless

10 This case is based on interviews med Karl-Christian Agerup, secondary sources, and the authors' own knowledge about how start-up communities function. The case has been developed for the book.

people in many start-ups in the 1990s, not only from Oslo but from larger cities in the Nordics and Europe too. However, the network was mobile, and slowly but surely the well-known entrepreneurs were brought to the university premises. Some were installed there because it was close to the university campus. In the initial phase, there was some trial and error.

"In the beginning, there were few cool companies and cool entrepreneurs. Not much happened either. So, then we thought, okay, we just have to create a kick-ass incubator, really, one that makes the entrepreneurs *want* to come to the Science Park," Agerup says of the first period. It turned out that the proximity to larger companies, the growing group of exciting personalities, and not least the proximity to the various research environments at the University of Oslo would be a shot in the arm.

The new venture capitalists Geir Førre, Jon von Tetzchner and Rolf Assev soon joined the community. "What happened then was that three or four more people suddenly arrived who wanted to meet together with Jon, Rolf and Geir. Eventually it became a pretty cool community," continues Agerup. Rent was set low. Start-ups could be there for NOK 200 a month. The aim was also to have a high turnover rate, which meant that new companies were constantly being onboarded. The idea was that those who eventually managed to stand on their own two feet would move out and move on.

StartupLab was established to create a meeting place for technology entrepreneurs, but with active advice from more experienced entrepreneurs. Nevertheless, it did not take long before the first venture fund was started, aimed at investing in the businesses of the entrepreneurs who had offices there. At the time, the venture community was still licking its wounds from the dotcom boom and the financial crisis. Nevertheless, Woxen, Agerup and the others managed to collect NOK 30 million by going round to their former investors. Then the ball started rolling. In the first fund, StartupLab contributed just NOK 1 million; there would be more later. Ownership of StartupLab is split 67% between employees and 33% to Oslotech, which is essentially owned by the University of Oslo, Siva, and Oslo municipality. The non-traditional ownership, consisting of entrepreneurs and public and private businesses, was probably quite demanding to handle at times. Regardless, the environment survived and has grown. Today, more than 200 people are located at the premises. Every six months, new people enter and others exit. "So, in a way, StartupLab was the starting point for the entire Science Park to change character. Everything is much more innovation-driven, and outside communities queue up to collaborate with the many young companies that are based there," continues Agerup.

A sandbox for development and innovation

After the community had settled, however, there was one essential thing missing from StartupLab. "We lacked the large companies," Agerup stressed. "We were looking for funding, we were looking for the first customer, but we were also looking for expertise and experience to help these businesses go out into the world. So, in a way, all three things were very good reasons for us to bring larger, more mature companies into the fold that we had created," he continues.

The price for a collaboration agreement with an established company was set at NOK 1 million per year. The amount was set high to ensure collective engagement from the partners, but at the same time sufficiently low to avoid innovation washing.

For the companies that signed agreements, this then became a question of how to best utilize an ecosystem of innovation companies. In retrospect, it is interesting to see that different models for collaboration were chosen. The situation of the various companies was then also quite different. Today, the partner network consists of Orkla, If, Equinor, NAF, DNB, EnTur, Posten, Schibsted, Telenor and the Møller Group. Topics such as mobility, energy, data science and infrastructure attract the interest of both start-ups and the more established companies.

There can be a lot to gain for the more established companies if the right models for collaboration in the development of new products and services are found. The term "regulatory sandbox" is defined as a controlled test environment for businesses that want to experiment with new products, technologies, and services under the supervision of the authorities. Considering that the Norwegian Public Roads Administration, Avinor and Oslo municipality, for example, are also involved as partners in StartupLab, one can see how this allows testing in the broadest sense.

The three main motives behind the established companies' cooperation agreements can be described as follows:

1. Corporate venture ambitions

Several of the largest companies in Norway have their own units for investing in corporate ventures. In short, this means that the companies use their own resources to invest directly in start-ups. Usually this is done by those who want to invest relatively small amounts in young, innovative companies where the growth potential is great, but there is also high risk involved. This is done through joint venture agreements and equity contributions in the companies.

Those who invest can also be obliged to provide advice within marketing, strategy and further development of products and services, and in many cases companies can also buy or test these. The investment can be considered a financial and/or industrial option.

The start-up company can benefit from the capital contribution, but also from the industrial expertise and brand position of the investor. The actual network of already developed products and services at the established company can also make it easier to gain access to further capital, growth, and value appreciation. Great demands are placed on such two-sided collaboration in order for this to be successful for both parties. In StartupLab, we have seen examples of both.

2. Practicing the agile working methodology

Although established firms use agile working methods and some have an agile organizational structure in all or parts of their business, there is little doubt that change processes and the implementation of new tools are more demanding in established firms. The work processes and culture have been engrained over decades. The decision-making systems are often hierarchical. Traditional waterfall methodology, with long and heavy development processes, is more the rule than the exception, and a silo mentality within the various business areas is often difficult to change. It is precisely for this reason that the large companies can use StartupLab, the employees, and the associated start-ups as an arena to establish internships for management and key employees.

There are several examples where employees in the partner companies have worked in the start-ups for shorter or longer periods. "We saw several times that curious employees in established firms did their utmost to understand how start-ups were able to get so much out of two millions, when everything they did themselves tended to end up costing at least forty. By working side by side, however, you could get the best of each other's work methodology," continues Agerup.

Entrepreneurs were also brought into the established firms to work side-by-side with employees in larger configurations. In addition, programs were carried out in StartupLab's premises. One of the most successful was the gatherings with the leading pioneers in Design Thinking from Stanford University. These carried out practical exercises and training with both entrepreneurs and business leaders. In this way, common experiences in design-driven innovation were gained. This was oriented around the person and/or the customer. The analytical approach was coupled with intuition and creativity. Together, the users' needs, expectations and challenges were mapped. Simple user testing and concept development were carried out and sprints were held. For many, these were a stimulating break from an otherwise traditional working day.

3. A source for learning and updating skills

A good example of the partner companies' learning opportunities can be obtained from the Møller Group. As one of the leading car groups in the Nordics and Baltics, the group is very concerned about the new business models that are being developed and are engaged with everything to do with mobility. Driverless cars, new ownership models, shifting power relations between dealers and car manufacturers and, not least, new government regulation are just some of the keywords.

The Møller group challenged the community of young companies at StartupLab. What characterizes the future of car travel? How can new technology be utilized within different transport scenarios? How to connect the vehicle's technological platform with the passengers' needs during the journey? Hackathons were conducted. Several dozen people from start-ups and the Møller Group worked in teams over a long weekend. Contacts were made and informal conversations were followed up after the gatherings. Many ideas came naturally. "A couple of them were actually invested in; these had high relevance for the group. It involved, among other things, an app for tourists that constantly brought up interesting facts about the places they were during their journey," explained Agerup.

Furthermore, DNB and Telenor started their own accelerator programs. With StartupLab as coordinator, entrepreneurs were invited in. "We are starting a program now. We are doing it together with these partners. And you got perhaps fifty, sixty or seventy potential companies who said that we would like to be part of this, and we picked out perhaps seven or eight of the most relevant ones", Agerup says. Telenor and DNB committed their own management resources to coach for a three-month period. "It became enormously powerful. And several of the companies were invested in by the partners. Insights were accumulated along the way. New constellations were created. It's fun," he concludes.

The Science Park, StartupLab and the University of Oslo – a reinforced axis

After the first accelerator program had been held between DNB and StartupLab, a snowball effect began to occur. The tech communities in the bank had become more curious about the most innovative trends within Data Science. The milieu in the Science Park was thus challenged to bring in the best people from the Faculty of Mathematics and Natural Sciences. StartupLab then organized the first "cutting edge" seminar for its partners in Data Science and Artificial Intelligence. Professors of mathematics and computer science were invited to lecture to the partner companies. Refresher courses were held and experiences exchanged. "It was a prerequisite that you could actually program in order to participate in the course," said Agerup. In this way, partner companies lined up selected, highly technically trained employees. They came from different environments in the businesses, but they shared a passion for making better use of their digital skills commercially. The participants were given an eight-week course with the leading research capacities at the faculty.

"I received thank-you emails for months afterwards. We had suddenly connected the university with some large Norwegian companies and given the university opportunities to be able to give something back – in relation to knowledge development and skills enhancement among groups outside the university. They were given access they previously hadn't had. Suddenly, the university became more relevant. It was an effect we didn't quite understand the significance of in the beginning, but which only came about along the way," continues Agerup. "It's a part of our history that DNB later developed a separate qualifying training scheme for its employees within Data Science. The plan was designed and coordinated by the faculty, and dozens of employees have thus been able to build a new technological competence profile."

StartupLab – a model for geographical dispersion?

According to Agerup, Norwegians are not as network-oriented as, for example, the communities around the incubators in the United States. "A very good example was the gathering of the well-known entrepreneurs at the start. Eilert Hanoa, Erik Bakkejord, Geir Førre and Jon von Tetzchner all invested a million each in our first fund, but they had barely met each other before. Absolutely incredible!", says Agerup, emphasizing that if they had been in California they would have met each other at least a hundred times at this point in their careers. There is therefore great value in building networks – between entrepreneurs, partner companies and research environments. An important question is therefore whether the model created around StartupLab is scalable.

We got the first answer to this in 2018. This is the year StartupLab was established in Bergen. Agerup is optimistic about the possibilities going forward: "I think that the idea and the basis can be copied in many cities. Especially in cities that have strong academic communities". He goes on to talk about a visit from the technology manager of a large institution in Israel, which can best be described as a combination of the Research Council and Innovation Norway. "We don't have this here. We do not have the type of innovation milieu at the universities where you can integrate entrepreneurs with established companies, finance and capital, students, and academia. The incubators don't even sit on campus in California, in San Francisco or Silicon Valley," he emphasizes.

A demanding exercise for the public sector

The role as manager of the Science Park was a public role with public tasks. At the beginning, Agerup asked himself if he had been given the right and the opportunity to continue being an entrepreneur in his new role. Could he continue to invest and collaborate in the non-traditional ways he had done earlier? Would the role of manager of the park shackle him hand and foot, so that his energy and creative power were drained? This was naturally regulated in the employment contract and dealt with by the board, which consisted of representatives of Oslo municipality, Siva, and the University of Oslo, among others. It goes without saying that the risk profile and incentive arrangements are very different in such institutions compared to entrepreneurial environments and start-ups.

The first test of the possibilities came after the first two years. StartupLab had been operating at a loss of NOK 5–6 million a year, and Agerup realized that this could not continue. The founders and companies in StartupLab were initially mostly concerned with themselves and their companies. Businesses entered and exited. Some developed in a positive direction, others stagnated or changed course. However, the integrity of the community was not protected.

At one point, Agerup said that enough was enough. This could not continue. He suggested to the board that the partners had to be held accountable. "We have to make sure that it becomes their company, not ours," he pointed out. The proposal was that the four partners could buy 67% of StartupLab for one krone. The Science park would retain 33%. The assumption was that they would manage on their own and be capable of surviving with a grant of NOK 2 million a year. This would turn the whole dynamic around. Income increased, the environment grew, and the partners worked better with both a greater number and a greater variety of different companies.

Giving away 67% of the company to four private partners was a difficult decision to make. However, none of the three strategic owners wanted to take on an unnecessarily large risk themselves. They wanted to support the model but not stick their heads out too far. "Through a smaller ownership share, one showed that one stood behind the ambitions, but for the public actors it was probably also a positive dynamic in that there was more than one party involved," concludes Agerup.

What can other environments learn from StartupLab?

In this case, we have identified three important reasons why the established firms sought out StartupLab as a start-up community. First, the collaboration with StartupLab gave the established companies an opportunity to get a handle on their corporate venture work. One of the things we have mentioned in Chapter 7 is that it can be difficult for established firms to collaborate with individual companies, and young companies are often difficult to work with because they are so different from the established ones. Through the programs in StartupLab, the companies mature, and it also becomes much easier to find companies that fit the established ones and not look for a needle in a haystack. Second, through collaboration with start-up communities, established firms are also exposed to the entrepreneurial culture and new ways of working, and if the established companies manage to mobilize their own organization to participate actively, this can spill over and build innovation capacity. Last but not least, communities such as StartupLab are an important source of learning about new technologies and trends and thus the development of the established companies' sensory apparatus and dynamic capabilities.

It is interesting to note how StartupLab not only added innovation capacity to established companies but also commercialized research that took place in the university. Although we focus primarily on the established firms, universities resemble established firms as they are largely organized in silos that often struggle to build bridges between research and application and commercialization of knowledge.

The insight from this case shows that there were several factors that were decisive for success. One was co-location, where the entrepreneurial communities and investors met in close physical contact with parts of the University of Oslo. To make this happen, key investors who could get the ball rolling and attract other investors were needed. Furthermore, locations were offered at a low price, making it attractive for young companies to try out ideas and create an arena where young companies, established companies, experienced investors and researchers could work together and test out new ideas. Without clear financial incentives that motivated the investors, this probably would not have been realized. And the fact that the partners were able to buy the majority of StartupLab (for just one krone) triggered a collective engagement and willingness to put their heads on the block and work to make the start-up environment a success.

CASE 7.2
WILHELMSEN'S COLLABORATION WITH START-UP COMMUNITIES[11]

The aim of this case is to illustrate the advantages for an established company of connecting with a start-up community in order to find the right partners. The case also illustrates how to deal with the back-end problem and linking the expertise of the established company to the start-up.

As a group, the Wilhelmsen Group is well advanced in the development of innovative partnerships and many of the more radical innovation initiatives take place in the New Energy Division. The corporation has entered into a collaboration with ThyssenKrupp to develop a solution for 3D printing of spare parts for ships, has partnered up with Kongsberg Maritime in the company Masterly, where they are exploring the possibilities for unmanned ships, is considering hydrogen investments in partnership with several players, including Equinor, and has invested in Loke Marine Minerals, an underwater mining company – to name just a few. Several areas in the Wilhelmsen Group work to develop innovative concepts and collaboration, and the parent company is conscious about stimulating some mutual competition between the slightly different skill profiles in these environments.

In this case, we will take a closer look at corporate venture investment in the division of the Wilhelmsen group that sells marine products and services globally. The corporate venture investment in this part of the group is about introducing, developing, and adapting a start-up methodology in a more traditional organizational landscape, and includes both the scaling of start-ups and the development of a framework for more open innovation. The aim has been to organize this work in a way that does not disturb ongoing operations too much.

Development towards open innovation

Like so many established firms, Wilhelmsen has experienced how difficult it is to achieve innovation in parallel with daily operations. The company has had several innovative ideas that it has spent several years trying to get off the ground, but the ideas have run aground due to lack of fit with the existing operations, processes, and systems.

> We have had a few flops there. We have toyed with it for far too long internally and tried to fit it into our existing system, instead of saying, this is a good idea, who can we bring in as a partner and how can we get

11 This case is based on conversations with two key people in Wilhelmsen that work with innovation in cooperation with start-up milieus. The case has been developed for the book.

> it out of daily operations. (Manager I in Wilhelmsen)

The realization has been that if the desire is to innovate, the innovation work needs to be separated from the daily operations and stand on its own feet. Whether it will be incorporated into daily operations at a later date is still an open question and will be a different assessment in each situation. However, trying to make it grow on top of daily operations is no longer an option.

In parallel with the corporate venture, there has also been a cultural change in the company. While the employees used to be very protective and kept the knowledge and insights internally, they have become more open to sharing knowledge not just with start-ups but also with industry partners.

> If you are not open to what challenges we see, or what a solution can contribute, really then, it is completely pointless. You have to be willing to share, and be willing to go into it whole-heartedly, or there's no point. (Manager I in Wilhelmsen)

The entire industry has to a great extent shifted its perspective on the industry towards an ecosystem where each actor has its own expertise and value creation can occur together. This coexistence will sometimes initiate a need to regulate the relationship between the parties, but not necessarily. Stricter requirements to deliver sustainable solutions have also triggered a realization that the challenges are becoming too large and too complex to be solved alone.

Contact with start-up environments

Although Wilhelmsen decided to increase its start-up collaborations, the question was how. It realized early on that it was pointless to search for small individual companies to cooperate with – the search would be too unfocused and time-consuming. Its solution was to contact several established start-up communities.

> Meeting and having a good overview of what is happening in the start-up and venture milieus is very time-consuming. We don't have dedicated resources to just work on this. (Manager II in Wilhelmsen)

In order to benefit from the collaborations, there were some central premises that had to be in place. First, it was important to make contact with start-up communities that had maritime expertise, and there wasn't exactly an abundance of these.

> One reason why it has taken such a long time to develop a position is that it has taken time to develop a global start-up community aimed at the maritime industry. (Manager I in Wilhelmsen)

Wilhelmsen found the strongest start-up community in Singapore – also known as the Valley of Shipping, where Wilhelmsen has a strong presence. It is no coincidence that Singapore has a strong milieu in the maritime sector. Singapore has a strong focus on maintaining the country's competitive advantage as a key port and has established a set of regulatory and economic frameworks that make it attractive to invest and start a business.

> It is definitely an epicenter for start-up communities with a maritime focus. I think it is a combination that there is a lot happening in Asia when it comes to technology and that Singapore is a hub where the West has met the East for many years. (Manager II in Wilhelmsen)

The choice of partner fell on Rainmaking, and through this start-up and venture community, Wilhelmsen has entered into collaborations with a few start-ups as well as invested in a venture capital fund that focuses on start-ups in the maritime sector. Rainmaking was established in 2007 by a group of smaller entrepreneurs who wanted to use their experience, tools, and mindset to help some of the world's leading companies tackle the big challenges.

Wilhelmsen has participated in two start-up cycles organized by Rainmaking. The first start-up cycle was focused on decarbonization, i.e., various measures to reduce the release of carbon emissions into the atmosphere, while the second was aimed at streamlining the supply chain. On the basis of these themes, Rainmaking used its network to search for and find companies. Out of more than three thousand companies, just over a hundred were identified as relevant. The list of these companies was made available to a bunch of industry partners, who then individually picked out and met the companies they found matched their business needs. There were four or five companies that stood out as particularly interesting to Wilhelmsen. These companies possessed relevant solutions or technology that could fulfill the Wilhelmsen Group's future challenges.

Together with the German terminal operator HHLA, Wilhelmsen has joined the venture fund Motion Ventures as an industrial anchor investor and partner. In contrast to the identification of individual companies that could respond to Wilhelmsen's identified challenges, this is more of an instrument for knowledge about what is happening and for keeping up to date with new technology and innovative solutions. The industrial partners have been given partial control of the fund by having an active voice in the selection of investments and contributing their industrial expertise.

In other words, Wilhelmsen used the contact with start-up environments not only to sense what is happening but also to seize the technology solutions and implement them in their own business when they are ready. However, not everything that happens in the maritime sector is of interest to Wilhelmsen. To get the most possible out of the companies, they had to respond to the challenges that Wilhelmsen identified in their own business.

Identification of strategic areas

Wilhelmsen spent time internally identifying pain points in its own business, in the interface with customers, and in the maritime service industry in general. It is easy to make mistakes and get excited by ideas that start-ups have, but if these do not match its own needs or are too far advanced for the shipping industry to adopt, then there is little point in investing in these innovation opportunities.

> We are very careful that at the bottom of everything we do there lies a fundamental understanding of what are pain points in our unique businesses. What do we want to solve? ... There is a great deal of cool technology, but it does not necessarily solve anything in our industry. (Manager I in Wilhelmsen)

Wilhelmsen benefits from collaboration with start-ups within decarbonization and streamlining the supply chain. Decarbonization is an area where the challenges are so great that it is not possible for any company to tackle it alone, but through collaboration, the readiness for taking these new technologies on board increases. An example of streamlining the supply chain is the sharing of data to optimize port circulation. Currently, however, this is an area with little information sharing between the different actors and few, if any, have a good overview. The result is inefficiency in many areas.

Many of the start-ups are not very familiar with shipping. With the focus on sharing data and the need for better data flow across the value chain, it is easy to believe that these are areas with great potential. And that's true, it's just not mature yet. The infrastructure to ensure the transfer, sharing and processing of large amounts of data on ships with the same type of capacity seen in other industries is not yet in place, and without this capacity, it is not possible to implement many exciting and innovative projects.

> There are many things that we see could be fantastic solutions, that we know we do not have a recipient for or that the industry is not ready. (Manager II in Wilhelmsen)

> Ships are not yet equipped with the same digital capacity that we see in other industries, but ongoing changes are taking place here. (Manager II in Wilhelmsen)

Even if this and other areas are not yet fully mature, it is valuable for Wilhelmsen to keep up with the technology and be able to act when the industry is more mature.

> There are many things that we know are extremely slow in our industry, but we see that these can be resolved

> in the long term ... So we put things on the back burner and meet with them and see how they develop. (Manager I in Wilhelmsen)

Internal sales and anchoring

In order for collaboration with the start-ups to be successful, it must also be anchored internally in the organization, i.e. the front-end needs to connect the back-end to the venture. Those who have first-hand contact with the start-up communities must act as intermediaries and connect Wilhelmsen's system to the start-ups. In order to succeed in this intermediation they need to have good insight into the various areas of expertise, whether these concern the business operations or marketing or sales.

> We facilitate a number of internal gatherings and try to build a comprehensive understanding of the value chain ... We have a pretty good overview ... we know who can do things. (Manager II in Wilhelmsen)

To get a pilot up and running there is a need to onboard a project team of people around the organization with specialist expertise in the various areas. The specialists are the ones who know what works and what doesn't. In Rainmaking's second start-up cycle, which concerned the supply chain, managers of these businesses were first connected, and in turn connected their experts.

However, it is not enough to simply connect the start-ups and the incumbent firm; the working methods and mentalities are often different, and a bridge must also be built between these to achieve well-functioning collaboration.

> Developing internally an understanding of the mentality in start-ups is one of the things we have found demanding. (Manager I in Wilhelmsen)

Just the beginning

Wilhelmsen is in an early phase of developing its systematic working methodology to attract and collaborate with start-ups, but is quite clear that this is the way forward in order to strengthen Wilhelmsen's innovation capacity within corporate ventures. While they contribute marketing knowledge and give start-ups the opportunity to scale their operations, the collaboration with start-up communities gives Wilhelmsen insight into what is happening in the outside world that is relevant to shipping, and the opportunity to seize technologies and solutions at a time when the company and the industry are ripe for this. And although the culture is developing to become more inclined toward sharing and open innovation, there is still a long way to go to bring the start-up mentality into the established operations.

Chapter 8

Partnerships

Partnerships can take many forms and can range from contract-based collaborations, such as licensing, to alliances that involve cross-ownership or joint ventures. There may be two or more parties involved, they may be between complementary actors and/or competitors, and within or across sectors. In Chapter 7 we explored collaborations with start-ups and start-up communities. In this chapter we examine partnerships in more general terms before delving into the particular features of different types of partnerships.

There is a great deal of research-based knowledge about partnerships, especially between two parties. Many partnerships, however, do not have innovation as their main goal, and since the aim of this book is to explore different way organizations can build innovation capacity, we will limit our focus to collaborations where this is the aim.

Partnerships can be used to try to *sense* what is happening in the environment, but first and foremost, they are important for *seizing* opportunities. This ability depends on the established business's ability to develop partnership skills. Whether the partnership creates *collective engagement* depends on how the partnership develops over time and to what extent the culture from the partnership spreads into the back-end of the established business. Through partnerships, the established firm can also gain access to *complementary* resources, allowing for faster scaling than if one had innovated alone.

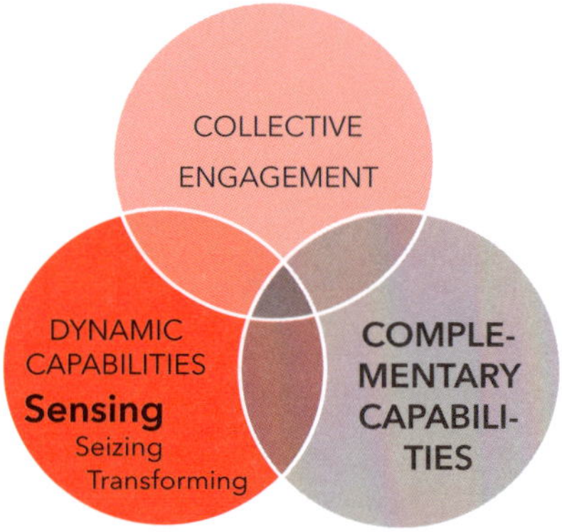

Figure 8.1 How partnerships can contribute to innovation capacity

We start by discussing factors that have been identified as vital for achieving success in collaboration between two parties. Then, we extend our focus to include collaborations that involve many parties, and finally examine co-operations between competitors and collaborations that cut across sectors. In the last main section, we take a look at the business cogwheels and discuss how different collaborations affect the established firm. To illustrate the key insights in the chapter, we introduce two cases. The first case is a collaboration between public, voluntary, and private sectors. This collaboration was put together during the outbreak of the Covid-19 pandemic to compensate businesses when the country shut down in March 2020. The second case is Vipps, which evolved from an internal innovation unit in DNB to a broader partnership, first by collaborating with the savings banks, and thereafter Nordic digital wallets.

Critical success factors for partnerships

The critical success factors for partnerships can be divided into three stages: experience from partnerships pre-agreement, strategic and organizational fit when negotiating the agreement, and governing the partnership post-agreement; see Figure 8.2.

Figure 8.2 Critical success factors in partnerships

Experience from collaboration

An important success factor for partnerships is the experience gained from previous collaborations (Gulati et al., 2009). This can be both experiences from other collaborations and experiences from working with the same partners. The general competence can increase the businesses' relational skills and make it easier for them to benefit from the collaboration. For example, by excelling in finding partners who complement the business strategically and organizationally, or by identifying which business models are best suited for the collaboration, or steering the collaboration and creating trust between the parties. For companies that have been relatively inward-focused, such expertise can be absolutely crucial to benefiting from the collaborations.

> We strive to work in partnership ... This is new for most people, they are not used to working with a partner, what they do is describe what they want, send it off and wait for the delivery. (Middle manager in an established firm)

Experience from collaboration can also be linked to the same parties, and this will enable the creation of trust between the parties. This was crucial in the compensation scheme case in this chapter, where an innovative solution was developed in only three weeks.

Strategic and organizational fit

Partnerships are useful because organizations gain access to resources and skills outside their own organization, whether these are dynamic or complementary capabilities. Importantly, what is usually referred to as complementary capabilities in partnerships (se figure 8.2) can be both dynamic and complementary capabilities in the way we have defined innovation capacity. Dynamic capabilities can for example be programming and technological skills at a young technology company, whereas complementary capabilities might be production skills or brands or other capabilities that go hand-in-hand with dynamic capabilities. These valuable resources will often take years to build up and cannot be purchased in a market. However, the parties can also benefit in other ways. In DNB's collaboration with 11:FS, a young British fintech company, it also benefited from learning about the recruitment processes by employing teams instead of individuals:

> They have a very good strategy, and it's also something I'd never thought of before ... They seek the best developers at other companies, and they also ask: who in your team would you take with you? So, they hire ready-made teams of people who have worked together. They have extracted so many tailor-made teams who already know each other ... They have a milieu; they know that they have each other. (Employee at DNB)

As in mergers and acquisitions, it will be essential to assess the organizational fit before entering into a partnership. Organizational fit encapsulates factors such as routines, cultures, and management philosophies (Lavie et al., 2012). Lack of organizational fit can be challenging if, for example, the parties have different leadership styles – say one is democratic, the other more authoritarian. Differences between cultures can be good if they complement each other, but if they are in conflict, it can be detrimental to the partnership. As opposed to mergers and acquisitions where one of the firms can be overtaken by the other, partnerships will require a continuous co-leadership from the partners, making it more important to resolve such conflicting differences at the outset. Partnerships can also be motivated by a need to share risks and costs. But collaboration can also be risky if a business is held up in a collaboration that leads nowhere.

Governing and managing the collaboration

If the partnership is to succeed, trust between the parties is essential. Trust means that one has faith in the other party in a situation where the other party has the opportunity to act opportunistically. Trust is not something that exists a priori – it needs to be built up over time.

There are several ways the parties can build trust in the partnerships. To create a common ground between the parties, they can invest time to build up personal relationships between managers and teams. Trust can also be built through resource commitments. One type of commitment that has received considerable attention in the alliance literature is relationship-specific investments, meaning investments that have no or little value outside of the collaboration. Partners can also show collective engagement by bringing their best and most qualified resources to the table – not just those that have free time on their hands or little alternative use. To build trust it is also important to have agreements that regulate information sharing and provide reassurance that the other party is not going to exploit the collaboration.

Sharing resources and skills is also often easier said than done. Capabilities can be tacit and socially complex, for example, when the capability consists of a product team working together. The entire team from one party may then need to be brought together with developers in the other party because knowledge will be generated in the interaction between the team members. In other cases, capabilities can be codified, making it easier to transfer to the collaboration partner.

Collaboration between many parties

When the collaboration consists of many partners, the complexity increases and thus also the risk of failing. Professors Barbara Gray and Judy Purdy (2018), who both have considerable experience as researchers on complex collaborations, argue that the framework for collaboration as well as the parties' contributions to it are absolutely vital to the success of partnerships between many actors. They identify the following success factors:

- The actors depend on each other to find solutions; no one can solve the problem on their own.
- A set of common rules, norms, and structures is developed over time.
- There is constructive trial and error through negotiations and consensus-building in order to find trade-offs that create value for everyone.
- The parties bring different skills to the collaboration and respect and learn from each other.

- All parties assume risk and are responsible for the result of the joint work.

Although complex partnerships share some commonalities, they also have some key differences which are important for managing the relationships. Professor Yves Doz, who has been studying alliances for decades, argues that the management needs to take into account whether there are alternative partners and how much relationship-specific investment is required (Doz, 2019). To explain this simply, we can start from a central player who wants to build an innovative platform for sharing data, but who needs several partners to make this happen. In this collaboration, there may be actors the central player is completely dependent on, while for other roles there are several alternatives. Say for example that a new platform for sharing health and socio-economic data across organizations is being built. The Directorate of Health controls access to many of the health registers and is the only party that can provide these data. It is also necessary to obtain socio-economic data, and these data can be provided by two different partners. While it will be absolutely essential partner to bring on board the first partner, there are alternatives for the second partner. These alternatives puts the central player in a less vulnerable position vis-à-vis these partners – at least at the start of the collaboration.

As people work together, develop the solutions, and combine data, they become increasingly invested in the collaboration. As more of the resources and investments become relationship-specific and have no alternative use, the more tightly the parties are joined together in a shared destiny and the less tempting it becomes to leave the partnership. If, for example, new registers are developed that combine health information and other registers, and the only place these combined registers can be accessed is through the new platform – this would be an example of a relationship-specific investment that has no alternative use outside the collaboration.

Alternatively, if the collaborations do not require relationship-specific investments, the actors are much freer to withdraw from the collaboration. For example, it could be that the Directorate of Health and one of the partners owning socio-economic data agree between themselves to link their registers. When the parties can use the resources in their own organization or in an alternative collaboration, it weakens the position of the central player.

In such a situation, the central player has two options: it may seek to build a common platform to strengthen collaboration and a feeling of collective engagement, or it may seek to attract and retain the parties by providing them with membership benefits.

Partnerships with more than two actors do not mean that everyone works with everyone all the time. Davis (2016) charted different constellations for collaboration between three parties and found three different patterns in how the collaboration functioned. Some collaborated in pairs, others had a form of *hub* and *spoke* collaboration with a central player – not unlike the central role shown above. But the last and most successful form was something Davis called *group cycling*, that is, they changed partners they were close to along the way. This illustrates that it is likely that not all parties are equally close in different constellations, and collaboration that changes focus over time can be good for innovation processes.

Collaboration and competition

In 1996 the economists Nalebuff and Brandenburger launched a new term, *co-opetition*, which paved the way for a completely new way of thinking about how many businesses compete and cooperate at the same time. In a new Harvard Business Review article, the authors wrote:

> In 1996, when we wrote about this phenomenon in business, instances of it was relatively rare. Now the practice is common in many industries, having been adopted by rivals such as Apple and Samsung, DHL and UPS, Ford and GM and Google and Yahoo. (Brandenburger & Nalebuff, 2021, p. 50)

One of the brilliant things about Nalebuff and Brandenburger's framework was that it opened up the possibility for businesses to have multiple roles as competitors, complementors, customers and/or suppliers.

The financial industry has long had a tradition of collaborating on joint solutions, even though there is stiff competition to win customers. BankAxept, which saw the light of day in 1991, is a prominent example of a successful collaboration on an infrastructure project where customers of Norwegian banks pay a fraction of the price on transactions in comparison to Visa and Mastercard. Another relatively recent example is the collaboration between several Nordic banks to create a joint company, Invidem, to combat money laundering. The company, which was established in 2019, collects data on people and companies, which makes it easier for the individual banks to detect money laundering. Invidem collects the data, but it is up to each bank to make their own assessments on customers.

Covid-19 also created a situation where competitors came together to deal with the pandemic. Two of the major big tech companies, Google and Apple, collaborated to create new technology that could track Covid-19. By sharing location data across platforms, the two companies enabled the authorities to develop apps that could notify citizens of close contact with infected people.

However, collaborating with competitors on innovations is more complex than collaborating with purely complementary actors. It is no coincidence that a nickname for such relationships is 'frenemies', a blend of friend and enemy. When entering into such collaborations, the first priority must be to take care that the Competition Act, which prohibits unlawful collaborations harmful to competition, is not violated. Finance Innovation, which we will discuss in Chapter 9 on ecosystems, has created a model to avoid this problem by involving a lawyer who is an expert in competition law in all projects where competitors collaborate.

But there are also several other conditions that are more complex when competitors collaborate (Hoffmann et al., 2018). It will often be more demanding to create a good, trusting relationship. As a result the parties may become more reluctant to share information and to provide their best resources because they are afraid that others will "steal" the ideas and act opportunistically. A company that was part of a multi-party fintech collaboration was afraid that the partnership would not succeed in its aim to come up with an innovative solution. It therefore hedged its risk by creating its own internal project. When this became known to the partners, trust in the collaboration evaporated, and although the project was completed, the solution they had jointly developed never gained momentum.

There are several ways the parties can try to overcome this lack of trust. To reduce the hazards of opportunism, the parties can adopt equity joint venture structures to align incentives, narrow the scope of the collaboration, or gain the mutual collective engagement of the partners' senior management (Gnyawali & Park, 2011). The parties can also choose to organizationally separate the managers or teams who are collaborating and those who are competing, a so-called bicephalous governance structure (Le Roy & Fernandez, 2015). A third option is to let a third party act as a broker in the strategic network to help partners to manage tensions (Fernandez et al., 2014).

Collaboration between private and public actors

Many public-private partnerships (PPPs) are routed in collaboration on physical infrastructure, but our starting point is collaboration on innovative projects. Such collaborations can take many forms. Today, there are many public-private project collaborations under the umbrella of smart cities. The overall goal of these projects is to use new technology and harness data in ways that increase well-being and reduce the risks of living in cities. There are also several collaborations on the sharing of data across public and private sector actors. One of the most successful examples in Norway, which will be further elaborated on below in the first case, is the collaboration between Tax Norway and Finance Norway, which has launched a number of projects, including a consent-based loan application generating estimated savings of NOK 13 billion.

Although public-private collaborations can bring great benefits and increase innovation capacity in both sectors, there have been a number of inherent challenges, and the series of failed public-private collaborations is long. Only one in ten collaborations deliver within budget, only one in ten delivers on time, and only one in ten realizes any gains (Ungureanu et al., 2019).

One of the most important inherent challenges is that the private and public sector are driven by different purposes. While private actors are driven by generating profits for shareholders, state and municipal enterprises have a public purpose and answer to the electorate. These different purposes are also reflected in the values of the employees. In the public sector, there is a greater proportion of employees with prosocial behavior, i.e., actions that are intended to support, help or be useful to other people. At the same time, it is not correct to present this as completely black and white, because within the private sector there has also been a trend towards pursuing sustainable goals that also take into account environmental and social impact – sometimes referred to the three P's: profit, planet and people. In the example above of the architectural firm 3XN, building an environmentally sustainable business was an important aim in establishing the ambidextrous unit GXN.

Public and private enterprises will also often have a different tolerance for risk. If data goes astray, it can be catastrophic for a public enterprise and lead to a minister being sidelined and the weakening of the population's confidence to report data. There have been several examples of data going astray at both the state and municipal levels. For almost two years, from early 2010 to November 2011, highly sensitive patient information from three Norwegian hospitals was stored on GE Healthcare's server in the United States and was not deleted for five years. In the municipality of Bergen, the commissioner responsible for kindergartens and schools had to resign in 2020 after a serious security error was discovered in the school app Vigilo, which was used for communication between parents, teachers, and childminders.

Public enterprises must also be careful that their collaboration with private actors complies with public laws, rules, and ideals such as equal treatment and legitimacy of the public enterprise. It is not without reason that we have strict regulations for public procurement. The aim is to avoid favoritism and to give business equal opportunities to compete for contracts.

Partnership and the cogs

The configuration of the cogs depends on the nature of the collaboration and to what extent the business is affected by the collaboration. Similar to collaboration with start-ups, in partnerships the established firm has to deal with one or more other sets of cogs outside its own organization.

Compared to collaboration with start-ups, it is likely that a larger part of the firm will be affected by the partnership(s), thus this type of collaboration will have a greater effect on the innovation capacity of the established firm. The most important cog that is affected in partnerships is naturally external relations, but other cogs such as management and governance, incentives, competence, culture, and ownership are also likely to be affected in the established business. The question of whether the partnership also involves *ownership* will vary. For some partnerships it will be appropriate to invest in the partner or partners, while in other cases the investments may be in a joint company. However, many partnerships will not be founded on ownership.

An important cogwheel in partnerships is the set-up for the collaboration, in other words what constitutes the *external relations* cogwheel. How close is the collaboration, how dependent are the parties on each other, and which and how much resources need to be invested? And how are the profits going to distributed when the collaboration is successful? In addition, how does one balance giving up resources and knowledge to build trust at the same time as maintaining (if desired) control over the most valuable assets? These issues reflect the challenges these collaborations pose for *management and governance* and the challenges for an established firm that can no longer make decisions unilaterally. Collaboration demands cooperation through a different form of governance that embraces management principles that instill trust and *incentives* so that partners share their (best) *skills* and resources.

Above, we showed that experience, both in general and from specific partnerships, was significant for how successful the collaborations are, and that in a *culture* that is secluded and introvert, it can be challenging to form successful collaborations. Most often, systematic work will be necessary if the established firm is to benefit from the collaboration and become more innovative, open, and collaboration-oriented.

CASE 8.1
COMPENSATION SCHEME 1.0 – AN INNOVATIVE COLLABORATION[12]

This case is intended to illustrate a complex and innovative collaboration – complex because there are many parties involved, cutting across sectors and working to a very short deadline due to a crisis situation. The insight from the case shows how important it is to reuse existing knowledge and components among the partners and select the right competencies to get up and running quickly. The case also shows how it is possible to challenge established decision-making structures, cultures, and working methods in the established firms to produce faster and more innovative solutions, albeit not entirely perfect in the first instance.

The beginning

On Thursday March 12, 2020, the Norwegian government introduced the most extensive and invasive measures ever initiated in peacetime Norway. Large swathes of the Norwegian economy were shut down and there were fears of a steep recession. Kindergartens, schools, and other educational facilities were closed. Cultural and sports events were prohibited. Restaurants, gyms, hairdressers, skin care and a number of other businesses were shut. All employees who absolutely did not have to go to work were sent to work at home, and no one knew how long the measures would last.

The government wanted to establish a compensation scheme to make up for the drop in turnover many businesses suffered overnight due to the precautionary measures. The idea was to offer financial compensation from the treasury. Some rough estimates indicated that the state would hand out NOK 50 billion to Norwegian companies. Each individual company would receive financial support based on its own size and its own drop in turnover. The challenge was that the state did not have an apparatus that could do the job; the Finance Minister cannot just put the treasury out on the street. The Ministry of Finance considered various alternatives and searched beyond Norway's borders, but could not find any satisfactory solutions.

Late on Tuesday evening March 24, a digital meeting took place which would be the start of an exceptionally complex financial technology project in Norway. The meeting was attended by Minister of Finance Jan Tore Sanner, Minister of

12 This case is based on the collection of data within the RaCE program and a project assignment on NHH's FinTech program. Data collection includes Tax Norway, Finance Norway including Bits, DNB, and the Ministry of Finance. The case is primarily aimed at understanding how it was possible to implement a solution in three weeks, and sheds little light on the political game and the negotiations between the employee and employer organizations and the political bodies.

Trade and Industry Iselin Nybø, Ole Erik Almlid (Director, NHO), Ivar Horneland Kristensen (Director, Virke), Hans-Christian Gabrielsen (Leader, LO) and Idar Kreutzer (Director, Finance Norway).

Idar Kreutzer saw an opportunity for the financial industry to contribute. He knew the Norwegian payment processing infrastructure well and suggested drawing on the well-established DSOP (digital public and private collaboration) between the Tax Administration and Finance Norway. At the meeting it was agreed that Kreutzer would explore the possibilities and report back quickly.

The following morning, Kreutzer called Eivind Gjemdal, CEO of Bits, the banks' infrastructure company for payment processing. The question was simple: "Can we help the state distribute money; can we solve this mission?" Gjemdal had to promise not to talk to anyone, this had to be kept strictly confidential. He was nevertheless allowed to involve a couple of colleagues with deep insight into the Norwegian payment infrastructure. During the day, the DNB New Tech Lab, led by Yngvar Ugland, would also become involved. Over the next two days, Gjemdal put together a seven-page document. This was Bits's proposal for a principal outline and DNB's proposal for practical money transfers. Kreutzer would present the plan to the Ministry of Finance on March 26 at 12 noon, and a press conference would take place at 8 AM the next day, Friday March 27. NHO, Virke, Finance Norway, and the Ministry of Finance met at the press conference.

The Minister of Finance was clear: We will create a solution; we will distribute the money. We must achieve this. Kreutzer followed up by saying that we will not only be able to create a solution, but we will also create it in three weeks. With a smile, he added: "But don't tell anyone."

Thus, the work could begin. The uncertainty was enormous. All that existed was a principal outline. There were no dedicated resources to do the work, no project organization, only a goal that one would go from concept to fully developed solution within three short weeks, which also included Easter. To succeed there was a need for a state administrative body which, according to the law, had the right to initiate payments on behalf of the State. Both Innovation Norway and Altinn were considered, but ultimately Tax Norway was chosen. It was quickly connected to the project.

The project had to develop tens of thousands of lines of code, but it also had to reuse and link existing services and infrastructure. The service had to calculate the amount of support and send the payment order to the bank automatically. The goal was that no persons should be involved from the time the applicant pressed "send application" until the money was in the account. Other requirements for the service was that it needed to: be transparent, be self-explanatory for the users because there was no large physical apparatus to help, handle heavy traffic, withstand scrutiny, ensure that no one got money illegally, and all development had to be conducted with (eventually) a couple of hundred people who were mainly working from home. At the same time as the service was being developed, legislative work had to take place and the framework for the scheme needed to be adopted by the Norwegian parliament.

Exactly three weeks and 13 hours later, there was another press conference. On Friday April 17, Jan Tore Sanner, Idar Kreutzer, and Hans Christian Holte, director of Tax Norway, met in the foyer of the Marmorhallen at the Ministry of Climate and Environment, where the government had moved its Covid press conferences. At 9 p.m., Finance Minister Jan Tore Sanner spoke. The first five minutes of the press conference was broadcast live. The message was that the service would be ready to receive applications at 12 noon the following day (the first applications were processed and accepted before ten minutes had elapsed.)

What might have seemed impossible had been realized and delivered. In the course of three weeks, a project had been developed which, under normal circumstances, the participants estimated would take 12–18 months to launch. How was this possible? Below, we will illustrate how the cogs between the collaborating partners were tightened to realize this ambitious project and reflect on what can be learned from it for established firms that want to build innovation capacity.

The tripartite collaboration

When the Ministry of Finance was given the mission of developing a compensation scheme on March 24, its attempt to find a solution was broad in scope. Denmark, among other places, was looked at, since it had already been working on a similar problem for a few days. However, it envisaged employing up to 500 people and establishing a separate organization.

> We started by seeing if others had done something similar, which we could draw on and which could save us time. We had communication with Denmark, which had stated a similar arrangement, but with manual case processing that would take a long time to both establish and implement … We wanted to solve this in a different, faster way, through automated case processing. (Leader in the Ministry of Finance)

Tax Norway received an inquiry from the Ministry of Finance about whether they would be able to develop a solution, and Tax Norway set itself the goal of coming up with a solution with delivery in May – far faster than any previous project – but its offer was put aside when Idar Kreutzer in Finance Norway envisaged developing a solution in just three weeks.

However, there was still a need for a party from the public sector, and Tax Norway was therefore brought in again, now as part of a larger constellation with DNB and Bits on board. Tax Norway was chosen because it is a well-functioning organization with considerable experience of large data projects, and there was also a large risk associated with paying out so much money.

> In order to achieve this, it was crucial that Tax Norway put large resources into the work. This is a formidable piece of machinery – around 400 people in Tax Norway were involved in the development and management of the scheme. (Leader in the Ministry of Finance)

> The Ministry of Finance saw that, in the worst case, this is a solution that could be abused. (Payment of) 20 billion a month, maybe more. Just paying the money out and then checking it at the back-end is very labor-intensive, but also difficult because the money quickly disappears out of the system. So, it (the Ministry of Finance) saw the need for a control regime. (Leader in Tax Norway)

The collaboration between Tax Norway and Finance Norway was not new. Through DSOP (digital public and private collaboration), the public sector and the financial industry, coordinated by Finance Norway, had collaborated for several years, including on the development of consent-based loan applications. DSOP contributed to Norway being in the forefront in offering electronic services through effective interaction, sharing of data, and automation that simplifies processes for citizens, the public sector, and the business sector. This collaboration created trust at the top because the senior managers knew each other. The employees in the project, however, had never previously worked together.

Finance Norway considered several potential parties, but chose DNB, which could offer a complete and close-knit team that is among the leading technological financial environments in the country. This team was used to agile ways of working and developing innovative solutions. As Norway's largest bank, DNB had also been central to all the DSOP projects, and the chairman of Bits, Finance Norway's subsidiary, had come from DNB.

Thus, there were three parties that were key to the collaboration: Tax Norway as the public party, Finance Norway from the voluntary sector with the subsidiary Bits on the team, and New Tech Lab from DNB from the private sector; see Figure C8.1.1.

The three parties also worked closely with the ministries and the new Digitalization Agency, which has Altinn (an internet portal for digital dialogue between businesses, private individuals, and public agencies).

Governance and management

The steering group for the project was Hans Christian Holte in Tax Norway, Idar Kreutzer in Finance Norway, and Benjamin Golding from DNB, who was also chairman of Bits. The project

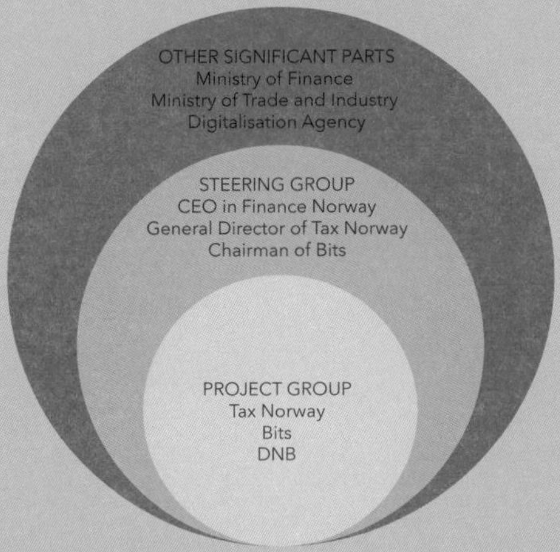

Figure C8.1.1 The collaborating parties in the compensation scheme

group included Odd Woxholt from Tax Norway, Eivind Gjemdal from Bits, and Yngvar Ugland from DNB. There were very short distances between the project group and the steering group, and they were in daily contact.

There were three very different organizations that contributed to this collaboration, and anchoring at the top was also different. Bits was a small organization with close relations between the senior management of Finance Norway and the Bits subsidiary. The new CEO of DNB, Kjerstin Braathen, was clear that she was lending her team of developers to the project, but the solutions they established had to be independent of DNB's infrastructure. She supported the team along the way and motivated them when things got tough. In Tax Norway, the solution would become part of its infrastructure and the agency would also handle the processing and control of applications. Hence, they could not just abort the project after three weeks. Tax Norway provided the most resources during the three weeks while the solution was being developed, especially when the solution opened up for businesses to apply for funds. Here, too, there were very short paths to the top, which distinguished this project from previous DSOP projects.

The three weeks that had been set as a deadline for the project created an external pressure, and this became an important premise for the management of the project both externally and internally.

The short timeframe provided the project with the power to withstand external demands and wishes. Politically, there was tension between those who wanted to prevent anyone from being paid money unlawfully and those who wanted the plans to be adapted for all industries to protect as many businesses as possible. The steering group checked whether requests from the government and the parliament could be implemented – and NHO and LO played an important role in aligning demands from the parliament with the project.

> On both (political) sides, there were well-intentioned proposals on the set of criteria. We played a central role the entire time by constantly checking whether this would be possible to verify digitally. Do we have access to the information, and could we manage to capture it with the algorithms we build or not? Then we could go back to the government and say that you can enter this criterion, but then it means that the payments would be issued in November. (Leader in Finance Norway)

Even as the politicians, organizations, and interest groups worked to adapt the regulations to their own needs, they were also perceived as supporting the project by creating legitimacy for the solution and instigating the rapid pace. The project group also felt that the outside world was on its side and was trying to manage the project to a lesser extent than it was accustomed to from other projects. It experienced an environment that was supportive and helpful. This did wonders for the progress of the project.

To speed up the decisions, responsibility and authority were delegated as much as possible.

> This was an extreme delegation of all tasks as far as possible; you have no other choice. How is a moderately intelligent person supposed to sit at the top of such a pyramid and make all the decisions? You have no chance. All decisions must go as far down as absolutely possible. (Leader in Bits)

Experienced employees were put in charge of the tasks, and decisions were made at a rapid pace without coordinating everything with the manager. The demand for speed also contributed to the fact that there was no time to have endless discussions about solving problems, so the solutions that were arrived at were pragmatic.

> Usually, you have such tough debates about whether you should use this or that (programming) language, or this or that framework, and it can often take six months before you agree on that ... We didn't have time for that here. We agreed that you use what you use, and we use what we use. So, we ended up with four different programming languages and technical platforms in the solution in the end. (Developer at DNB)

Given the time pressure, there was no time for lengthy anchoring rounds between the parties. Decisions had to be made and stuck to; there was no time for do-overs. Although the parties were prepared for the possibility of heated debates during the meetings, the attitude throughout was that this had to be solved.

Since the meetings took place online, many people could be present at the meetings at the same time. This created a good flow of information for the project and meant that there were shorter distances between the three parties and between the project and the steering group.

Division of work

During the project, there was considerable uncertainty about what should be delivered, which requirements should be satisfied, and especially which party should deliver the different pieces of the puzzle. The solution that Bits put on Idar Kreutzer's table gave DNB a greater role than what would eventually become the case, and the idea was that Tax Norway would be brought in to provide data to Bits and DNB. However, Tax Norway had also drawn up an outline for a solution through its input to the Ministry of Finance, where the control aspect was better managed. As a public agency, Tax Norway also had far greater opportunities to connect to other public registers and check for matters such as corruption and financial fraud.

> We had never worked together before; we didn't know each other. It was a difficult situation when two different players have been given the same mandate, and DNB and Bits had come quite far in outlining their solution. (Leader of Tax Norway)

> We relied on getting a copy of public registers and extracting the information ourselves to process the application and pay out the money. So that's what the first system was based on. (Developer at DNB)

Even if the parties had a fundamentally different point of view, they quickly managed to reach an agreed solution. The time pressure played a significant role, but the fact that clarifications would take place at the lowest possible level also helped.

> Over the weekend we agreed that we would combine the concept that the financial industry had proposed with our concept – which was more of a management and control regime – but we stuck to all our deadlines. (Leader in Tax Norway)

> Everyone wanted this to succeed. We're going to launch it, and we just have to figure it out. And professionals talked to professionals. It helped, then you find solutions. (Leader in Tax Norway)

The solution that the parties arrived at on the first weekend drew on Tax Norway's resources and experience. In this solution, Bits provided the open information site Kompensasjonsordningen.no (CompensationScheme.no), DNB created the application portal with a self-service solution, while the case processing – both automated and manual – was handled by Tax Norway.

The work processes

In order to be able to launch the solution in three weeks, an overall timeline was sketched out with one week for programming, one week for testing, and one week for production setup. The team worked quickly and after only five working days, they presented the first pilot to external stakeholders.

The calendars of key people were fully accessible for this project. Discussions and clarifications that normally took weeks and months were completed in hours. The fact that large parts of the project took place during Easter (a national holiday in Norway) also meant that it was easier to free up time for the project.

The meetings within each organization and between DNB, Tax Norway, and Finance Norway/Bits were largely carried out digitally. This meant that people who were located in other places in the country could easily be connected, and it did not take much time to move between meetings. One participant in the project experienced that Teams was not fast enough for individual clarifications and used the telephone. The meetings were conducted at all times of the day, also on the weekends and throughout Easter.

People were incredibly helpful and were available at any time of the day. Tests were done in slots in the middle of the night, the project staff worked 24/7, and no one seemed to have any qualms about calling late at night or at the weekend for help and clarification.

> There were inhuman amounts of work. It is not often that you have regular meetings in Outlook at 12.30 AM in the public sector during the Easter holidays. This went on around the clock ... I don't think anyone dared to count the hours. (Leader in Tax Norway)

Even though the project required a great deal of coordination, in the first phase the various teams worked independently of each other. In DNB, the team continued to work according to (ultra) agile methodology, and around ten people from the New Tech Lab and Open Banking in DNB worked closely together. The big difference was that they had to work three shifts instead of one.

In Bits, there was a smaller team that worked closely together; it had shorter decision-making paths and did not work according to any special methodology. Cases were settled bilaterally between people with a minimum of formality, and there was a dividend for taking chances and stepping on the gas.

In Tax Norway, the team also applied agile ways of working, but in contrast to earlier projects, the lawyers and developers worked side by side. Normally, the lawyers would develop the legal text first before the developers were connected.

> What was nice was that we had a tight link between those who worked on the legal framework and those who worked on the solutions ... The fact that they were so close to each

> other and started at the same time, that's unique. Normally in the public sector you create the regulations and then you create a solution ... But now we were able to ensure that we had implementation-friendly regulations ... (Leader in Tax Norway)

The tax authorities also used the opportunity to invent new, creative solutions and try out new technology. They created a transparent solution that showed all the companies that would be receiving funds and based this on tips about companies that should not receive public money. They also worked to increase the proportion that could be cleared automatically using artificial intelligence and incorporating learning loops into the manual case processing procedure.

On Wednesday, halfway through the sprint, the project experienced a hiccup. The steering group was urgently summoned with the message that a problem has arisen which was likely to mean that the deadline would not be met. The situation was a combination of a technical problem and an access problem which turned out to be a Gordian knot. The steering group met late in the evening without finding a solution, and everyone slept badly that night. At 9 a.m. the next morning, they were told that this had been resolved in the middle of the night: "Well we sat and worked through the night anyway, so then we might as well work on this problem across the teams." This illustrates the team spirit and stamina in the project.

From the time the parties met on the March 28th until the April 1st, when the final mandate with design, roles and responsibilities was clarified, there were many, and frequent, changes in architecture. The regulations were continually being developed and there were many interest groups who were seeking changes.

> We rewrote the solution ... about every other day until launch. (Developer at DNB)

The demand for speed also meant that there was no time to file the regulations and solutions so that they would be perfect. This was challenging for Tax Norway, which is the controlling authority, and for the Ministry of Finance, which is concerned with 100% fairness and equal treatment.

> I spent quite a lot of time on internal communication about the fact that this is a different arrangement than what we usually establish in the Tax Administration. We had to control this, but it had to be as fully automated as possible. It had to be verifiable, but on different criteria than what we usually use. (Leader in Tax Norway)

Seasonal companies and special cases such as zoos and circuses were added to the next phase; now it was about solving the needs of the majority of companies and working according to a good-enough methodology.

> In the public sector, there is more fear of making mistakes, so one hesitates quite often. It makes things come to a standstill. In this project, there was very good decision-making power; daring to give a mandate and make decisions. (Leader in Tax Norway)

> We made the large plan, and then we gradually allowed these special cases. There were quite a few things that we had to deal with somewhat later, so we had a bit of an MVP (Minimum Viable Product) mindset. (Leader in Tax Norway)

At the same time, there was a high risk in the project and testing was not possible as is common within agile ways of working. Thus, there was also more at stake, even for the team from DNB who was used to working under tight timeframes.

> Building things in three weeks is not that scary ... What was scary, of course, was that we couldn't fail, there was no other alternative. (Leader in DNB)

On Tuesday April 14th, testing was finished and a pilot was in production. From this week, joint stand-up meetings were also held between DNB and Tax Norway. The purpose was to synchronize across the board and move from everyone working independently to working in teams across the board.

> What was really cool to see was that the people (from Tax Norway) who helped build this had a completely different attitude ... It was like, well, zero stress, just send me an email, or just do something about it. I had daily conversations and e-mail exchanges with them, and we were able to test and check out interfaces ... and reconcile these continuously. So, they became part of the team too. (Developer at DNB)

Technological infrastructure

In the outline for a solution that was drawn up by Finance Norway on behalf of the Minister of Finance, Bits and Finance Norway reviewed what was possible to reuse from what they already had in-house. Kreutzer considered that through the DSOP, arrangements had been established that could be reused. Finance Norway had the KAR register, which links organization numbers and account numbers, Tax Norway had all the necessary information to be able to make qualified evaluations of the applications that would come in, and if these were linked together with the Brønnøysund registers, that was everything necessary to process it digitally.

Therefore, the compensation scheme would be built on existing registers and common components. This made it possible to check the applicant's identity and the applicant's authorized relationship for the actual company, the information about the company's turnover level and decline, together with confirmation that the organization number and the account for the payment of the funds actually corresponded. Furthermore, established channels, such as information via Altinn and payment processes, were reused via an established bank connection under the Government's Group Account arrangement.

In addition to using existing infrastructure, solutions or parts of solutions that were developed previously were also copied.

> The tax authorities had created many similar solutions in the past. We had the advantage that we could lean heavily on solution patterns, we could copy parts of the solutions ... We could copy things we knew would work and thus get up to speed quickly. (Leader in Tax Norway)

This meant that the project could take advantage of registers and components that already existed and also reuse bits of solutions that had been developed previously. This was absolutely essential for delivery in three weeks and was also the strength of bringing parties together to the table who had experience of using these components.

Motivation

Even if the parties had previously worked together in the DSOP, this only applied to the top of the steering group. No one in the project group had met each other before, and there was no time to build trust in the team before starting work. Moreover, the task to be solved was unlike anything that had ever been solved before, and a successful solution would be able to keep large parts of the business world afloat through the pandemic.

> Now we were not going to create a future, now we were going to ensure that there is a future at all – for the companies, the employees who worked there, and their families. Being able to help people sleep well at night – that was what motivated us. (Leader in DNB)

> What we said when we talked about this internally was that Norway is in crisis and the financial industry is part of the solution ... This is our opportunity to be involved, responsible and demonstrate what we can achieve. (Leader in Finance Norway)

Everyone said yes immediately, even if they were deeply involved in other tasks. The understanding was that you just have to do this and throw yourself into it, and actually many of those sitting on the outside wished they were part of the team.

> It wasn't an option not to say yes. Everyone understood this was

important. Then it was just a matter of rolling up the sleeves and getting started. (Leader in Tax Norway)

The task was also highly complex, with few guidelines and three parties who had to learn to understand each other in record time. DNB's team was used to working quickly, but the publicity and extreme stature of this task put extra pressure on the entire project group. And there was no talk of not working hard around the clock for the project. Easter holidays, weekends, and certain nights would be sacrificed without anyone having to ask.

> Everyone involved was a bit giddy. This was new for many, and it went so fast. We noticed that those who were responsible for building it thought it was really fun, and that meant that they worked much more than they otherwise would have done; some of us had 20-hour working days. (Developer at DNB)

None of the people involved in the project knew whether they would get anything back in terms of salary or time when they began work on the project. They could hope that if the project is successful the recognition could lend weight in future salary negotiations, but financial reward was not what drove the project group to deliver.

In addition, there was a little healthy rivalry between the development teams, as Tax Norway wanted to show that their team was as good as DNB's.

Competence

Three key people in the project were Eivind Gjemdal from Bits, who had considerable experience from the development of banking systems and services from the time when both BankAxept and BankID were part of Finance Norway (and not Vipps like today), Odd Voxholt from Tax Norway, who had invaluable experience from countless digitization projects, and Yngvar Ugland from DNB, who was a serial entrepreneur and built up the key team New Tech Lab, a group of experts in innovative thinking and radical project implementation.

When Kjerstin Braathen offered DNB's resources to Finance Norway, she could do so on the basis that the New Tech Lab is a complete team of developers who work independently from the rest of the bank. Yngvar Ugland was clear that he needed to bring the whole team into the work. They knew each other and were used to developing innovative projects in record time. DNB also chose to draw on the Open Banking team in DNB, and in total they were about ten members of the team working on the compensation scheme.

In Tax Norway, they were given the "Gold Card", i.e., they were free to bring in the best resources for the project and free them up from current tasks.

> This was like running a project with a Gold Card; I highly recommend it. I could pick from the top shelf. (Leader in Tax Norway)

There was a deliberate selection of employees. There was no room for someone who could not deliver or for someone who loves to discuss matters at length before making decisions. When possible, the selection was directed at people who had the experience of working together. People who had worked together before have confidence in each other, and time is not wasted on unnecessary clarification and discussions.

> I brought X with me. I know exactly what he stands for, we can clarify things very quickly, we don't need to say much, we understand what we are talking about. This is crucial when you are short on time. (Leader in Tax Norway)

Many consulting houses knocked on Finance Norway's door wanting to offer their services and gladly work for free. However, the assessment was crystal clear. You have to build on teams that know each other and have experience that can be used directly in the project.

> Had this competence been in India (outsourced), you could just forget about it. Tax Norway, Bits, and DNB had the expertise in-house. You could never outsource this to a consultancy. (Leader in Bits)

Compared to DNB and Bits, Tax Norway drew on a large number of employees – several hundred people were involved in the work. The project group, which consisted of 20–25 people, has good support in Tax Norway's IT environment. As the solution approached production, case managers were connected to handle the manual applications.

In Bits, the need for resources was solved with internal resources and extensive use of overtime. It drew on the most experienced employees who could work quickly and independently. The expertise that had been built up over years of responsibility for the financial industry's payment structure was now worth its weight in gold.

Can others learn from the Compensation Scheme 1.0?

There is little doubt that the circumstances surrounding the creation of the first compensation scheme were completely unique. It occurred during the early stage of the Covid-19 pandemic, when uncertainty was sky high and the fear that large parts of the Norwegian business sector would collapse was tangible. It is such a unique situation that caused managers and employees in Tax Norway, Bits, and DNB to persevere throughout weekends and holidays and make themselves available around the clock.

Fortunately, such situations do not occur often, and organizations cannot be rigged to deal with such crises permanently. But we can still learn from the ambitious and successful project for established firms that aim to build innovation capacity.

One of the most striking features of the compensation scheme was the speed of decision-making. Decisions were characterized by short decision-making channels to those in charge at the top, with as much as possible being delegated, new virtual meeting places enabling quick meetings across scattered locations and disciplines with little advance notice, and the strict selection of participants.

Of course, senior management cannot be fully operational and available for all projects at all times of the day, but there are some decisions that are more important than others. Gathering decision-making power and professionals in the same forums is something that DNB has experimented with in its key teams (see the case about DNB in Part 1). Here, the CEO or others from senior management sit together with experts and make decisions on matters for which there is no time to get stuck in the hierarchy. In order not to completely overwhelm senior management, one must also be selective where one implements such a model and also be aware that responsibility is delegated as far down as possible.

The advantage of interdisciplinary teams was discussed in the chapter on agility earlier in the book, but there are two additional aspects worth noting from this case. First, it is much easier to gather many employees on virtual platforms and ensure that everyone is informed and can provide input. The other important lesson is the interaction between lawyers and developers in the development of new solutions. This is particularly relevant for businesses in the public sector, which can often be swamped by a new set of regulations passed by the Parliament that does not consider how easy it is to code and implement regulations into new and existing systems.

The experience from the case also shows that when professionals are put together, they are good at finding solutions and putting aside the prestige of who does what. In this case, it was made easier by the fact that there was considerable external pressure, but pragmatism such as what we saw here can also be found in other collaborations, for example in other projects in the DSOP.

It is difficult to imagine that the incredible motivation found in this case could be copied to other situations. However, it is interesting to note that the motivation was also largely directed towards the task to be carried out, not just the external circumstances. Many employees are driven by an inner motivation on the task itself, and the more difficult this is to solve, the more motivating it becomes. Setting a framework for those who are engaging in innovation can therefore be as much about the tasks as the economic reward. It is no coincidence that, between all its other projects, the consulting company Cowi selects projects that are incredibly ambitious and complex, such as building the world's longest bridge, to give its employees something to sink their teeth into.

When developing a completely new solution, it is easy to think that everything has to start from scratch, but kompensasjonsordningen.no made major changes to existing registers and common components, or parts of technological solutions that had been developed previously. This is in line with what can be found in new, modern innovation environments where one connects to the cloud and retrieves bits of code that have been developed before and put them together in new ways. In other words, reuse is key to rapid development.

At least as important is the experience the employees bring to the collaboration. Without the experience Bits had from payment processing, DNB had from designing code for demanding and innovative projects, and Tax Norway had from handling large and complex IT projects, the compensation scheme would probably not have taken off, at least not so quickly. The competence the employees relied on, and the confidence they had in each other, was absolutely decisive.

Last but not least, this case has something to teach us about the value of setting ambitious goals and frameworks around a project. In Finance Norway it was considered that if the deadline had been three months instead of three weeks, then yes, it would have taken three months, and the sense of being busy would probably have been as great as it was with the three-week deadline. In other words, ambitious goals are an important driver of innovation.

CASE 8.2
VIPPS – GOING ALONE OR PARTNERSHIP?[13]

The story of Vipps stretches back to December 2014, when DNB decided to develop the first Norwegian digital wallet on its own. The mobile payment solution was called Vipps and DNB's own employees came up with the name after a short brainstorming session. Vipps was 100% owned by DNB and it had been developed and introduced to the market in less than six months.

In 2021 Vipps is used regularly by over four million Norwegians, and it has become a Norwegian verb of its own that has been incorporated into dictionaries. At this time, it was announced that the company planned to join forces with MobilePay in Denmark and Pivo in Finland. Vipps was taking the step to become one of the major Nordic mobile players .

A lot has happened along the way: from a solo run in DNB to collaboration with other Norwegian banks, from a pure digital wallet to digital ID and infrastructure ownership, and from Norwegian to Norwegian-Danish and Finnish. Nevertheless, the story goes on. Nobody quite knows what Vipps might become, or how the competition against theses global giants will end.

Are we at the beginning of a successful journey, or are we near the end of something that was short-lived? Will the company, which is currently valued at several billion kroner, soon start to show a profit on the bottom line? Will the growth continue to new countries and markets with even more products in their portfolio, or will Vipps disappear off the radar of global players such as Apple, Facebook, and Google? Are several hundred Norwegian, Danish, and Finnish bank owners able to steer this ship forward effectively – towards Nordic, European and global growth?

In this case, we are primarily concerned with the strategic choices DNB faced in choosing partners, but also the choices that led to DNB withdrawing from one of the partnerships. We describe the history behind the development, and the drivers for different strategic choices as well as the choices made by the boards and senior management in the companies involved. There have been many actors involved along the way: telecom companies, banks, payment and infrastructure companies, and government actors. In times of ever new players, disruption, and changes in regulations, the company will undoubtedly still face with demanding choices – choices where the outcome remains unknown for a long time, and which can lead to continued growth or decline.

13 This case is based on an educational case developed for NHH Executive written by Rune Bjerke, Carl Christian Christensen, Christine Meyer and Inger Stensaker together with Rune Bjerke's own experiences and reflections.

Divorce or fidelity?

Two former CEOs of DNB and Telenor (Svein Aaser and Tormod Hermansen) were both innovation- and growth-oriented. Aaser had set up a separate innovation unit in DNB in the early 2000s, and Tormod Hermansen invested in powerful growth in Bangladesh and Pakistan – also in similar bank services. The senior managers met frequently and developed models for a possible product collaboration between the companies. The collaboration was formalized through the creation of various jointly owned companies such as Doorstep and Valyou.

In the dot.com period around the turn of the millennium, the idea of closer collaboration between banks and telecoms was considered on several continents. Nevertheless, cross-industry mergers failed to appear, perhaps primarily because of the numerous IT and dot.com collapses immediately after the turn of the century. Nonetheless, the IT development environments in companies across industry boundaries had established closer contact and collaboration. In most cases, they were also large and important customers of each other.

Aaser's and Hermansen's successors, Fredrik Baksaas and Rune Bjerke, also believed in cross-industry collaboration. They continued to build relationships and also explored new forms of interaction. While employees further down in their organizations might prefer to challenge each other, strategic choices were made at the top of both companies about continued collaboration. Most agreed that an exciting area of opportunity was to be found in the boundaries between the two companies.

Senior managers and innovation environments in DNB and Telenor met regularly. The purpose was to develop visionary products and services together. Resources were made available, and the aim was to simplify payment services for customers. The idea was to develop something that could have a global impact. The boards of the two companies actively supported this collaboration.

A tangible result of this collaboration was the payment service SmartPay, but it proved unsuccessful and was restructured in 2006. In the meantime, Telenor and DNB worked on other solutions, both in Norway and internationally. The companies mainly worked on payment solutions in Norway that were closely linked to their own services, for example prepaid cards and SMS-based services, as well as identification services such as ZebSign.

ZebSign was later sold to BBS (Bank Payment Central, later Nets and today part of Mastercard) which laid the foundation for BankID on mobile phones. At the time, BBS was much better suited to using and scaling the technology. Later, this became part of an ID solution for more than 150 banks in Norway – with a steadily expanding area of use. The income from the sale of ZebSign paved the way for continued collaboration between Telenor and DNB. Consequently, this technology took on a more strategic role.

BankID for mobile phones took time to develop and was ultimately launched in 2009. This was considered a successful and tangible collaboration between banks and telecoms, and a considerably simpler solution compared to the previous code chip solution used for BankID.

With this in the back of their minds, the companies took the collaboration a step further – to payments and transactions. A joint company, Valyou, was created to develop an NFC (Near Field Communication) solution. This involves communication via an electromagnetic field at very short range – in this case to trigger payments wirelessly via mobile phones in close contact with payment terminals in stores. This had to be embedded into the mobile phone's SIM card – not in the mobile phone and not in the payment terminal. The idea was that whoever owned the SIM card was in possession of the customer and thus the customer interface. At that time, this was a solution that neither Apple, Google nor other companies had developed. Valyou was therefore the first company in the world to make it possible to pay wirelessly with a SIM card. In 2014, Bjerke paid for a Snickers in Hong Kong by holding the mobile phone three centimeters above the terminal, and later that year the two CEOs were on the news broadcasting a pilot project in Oslo South where they bought hot dogs at a Narvesen kiosk.

Telenor's managing director, Fredrik Baksaas, believed that a person-to-person mobile phone payment solution would be the next stage in the development. Transactions in stores should be prioritized. The pride in the company's management was great. This could become a global solution with Norwegian technology and ownership. Further down in the organizations, the enthusiasm was likely somewhat more reserved.

The decision to go it alone

On May 7, 2013, Danske Bank rolled out MobilePay in Denmark. The application was developed in-house and 100% owned by the bank. The launch had had a great impact and paying via mobile phones and in-store terminals soon became a popular method of payment. The app also allowed peer-to-peer payments using mobile phone numbers. At the time, there were only a handful of similar applications available in Europe, none of them particularly powerful, and MobilePay was the first digital wallet that made a massive impact on a market. Other banks in Denmark were shut out of this success, while Nets, which at the time owned the popular payment card Dankort, was in the process of developing its own wallet.

At a meeting in the summer of 2013, Valyou's administration presented the Danish concept to the company's board. In addition to the two CEOs of DNB and Telenor, the board consisted of key employees in the two organizations. MobilePay's own solution was viewed as very interesting and user-friendly, but according to the participants it lacked the uniqueness that Valyou had in its solution, namely NFC technology embedded into the SIM card itself. Instead, MobilePay had developed separate terminals with an integrated in-store radio unit. In addition, there were also rumors that the radio transmission protocol that was used in Denmark to send and receive data wirelessly between the devices was not functioning properly. Despite this, the number of users in Denmark continued to grow exponentially.

On the eve of 2014, Rune Bjerke received an unexpected inquiry from the Norwegian country manager of Danske Bank. The question was abrupt: "Should we collaborate on the rollout of MobilePay in Norway, Rune?" There was no doubt that this was an inquiry rooted in Denmark – in the board and senior management of Danske Bank. The question was not answered there and then. There was also no explanation for the motives behind this cooperative spirit. However, it became clear that important choices had to be made at DNB. Collaboration with the Danish competitor? Break with Telenor? Develop a digital wallet on its own? Continue as before?

The board and management of DNB chose to focus on development under its own roof. In the first phase, the collaboration with Telenor could continue. Of course, they realized that the break would come if the development of their own digital wallet was successful. If Valyou succeeded in the market while development was taking place, the internal venture could be aborted. However, it was difficult for DNB not to inform its long-standing partner, Telenor. Although the break was not immediate, going alone with the digital wallet was a break with the good spirit of collaboration. The Danish MobilePay solution had, after all, been presented to the joint collaboration body, Doorstep.

Why, then, did DNB choose to develop something for itself, without informing Telenor? Why not join forces with Telenor this time too?

A question of timing

The most important argument behind DNB's choice was the timing. The invitation from the Danes indicated that MobilePay would be coming to Norway anyway. The technology circles in DNB assumed that it would take a minimum of six months to successfully convert the Danish solution to Norway. A launch under its own auspices therefore had to take place by the end of May at the latest. All players knew that in the development of digital wallets there was a clear first-mover advantage. The first player to launch had good opportunities to take the entire market. This had been well documented in Denmark. In DNB, the Danish invitation was seen as half-hearted. DNB had marketing and distribution power with close to 25% of the market share. Danske Bank had the technology, but not the customers. In DNB, it was feared that a collaboration would make the Danish competitor stronger, while DNB's own interests would suffer. It feared ending up as a little brother in a Danish-Norwegian collaboration, where ownership of the technology lay in Denmark.

In 2014, it took an average of 18 months to complete a typical IT project in DNB. In order to succeed in shortening this time to less than six months, the project would have to receive full focus and support. Internal colloquium groups or laborious interaction with Telenor were viewed as time sinks that would make it impossible to achieve the necessary progress. Therefore, DNB went full speed ahead, but did so alone. Without a business rationale and with enormous risk, interdisciplinary resources were recruited internally. The project was given autonomy and great freedom, but with a direct line to the executive directors for IT and Personal Banking and to the CEO. The board and senior management gave their full support. Resources were made available, and the project was given such high priority internally that other units working on innovation projects objected – to the extent that they understood what was happening. As few people as possible could know about the project. DNB's competitors could not learn that it had chosen to go it alone with its own digital wallet.

Vipps is launched

On May 14, 2015, Vipps was launched. The decision to drop Valyou was made at the same time, but only publicized in October. The break with Telenor was therefore a fact. "After a comprehensive assessment, Valyou's owners have chosen to close down operations in the company. The reason for the decision is that the desired growth of consumers has not been achieved, and that the rate of roll-out of new terminals in the stores has been too low. It has also not been successful in engaging the required number of banks and mobile operators in the solution", an announcement on the Valyou website stated. In Telenor, it was believed that SIM cards were the technological key to transactions. In Denmark and other countries, it had been shown that the telephone number was the solution. DNB's own assessment was that the SIM card path would be a long haul – if it could ever succeed at all.

Valyou had initially been backed by the two market leaders, DNB and Telenor. In total, the customer base amounted to over three million people. However, the position was demanding. The product demanded too much. Too few banks and telecommunications operators entered into binding partnerships. The old payment terminals did not support SIM card integration. And most importantly, Apple refused to open up the solution in its operating system. The perfect customer thus had to be a customer of DNB *and* Telenor, the terminal in the store had to be relatively new, and Android mobile phones were a must for those who were going use Valyou to shop. The overall market potential in Norway at the time was 5–15%, not an attractive market position to bet on as the world looked then.

Four months after launch, Vipps already had a million users. In August of the same year, Danske Bank launched MobilePay in Norway. Later that year, Sparebank 1 Gruppen took over mCash and its rights in Norway through the acquisition of a smaller fintech company, and launched its own solution in the market. At the end of the year, there were close to two million users of Vipps, but also three digital wallets fighting for the Norwegian market. Vipps had a big lead.

When a new mobile application is launched, there are two decisive factors in particular that determine the rate of speed and success – the power of distribution and the application's characteristics. Vipps was well positioned. It had an owner with close to two million personal customers. DNB had 25 000 incoming phone calls to its call center every day and had over 10 000 employees in Norway. The product was also a simplifying innovation. As mentioned above, money could be transferred directly to family, friends, and shops merely buy using the recipient's telephone number. Bank affiliation and account number were no longer important.

A large amount was invested in marketing in the first phase. Campaigns were run on social media. Selected employees with large networks received smaller amounts to send to friends and acquaintances, who in turn had to download the app for the money to be transferred to their own accounts. DNB's customer center suggested that customers who called in should download and test out Vipps. Four months later, the head office was filled to the rim with employees celebrating one million downloads.

Danske Bank did not have the market power in Norway that it had in Denmark. With less than 5% of the retail market in Norway at this time, it would have been hard to roll out the solution successfully. It can be argued that Telenor, with its customer base on top of DNB's, could have provided double the distribution power. However, Telenor was a telecoms corporation, not a bank, and a financial product was likely to be a harder sell. It would also have been harder to argue for something that it only partially, not fully, owned.

A shot in the arm

DNB badly needed an upturn after the financial crisis. Several years of unrest and recession, interest rate increases, data problems, new regulations and restructuring had eroded self-confidence and collective engagement in the organization. Even though Vipps consumed substantial resources internally, it did not take long for success to be realized and for pride and collective engagement to spread throughout the organization. This was a technological innovation owned and developed by DNB, and a story that could be used in any customer dialogue that dealt with payment, technology, and new industry trends. The culture at DNB was given a boost that no one had planned or even dared to hope for; at last, the bank was on the offensive and would be able to capitalize on this success for many, many years to come.

There were also important differences between the cultures at Telenor, DNB, and Danske Bank. A collaboration with Telenor or Danske Bank would not have afforded DNB the same power. Differences between the firms would also make it difficult to develop solutions together, making it harder to build up the same pride and enthusiasm across the board. Telenor was more internationally oriented. Danske Bank was bigger and stronger than DNB at the time. Equality and common interests would be difficult to develop.

On the other hand, the development of Vipps led to DNB becoming more technologically savvy. The need for greater technical expertise was suddenly understood by everyone. The hundreds of Indian IT engineers who had contributed to its development were highly appreciated. However, DNB could not rely on extensive external labor in the long run. Because of Vipps, DNB changed from within. There was a greater emphasis on new skills and more focus on developing as an agile technology company instead of a traditional bank. Vipps prodded the bank to reconsider its culture, organization, skill set and collaboration with others.

Emerging unrest

In 2014, DNB chose to go it alone rather than partnership and collaboration. The concept of *frenemies* had not taken root at that time. In the first two years of Vipps' history, its staff enjoyed the rush of victory. However, there were strategic threats at the top of the organization. The two competitors were still in the market. Nordea, Gjensidige, Storebrand and Skandiabanken had joined MobilePay. The savings banks bet heavily on mCash. They had resources and endurance. This was in full view at a Bruce Springsteen concert in June 2016. In front of 25 000 spectators, Vipps CEO Rune Garborg saw large mCash banners all over the stadium. To skip the queue to buy beer and mineral water, concert-goers could download the competing app. DNB's opponent had shown creativity and strength. But fortunately for Vipps, the attempt was not entirely successful. Telenor had too little capacity in its mobile network to deal with the peak in demand. Many attendees could neither download the app nor buy beer. Nevertheless, it unsettled DNB's top management.

The board and group management speculated that the two contenders would find a way to work together. In that case, the competitor(s) would be almost as big as Vipps. DNB knew that the definitive breakthrough for Vipps would only become a reality if the entire population were active users. In other words, there were two competing apps standing in the way for DNB's vision. Internal discussions at DNB began to consider collaboration with the competitor(s). The term frenemies was used more frequently in the presentations to the board. Why not make friends with DNB's enemies?

An historic banking collaboration

The Norwegian digital payment infrastructure had been systematically built up since the 1970s, when banks and the postal service began cooperating ever closer and better on standards, technologies, and frameworks for cards and transactions. The Norwegian banking collaboration is one of the most extensive and successful in Europe. The payment system is still independent of the global giants and today is owned by the banks in Norway – via Vipps.

Thanks to the long-term collaboration, checks and cash were phased out much faster in Norway than in most other countries. People in the United States still write over 15 billion checks a year, and the US Postal Service derives over 20% of its revenue from checks sent through the mail.

In Norway, the collaboration has provided superior online banking solutions, particularly efficient transactions between individuals and companies. Until 2013, digital identification (BankID) and the transaction infrastructure, BankAxept (BAX), were parts of the industry federation Finance Norway.

That year, the business was separated from Finance Norway into two limited liability companies with the banks as direct owners. The main rationale was to commercialize the infrastructure, increase investment capacity, and invest more heavily in further digital development.

In 2021 more than 80% of transactions in Norwegian stores were processed via BAX. Digital identification for online banking, health services, tax returns and other public registers was via BankID. These were technical solutions that were fully equivalent with the best available in the world, including those offered by Visa and Mastercard.

It is particularly customers and terminals at the user sites that have benefited from the national infrastructure. Payments via BankAxept are carried out free of charge for private customers and are very reasonably priced for the user locations. The banks' income mostly comes from traditional products such as loans and deposits. Cash Management (cash handling and payments) was most often considered the "heart" of the banks' ecosystem, but was rarely defined as an important part of the banks' value chain.

On several occasions the Central Bank of Norway had expressed a clear opinion that the costs associated with the infrastructure should be charged to a greater extent directly to customers. This would provide better incentives to continue investing in infrastructure. This was also a key driver for the reorganization in the area of payments. Nevertheless, the collaboration between the owners of the companies was somewhat crippled due to tensions between the Norwegian-owned and the foreign-owned banks. At the same time, the administration in BankAxept wanted to develop its own solutions – in competition with the banks, and especially their payment applications, Vipps, MobilePay and mCash. In DNB, there was a stronger orientation towards the interests of the Norwegian banks. It was hard work, but little progress was made along the way.

Historically, there had been a long-standing banking collaboration, a separately owned and independent infrastructure. The traditions were in place. Nevertheless, collaboration had gradually weakened after the financial crisis. Too little was being invested and diverging interests among the banks led to friction. Could Vipps be used as a tool to unite the collective interests of Norwegian banks?

Frenemies

Internally in DNB, the fear was that MobilePay and mCash would join forces, and this led to new strategic discussions within the bank. To combat the Danish digital payment wallet, DNB's Vipps could join forces with the Norwegian savings banks. This could also lead to smoother decision-making processes in the financial industry's main organization, Finance Norway. Here, DNB often lacked support from the other Norwegian banks. In addition, it could make the collaboration in BankAxept and BankID smoother.

Should DNB really invite the savings banks on board? Vipps had been such a successful rollout. The market position was strong. After launching on May 30, 2014, it took just ten days to connect 100 000 users. It reached a million within four months. And now, towards the end of 2015, Vipps was storming towards two million users. Its victory didn't need to be shared with others, did it?

There was still something missing. The desired connection between Vipps and the rest of the Norwegian payment infrastructure was repeatedly being postponed. DNB was more dependent than ever on the expensive services of Visa and MasterCard. Vipps lacked BAX. Vipps lacked an immediate payment solution from account-to-account. Vipps lacked enthusiasm from the rest of the banking sector in Norway. And Vipps lacked a platform for further expansion abroad. In addition, the purchasing power vis-à-vis the organization processing the transactions, Nets, was weakened by standing alone.

Could the savings banks that owned mCash initiate collaboration with the Danish-owned MobilePay? The fact that Storebrand, Gjensidige and Nordea had chosen to collaborate with Danske Bank had made the competition even tougher.

This dilemma was discussed on numerous occasions amongst the board and management. Although there were strong voices that wanted to continue going it alone, the board and management were open to exploring different partnerships through which the success of Vipps would be shared with the other Norwegian banks. The board finally agreed to reach out to the regional banks. Vipps, mCash and MobilePay were all losing money every single day. It was expensive to subsidize this friendly payment service.

But was it right for DNB to share its success with others? 100% ownership ensured speed in the development of the services, and this could be reconciled with highly efficient decision-making processes. The experiences from Finance Norway and the former multi-bank ownership of the payment company Nets were good examples of the many management challenges shared ownership implied. After many discussions and differences of opinion, the board and management realized that there was only one thing to do: its CEO picked up the phone and called.

"– Hello, it's Rune (Bjerke – CEO, DNB). I'm calling you to ask if you want to remain Norwegian – or if you want to end up in Denmark." The good-natured laugh from the CEO of Sparebank 1 SMN, Finn Haugan, echoed through the iPhone. SMN was among the largest owners in mCash. This was not a spontaneous laugh. It was a sign of relief that provided the answer to the ongoing discussions in the Norwegian savings banks.

However, the invitation to partner up also raised many questions. What ownership stake was envisioned? How would they value Vipps's successful history? Would it be possible to keep up the pace of development in a jointly owned company? Did the savings banks have the muscle to invest internationally? And not least, would they be willing to consider the role Vipps could take in the future in Norwegian payment infrastructure?

After Bjerke spoke to Haugan, Danske Bank expressed its interest in joining forces again, but now with a much weaker starting point than in the previous round. This time, DNB had the opportunity to be in the driver's seat and dictate the terms to a greater extent. Such an important and international partner could be vital in establishing an international position and taking up competition with the major players such as Apple and Google in the Nordic market. What at that moment seemed to be a simple choice suddenly became a more complex one.

It ended with the board supporting the broad, Norwegian alternative. National competitors would be invited into Vipps. The historic collaboration on infrastructure would be continued – with Vipps as the common denominator. The price that DNB had to pay – giving away the majority of the company – was high. On the other hand, the Vipps's potential to reach a market value of NOK 1 billion came into sight for the first time. However, the big question from now on changed: Was it possible to maintain this speed? Would someone be able to unite the interests of Vipps's more than a hundred owners so that the company could continue to prosper? Would the Norwegian savings banks participate in further investments outside the country?

Two new marriages in sight!

After DNB invited the savings banks in as owners of Vipps, Vipps merged with BankID and BAX in 2018. On January 11 of the same year, MobilePay closed its operations in Norway. Through the merger between Vipps, BAX and BankID, there were even more owners of the new company. In addition to all the Norwegian banks, Danske Bank and Nordea also joined as a result of their previous positions in BAX and BankID. Thus, through Vipps, the historically close collaboration on payment solutions in the Norwegian banking market had been restored. However, the digital wallet had become so much more. In-store payments, invoice payments, online shopping, digital ID, transactions and eventually also mobile telecommunications.

In 2021, DNB still holds the largest share in Vipps, at 45%. The services continue to grow in Norway. Vipps has over four million users. Vipps makes money particularly on online shopping and direct payment in stores, but still makes a loss on peer-to-peer payments. Even if the bottom line is still not in the black, recent developments show that this is only a matter of time. The moment Vipps decides to stop growing, the company will make a profit. But is there really any alternative to growth?

The big game between the global and regional players

International players, giants like Apple and Amazon, but also neo-banks, are gaining an increasingly stronger foothold in the market. Neo-banks such as Monzo, N26 and Revolut issue plastic cards based on customers filling the card with money before paying. Once customers have a card, they get access to the services. The neo-banks undercut the traditional banks and offer cryptocurrency trading and other innovative services. In Great Britain and Ireland, neo-banks have gained a solid hold on customers, largely because traditional banks have been caught napping during the development of mobile payment services. In Ireland, for example, Revolut has become one of the dominant players in online transactions.

In the Nordics, Klarna has a strong grip, earning a position as the leading player in online shopping. The company has been awarded banking licenses in an growing number of countries, including the United States, and makes money particularly in deferred payment (credit) for online shopping. During the pandemic, online shopping saw robust growth all over the world and it looks like this growth is being sustained. When Klarna is rolled out in new markets, a new global payments player is created. In 2021 Klarna was valued at close to NOK 400 billion – significantly higher than the market value of DNB. Not long ago, Klarna was a small fintech player focused on online shopping. In the beginning, its solutions were paper-based. In short, its focus was on deferred payment. Over time, its solution has become more and more digital. Today, in 2021, the app and payment solutions probably have the best functionality and checkout solution in the market, and growth continues.

In April 2018, Apple Pay was launched in Norway as the provider of what was at the time the only in-store payment solution in the country. Apple Pay's business model is a clear threat to Vipps and the Norwegian banks. Norwegian banks chose different response strategies; some were loyal to Vipps, others chose Apple Pay, and a few chose to partner with both. At the same time, there is great uncertainty about how the mobile wallet will develop in the future. Are we moving towards a card and cashless society? What advantages and disadvantages does further technological development bring?

Vipps is also developing a number of other services, and online traffic to the banks is increasing because Vipps is helping to remove paper invoices. Twenty-five% of invoices in Norway now go through Vipps, and business-to-consumer transactions make up an increasingly large part of the transactions in the Vipps system. In the coming years, integrated business models related to online shopping and home delivery are also planned. Vipps is working to find its role in future ecosystems.

At the same time, data is emerging as the new gold standard. Big tech firms such as Google, Facebook, Apple, and PayPal base much of their business model on access to data. They are used to handling large amounts of data and developing innovative services that customers want at terrific speed. Chinese players like Alibaba and Tencent are far ahead in their use of transaction data via their ecosystems.

By gaining control over payments, Apple has expanded its future business opportunities. It has entered into a collaboration on a digital personal bank in the United States together with Goldman Sachs, which plans to invest further in Europe. Although today Apple makes money from each transaction via its mobile phones by taking a commission from the banks, there are several players who do not make money from the transactions themselves, but from the data and the sale of advertising. Vipps therefore meets players with fundamentally different business models, making the competitive landscape very challenging.

The Norwegian banks that collaborate with Vipps still have access to the transaction data and thus a basis for being able to retain and develop their customer relationships further. The value of data only seems to accelerate. Whoever controls the most sets of data, and whoever can make use of this, has a unique platform for growth and value creation. The transaction data of the banks and payment companies are especially attractive to the global players. During the pandemic, we saw concrete examples of how Vipps's data sets could be used by authorities and the central bank. The scope of transactions within various geographies and industries could be followed continuously. Vipps became a thermometer for the pace of the economy.

Vipps, like the banks, is in a market that depends on customers' trust. It is therefore important to comply with GDPR, the new data protection regulations from the EU, and build trust through secure identification solutions.

The money-laundering scandals that have afflicted several of the Nordic banks have also created increased attention on the need to know your customers. Vipps has been concerned with developing competitive advantage in digital identification, and the ID-product shelf is growing. One challenge is that the giants seem to be less vulnerable to breaches of the regulations and both financially and in terms of reputation can afford to pay the occasional fine.

Vipps becomes Nordic

Already in 2019, Rune Garborg was continuing with new strategic moves. Together with the CEO of DNB, renewed contact was established with Danske Bank. It would turn out that Vipps had succeeded better than Danske Bank in its investment in online shopping and corporate payments. In Denmark, growth had come to a stop in several of the product areas. The conversations clearly showed that the little brother had become the big brother. Vipps was earning more from its customers and was growing faster. The comprehensive banking collaboration in Norway had proved more effective than Danske Bank's solo run in Denmark.

However, few people still believed in a Nordic consolidation, especially because DNB and Norwegian banks had withdrawn from a Nordic collaboration on real-time payments across national borders – P27. But Rune Garborg and Kjerstin Braathen did not give up. The many conversations over several years eventually yielded results. In the summer of 2021, a plan for collaboration was announced. The digital wallet in Vipps was to be separated and merged with MobilePay in Denmark and Finland. In addition, the Finnish owner of Pivo, another Finnish payment operator, was invited in with a 10% stake. Vipps retained 55% of the company. The rest of Norwegian Vipps would be kept out of the transaction. Garborg would become CEO of the Nordic company, and Braathen from DNB would become chairperson of the board. After the European Commission (EC) raised doubts about the transaction, Finland's Pivo chose to back out of the merger. The reasoning behind the commission's concerns was that Denmark's MobilePay and Pivo were the two major players in the Finnish market. The merger between MobilePay and Vipps was approved by the competition authorities in 2022.

What can others learn from Vipps?

This case illustrates some of the strategic choices behind partnerships and how different choices can help to open up and close down future options. Partnerships have many advantages because they provide access to resources, but partnerships can also be difficult to manage because no single organization has full control over the decisions.

The partnership between DNB and Telenor was a fruitful collaboration for a long time, the parties had complementary competences, and the collaboration led, among other things, to the development of mobile BankID. When DNB set out to develop a new digital wallet and the senior management team assessed a time window of six months, the Telenor collaboration was deemed unviable. This was based both on *collaboration experience* and the development of Valyou. The DNB management also saw the challenge of *managing* such a rapid development course in two teams.

Danske Bank also had a digital wallet but was a *competitor* that at the time was stronger than DNB. The option of entering into a collaboration that could lock up DNB's marketing opportunities in the future was considered unattractive. DNB therefore chose to go it alone and put all of its efforts into succeeding in the development of a new digital wallet. Through the development of Vipps, DNB built innovation capacity. It developed new and *agile* ways of working, was able to recruit *technological competence*, its *culture* was drawn in a more innovative direction, and Vipps created collective engagement among its employees. It was therefore not an easy decision to invite the savings banks into the ownership side. This meant that DNB lost one of its most valuable innovative brand names, and many skilled employees went over to Vipps. On the other hand, it strengthened the chance that Vipps could become the winner in the Norwegian market, in addition to merging with the important *complementary* banking infrastructure that had been built up over many years of banking collaboration. But there was also a significant risk in managing the collaboration with so *many partners* on the team and a real danger that the speed of development could be lost.

However, Vipps has not stood still, and in 2022 Vipps became part of a Nordic constellation with Denmark's MobilePay. Will Vipps be on safe ground with its new Nordic partner? Is the Norwegian payment infrastructure the backbone of future transactions? The answers to these questions are no easier than the strategic choices Vipps and Norwegian banks have already made. No one remains on safe ground for long periods of time. New players are constantly coming up with improvements and new concepts. The big ones keep getting bigger. Regulatory changes create dynamism in the markets and the technology improves continuously. Only a company that is at the forefront is sustainable over time – a company that has sufficient innovation capacity and the will to continuously develop further.

Chapter 9

Ecosystems

Ecosystems are often associated with biology and coevolution, where different species interact and influence each other in ways that drive adaptation and development. James Moore (1993) believed that biology could provide a different understanding of how innovations are developed as firms interact, cooperate, and compete across industries and sectors. As with biology, economic (business) ecosystems do not stand still, but rather emerge, develop, and renew themselves or die in interaction with other actors. Since Moore's pioneering insight, research on ecosystems has gone through exponential development (Bogers et al., 2019; Shipilov & Gawer, 2020). Although this impressive evolution of the field has increased knowledge of ecosystems as a phenomenon, there continues to be considerable confusion and uncertainty about how to define ecosystems and how managers can navigate through such systems.

Ecosystems allow firms to specialize in areas where they have a (competitive) advantage. An ecosystem can strengthen a firm's abilities to sense and seize innovation opportunities for the established firm because of its connections to other parties in the ecosystem. Through ecosystems, firms can also access to complementary capabilities from other actors. This enables the firm to scale and develop innovations more quickly.

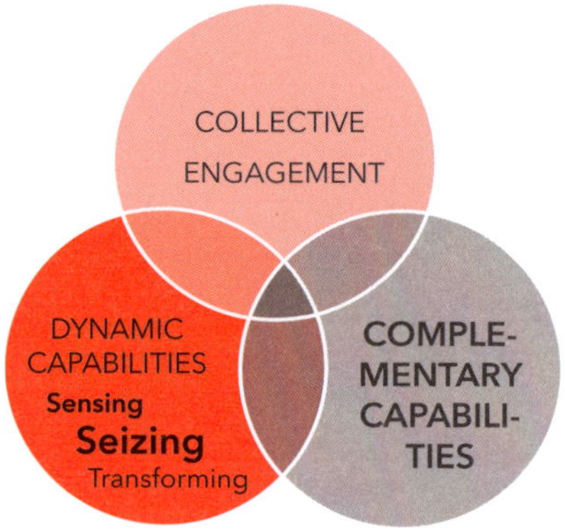

Figure 9.1 How ecosystems contribute to innovation capacity

In this chapter, we explain what an ecosystem involves and illustrate different types of ecosystems. Furthermore, we explore how different types of actors can navigate in the ecosystem. We introduce Alibaba as a case to demonstrate how an ecosystem can emerge and develop over time.

What is an ecosystem?

An ecosystem is perhaps one of the most difficult concepts in this book. It is a rapidly developing field, and new research constantly presents new understandings and insights. In contrast to the related but more established term "industry clusters", there are many different definitions of ecosystems, and the term is often used rather broadly and imprecisely. At the same time, there is little doubt that ecosystems are different from pure partnerships, even when they include many parties. And while clusters are confined by their geographical proximity and industry, ecosystems typically span across industries and geographic locations. We draw on leading researchers to introduce the concept and provide a glimpse into an exciting and prospering field.

In contrast to partnerships, discussed in Chapter 8, there are usually no clear organizational boundaries for an ecosystems. Therefore, it can be difficult to determine which actors to include and which to exclude from the system. It might be easier to define which actors are close to and at the core of an ecosystem and which actors are more peripheral. Unclear boundaries also mean that organizations in an ecosystem can co-exist without having a contract that regulates the relationship between them. Moreover, ecosystems vary in their degree of openness.

A good illustration of how difficult it can be to determine these boundaries is the Norwegian fintech ecosystem Finance Innovation (FI). Finance Innovation is a member organization whose purpose is to promote innovations in banking and insurance. Many associate Finance Innovation with an ecosystem, but is that correct? Finance Innovation is a member organization, and in 2021 there were around 90 members. Membership gives access to Finance Innovation's resources at two levels. At a higher level, the membership provides access to networks, a place to meet and work, and entry into seminars and other events. On a project level, Finance Innovation contributes legal and technical expertise. These projects are initiated by the members, and they decide who to include. Finance Innovation does not exclude participation in individual projects by organizations outside of its membership. As an illustration, a project on insurance fraud had members both inside and outside of Finance Innovation. This shows precisely how difficult it is to set boundaries around the ecosystem and that the ecosystem in this case can extend outside the membership.

Professor Michael Jacobides from the London Business School, one of the most prominent researchers in the field, defines ecosystems as "a set of actors with varying degrees of multilateral, unique complementarities that are not fully hierarchically controlled". (Jacobides et al., 2018, p. 2264).

Ecosystems are particularly focused on relationships between actors that are interdependent and complement one another. Complementary means that they produce more value together than they do individually. In contrast, when organizations compete, then one firm's product becomes less valuable because the customer has an alternative. When complementarities are unique, coordination must be done by the producers before they are sold in a market. Examples of complementary products could be a cup of coffee and a croissant, or a cup of green tea and chia pudding. You can buy these separately in a market; you don't need an ecosystem to produce these combinations, hence they are not unique.

Ecosystems make sense when the coordination cannot be solved in the market. At the same time, the products/services offered through an ecosystem typically do not require as strong coordination as in an organization or close collaboration. This led Altman, Nagle and Tushman (2021) to launch the concept of *the translucent hand* to describe the coordination of actors who are located somewhere between the invisible hand of the market and the visible hand of hierarchy.

Ecosystems help coordinate organizations that are related, but at the same time autonomous and independent. As mentioned above in Chapter 8, the actors might be both competitors and working partners. In its simplest form, actors coordinate their actions to make the pie bigger, but compete for a share of the pie. In more complex relationships, the actors cooperate and coordinate some deliveries, but act as competitors in others (Hannah & Eisenhardt, 2018).

Ecosystems have a modular architecture somewhat like Lego bricks, where different components can be developed and produced by different actors with limited need for coordination. The various companies can design, price, and in other ways decide on their components as long as they interconnect with others in agreed and predefined ways.

Some components will be unique in the sense that only one actor can produce them, for example a component protected by a patent. Potentially, this will provide the actor with a powerful position in the ecosystem. This means that ecosystems are prone to bottlenecks in some of the components (Hannah & Eisenhardt, 2018). These bottlenecks can create challenges for development and growth of the ecosystem. The exploitation of these bottlenecks depends on whether the components can be replicated or substituted. If so, attempts to exploit bottleneck positions can incentivize others to begin to produce the component or new players entering.

The relationships between actors in the telecom industry closely resemble an ecosystem. A prerequisite for the actors to enter the industry is that they have access to roam in (each) other's network regardless of whether they have their own network or not. Roaming prices have been a recurring theme between the parties and for the supervisory authorities, and high prices have spurred the building of replicate and competing networks. However, within the frames of roaming agreements, each player is free to develop and price their services to customers.

Different types of ecosystems

The research literature distinguishes between three different types of ecosystems: business ecosystems, innovation ecosystems, and platform ecosystems (Jacobides et al., 2018).

The business ecosystem maps the community of different actors that impacts a focal firm and its suppliers and customers (Teece, 2007). The actors can be various organizations, institutions, and individuals. Business ecosystems will often cross industries and include competitive as well as complementary relationships.

If we set our eyes on the wider circle of actors, Vipps (see case after Chapter 8 on partnerships) can be portrayed as a business ecosystem. In Figure 9.2 we have drawn Vipps's ecosystem before its merger with the Nordic digital wallets.

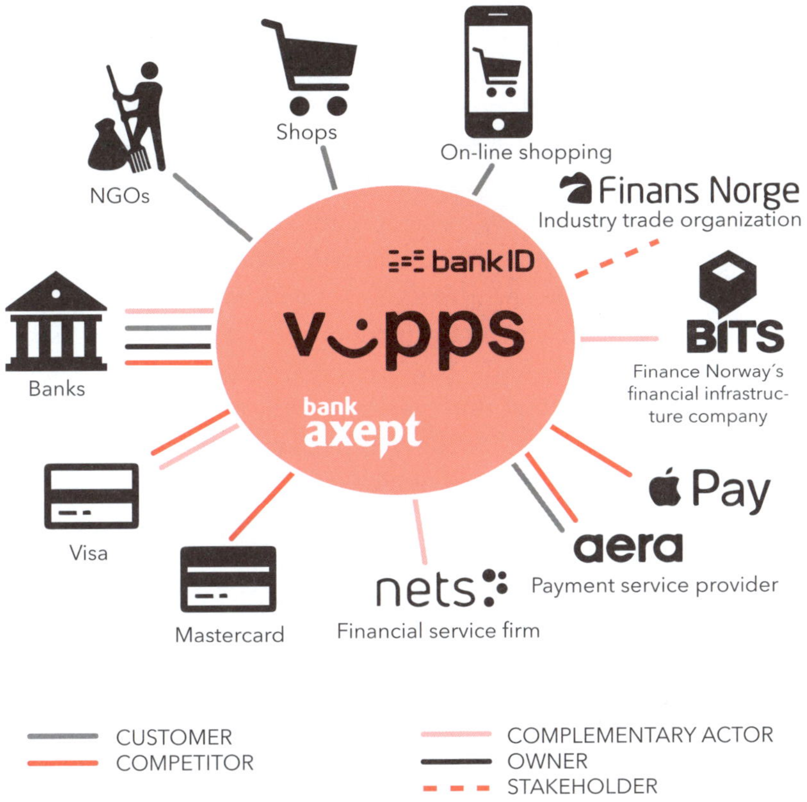

Figure 9.2 Overview of Vipps's ecosystem in 2020

The *innovation ecosystem* focuses on a focal innovation and the set of components and complements that support it. This type of ecosystem can be described as a collaborative arrangement where different actors to come together and create new innovative solutions or products (Adner, 2006). The innovation ecosystem is closest to Moore's description of parties who co-evolve and co-create. Through this lens, an attempt is made to understand how independent actors interact to create and commercialize innovations that serve their end users – and their coordination within the ecosystem is absolutely essential for the innovation to be successful. The development of standards for mobile networks, ranging from first-generation NMT to 5G, are examples of such innovations and standards that have been developed in an innovation ecosystem.

The *platform ecosystem* is (similarly to the business ecosystem) often based on a focal company. This ecosystem consists of the platform itself and the complementary actors that make the platform valuable for the consumers (Ceccagnoli et al., 2012; Gawer & Cusumano, 2014). By connecting with the platform, the complementary players can drive innovation on the platform and gain access, directly or indirectly, to the platform's customers. A good example of a company that has seen the benefit of developing its platform into an ecosystem is the gaming company Valve.

Steam is a digital gaming platform developed by the gaming company Valve, and was launched in 2003 to support sales of Valve's own online games. Shortly after, Valve users protested loudly when Valve tried to force them to use the platform to access the games. This was early in the development of a new platform, and at this point the functionality was mediocre. In order to rally the gamers and develop the platform into something more valuable, in 2005 Valve opened up so that third parties could also distribute their games through the Steam platform, with the continued requirement that only Steam would publish the games. In 2008, with the launch of Steamworks (a software tool that allowed anyone to configure, manage and run games on the platform), Valve took another step and offered game developers and users closer access to the platform; from only functioning on Microsoft Windows, Steamworks was also launched on macOS, Linux, and mobile platforms. Through freely available APIs, developers could integrate many of Steam's functions through Steamworks into their games and anyone who wanted to publish games through the Steam platform. Many gamers also chose to jump over the fence and become producers. Through these successive steps, Steam developed its platform to include more and more complementary actors to innovate and create new gaming experiences. In 2021, Steam had 132 million monthly active users and had gone from launching only seven games through the Steam platform in 2004 to increasing the number of games to over 10 000 in 2021 (source: Statista, March 19, 2023).

Different roles and how to navigate within the ecosystem

One of the great things about ecosystems is that they provide insight into the complex and different relationships between the actors. In the example with Vipps above, many of the banks are owners, customers, suppliers, and complementary actors, while voluntary organizations are customers of Vipps, and governments have a role as regulators. The major grocery stores are customers, such as Coop and Norgesgruppen. Meanwhile these firms are also building a (potential) competitor to Vipps through Aera – a company whose aim is to protect the grocery stores' interests in payment processing. Such complex relationships, which are also full of contradictions, create dynamics in the ecosystem, and any attempt to exploit a position can easily backfire. Therefore, by mapping the various actors and their relationships in the ecosystems, complexities and interactions are revealed.

The roles can differ depending on the type of ecosystem in question. Platform ecosystems typically involve a clear leadership role with the platform owner. The platform owner builds the overall architecture and creates rules for other actors who want access to the platform. The challenge for the platform owner/leader is to establish models that ensure that many actors benefit from and/or enjoy being associated with the platform (Schmeiss et al., 2019). For many platforms, there will be significant network effects. The more people who use them, the more each user will benefit from the platform. The challenge in this type of platform ecosystem will be to attract players to the platform in an early phase when it is of little value to the users, as illustrated in the example with Valve above.

There are three central mechanisms in platform ecosystems for governing the ecosystem: access, control, and incentives (Schmeiss et al., 2019). First, the platform owner/leader can decide who gets access to the platform and what kind of rights they have. In Valve's contracts, different subscribers have different rights. Second, there are also clear guidelines for what cannot be published on Steam, including content that exploits children in any way and programs that unlawfully attempt to acquire sensitive information. The control defines which rules apply to interaction between the actors. For example, in Steam Community Market the company has built in functionality that enables buying and selling between users, but then on the condition that Valve has control over the transactions. The last mechanism is to build in incentives to make active use of the platform and to innovate. By launching Steamworks, Valve created incentives for users to create games on Steam's platform while at the same time giving Valve control and significant business opportunities.

In open ecosystems it does not make sense to talk about access, and the boundaries regarding which actors are part of the ecosystem (or not) also become more difficult to define. On the other hand, this is the main advantage of open ecosystems, as actors can gain autonomy and control over their own ideas and interact without limitations from a leading platform owner/organization (Baldwin, 2012). In these ecosystems, it is not possible to exercise hierarchical control, but this does not mean that central actors in the ecosystems are without tools. Some relationships can be formalized through contracts, other relationships can be incentivized by making it attractive to participate in the ecosystem. Vipps's free peer-to-peer payments, for example, was an important feature in attracting consumers to use the app. Although Vipps did not earn money from these free services, they created ripple effects for other actors in the ecosystem that provided profits in other areas.

There are also important differences between business and innovation ecosystems. In business ecosystems, the focal firm usually has limited control over who is included in the ecosystem. Parties that exploit the ecosystem and maximize their profits at the expense of others can destroy the ecosystem or increase the risk of replacement by other ecosystems.

In an innovation ecosystem, the actors are bound together by a common fate, even if they have different perceptions of revenue sharing. The fact that they have common goals provides a driving force for the collaboration. At the same time, such ecosystems can be more complex because they involve many actors, particularly if there is no central actor. When many actors are involved, it is also more difficult to find effective forms of governance that balance speed and democracy. Therefore, managing this type of ecosystem is not unlike that which we find in complex partnerships.

Ecosystems and the cogs

Similar to the other organizational solutions that open the boundaries of innovation, external relations is an important cog in the wheel. But ecosystems also affect governance and management, competence, incentives, and culture in the established company.

Depending on the type of ecosystem, the cogs will be affected in different ways. In the business ecosystem, the focal firm will be surrounded by a number of actors who influence the business in addition to the customers (*external relations*). In the innovation ecosystem, the central unit is the innovation and in platform ecosystem, the platform itself constitutes the center.

All three ecosystem types will require *transparency*, *governance*, and *management*. By being dependent on others, it is no longer possible to make unilateral decisions. When the aim is to co-create and grow the ecosystem, it is generally important to ensure that the parties make a profit or benefit from being a part of the system. This requires *tolerance* for tensions and versatile management models. It is also likely that the *competence* in the business will be affected both because of the opportunity to specialize, and gain access to competence that matches/balances one's own. In order to stimulate other parties to become part of the ecosystem, it may also be necessary to look at the *incentives*, and perhaps share proprietary knowledge. Thus, it is also likely that the *culture* will be influenced to become more open and sharing.

CASE 9.1
ALIBABA[14]

In this case, we will illustrate one of most known global ecosystems, China's Alibaba. Alibaba's core is e-commerce platforms, but the ecosystem also includes almost every imaginable support function for online-shopping such as payment, marketing, cloud storage and logistics. Our purpose is to show how the ecosystem functions and how it has grown since Alibaba was established in 1999 until today. We will also show some of the challenges Alibaba currently faces, as well as the opportunities Covid-19 provided for expansion. The case illustrates how growth in an ecosystem depends on complementarities and key synergies as well as strong control and coordination.

The ecosystem

Alibaba was established in 1999 by a former English teacher, Jack Ma, from Hangzhou in China. The vision behind Alibaba was to enable smaller companies to compete with the large established firms through the use of the Internet and new technological solutions. In March 2021, the company reached a milestone of over 1 billion customers, and the goal for 2036 is to double the number of customers to 2 billion (Alibaba's homepage, May 2021). Over 50% of all retail sales in China in 2020 occurred through Alibaba's platforms (source: Investopedia, January 18, 2021).

The roots of Alibaba go back to 1995, when Jack Ma established ChinaPages.com (Tan et al., 2009). China Pages was a small business that offered web services to local Chinese companies. This was before the Internet became known among the Chinese population, and Jack Ma convinced Chinese companies of the value of creating websites in English. China Pages did the translation job themselves and then communicated the information to partners in the United States who developed the websites. Eventually, China Pages acquired the necessary technical skills to develop the websites itself. When Jack Ma left China Pages with his development team of eight in 1997, they were selected by the Chinese government to develop China Market, an online portal directed at global companies aiming to do business in China. Jack Ma's experiences from China Pages and China Market made him realize the global potential that lay in lifting the horde of small and medium-sized businesses into a new technological era.

Alibaba started as a simple ecosystem where the business idea was to create a platform that connected the countless small and medium Chinese enterprises with companies all over the world. Even though B2B platforms existed in 1999,

14 The case on Alibaba is based on secondary sources and has been written for this book.

the cost was an effective entry barrier for the Chinese SMB segment, and the companies also needed support to transform their business from a pure brick-and-mortar business to online shopping. In addition, from its detailed comprehension of Chinese business practices Alibaba had a local knowledge advantage compared to the global players. Jack Ma's apartment was the birthplace for development of Alibaba, and in the beginning, Ma and the entire development team had a combined income of 73 US dollars a month.

Alibaba quickly gained a grip on the giant Chinese SMB market and within a few years became a dominant player in B2B online commerce. Eventually management saw substantial business opportunities in selling directly to consumers, and Alibaba established several web portals for B2C. But the biggest threat to their business model came from search engines like China's Baidu and Google. In 2005 Alibaba therefore bought Yahoo China. The goal was to create its own search engine and block the leading search engines from indexing the database for Alibaba's own shopping platforms. Therefore, buyers would have to go directly to Alibaba's platforms to gain access.

As technology made it possible, more and more activities in the value chain that supported the core business were moved to digital platforms: marketing, logistics, technology support and cloud services, payment processing, and financing. Several of these created fertile ground for new business adventures and eventually developed their own complete ecosystems. One of the most famous is Alipay, now Ant Group, which Alibaba chose to spin off in 2010.

With adventurous growth, the close relationship Alibaba previously had with the individual members of the ecosystem came under pressure. Consequently, Alibaba realized that it had to develop the ecosystem to become self-organizing and to a greater extent facilitate the development of connections between members. As a result, in 2006 it bought Koubei.com, one of the most popular Internet portals for reviews of lifestyle products. The goal was to get members to spend more time in Alibaba's sphere and develop relationships among themselves. Moving more of its support functions to the Web and developing a technologically advanced decentralized infrastructure, Alibaba evolved from a mere hub-and-spoke (junction point) to a self-organizing ecosystem.

Jack Ma and his team was set on building an ecosystem and developing strong relationships with all members of the ecosystem. A senior executive at Alibaba explained it this way:

> Our ecosystem is the key to our success … We have a close relationship with our (ecosystem) members … we know their needs and we are able to meet their needs quickly and effectively … this strengthens our members and enables them to contribute to the collective good … It is a virtuous cycle. When the ecosystem prospers, everyone (within the ecosystem) prospers. (Quotation taken from Tan et al., 2009, p. 9)

Alibaba's ecosystem is in continuous development, and Alibaba has expanded into ever-new industries such as entertainment and social media and, among other things, invested in Weibo and Youku Todou, China's answer to Twitter and YouTube, respectively. Today, it is difficult to identify and systematize the jungle of actors that are part of Alibaba's ecosystem.

Governance and management

Jack Ma was a big fan of Jack Welch, and Alibaba's strategy and organization bear clear signs of General Electric (GE) (Wulf, 2010). There has not been an overarching strategy for the Alibaba system – each business area has developed its own strategy and competed with the others to achieve the best results.

> Business area presidents must have the freedom to do what is right for their business. I want the business areas to compete with each other ... and focus on being the best within their businesses. (Jack Ma referenced in Wulf, 2010, p. 7)

To encourage competition and independence, Ma established separate board and senior management for each business area. The philosophy was that the business areas should pursue their own interests, not Alibaba's. For example, when Alipay was established, its goal was to become a leader in payment processing. This required it to establish its own customer base for online shopping. But those customers could just as well be on platforms that competed directly with Alibaba's own.

The internal competition meant that Alibaba potentially missed out on synergies between the business areas, and it also created tensions between them. Nonetheless, Ma made the leaders responsible for sorting out disagreements among themselves. He was also clear that rather than hunting for synergies, he prioritized the development of the companies in a tough and unpredictable competitive climate.

> We sacrificed forced synergies in order to quickly pursue subsidiary opportunities ... Since you don't know where the competition is coming from and firm boundaries are changing quickly, suppliers and partners can develop into competition overnight. Only the paranoid survive ... that is why Alibaba's decentralized model holds up in fast-growth settings. (Joe Tsai, CFO of the Alibaba Group, referenced in Wulf, 2010, p. 8)

To keep Alibaba together in a time of exponential growth, Jack Ma developed a strong HR function that guarded the core values and ensured continuous organizational development. The core values are still strong at Alibaba, and today these are (source: Alibaba's homepage 2021):

1. First customers, then employees, then owners
2. Trust simplifies everything

3. Change is the only constant
4. Today's best results are tomorrow's standards
5. If not now, when? If not me, then who?
6. Take life seriously, but be happy by working

Ma rotates managers of the business areas. Senior management is deeply involved in the strategic plans of the individual business areas. To create extra motivation for the employees, Alibaba offers them stock options. When this was introduced, it broke with Chinese culture, but the recipe has proven to be successful, particularly in the parts of the company that are listed on the stock market. For the unlisted companies, workers are offered employee stock options (ESOs) in the unlisted Alibaba, and the higher staff rise in the ranks, the more remuneration becomes based on performance. The challenge, however, is that the value of these shares was more fluid, and difficult to sell should staff wish to leave the company (Wulf, 2010).

In 2018, it became known that Jack Ma would hand over the helm to his successor Daniel Zang from 2019 and retire from Alibaba's board in 2020. Daniel Zang was well known; he had been at Alibaba for over ten years and was Ma's hand-picked candidate. Moreover, Ma has continued to be part of Alibaba's 38-member overall management committee and still has a stake of over 6% (Kuo, 2019).

Trading platforms and complementary players

Alibaba has many different trading platforms, each with its own business logic. Some of the largest are Alibaba.com, Taobao and Tmall. Alibaba.com, established in 1999, was the first trading platform with the B2B segment as its target group. Alibaba receives income on the platform through a fixed annual fee from the sellers as well as sales commissions. Suppliers can also pay extra for better exposure.

Taobao, which means treasure hunt in Chinese, is the other major marketplace platform focusing on B2C. Taobao was established in 2003, and in 2021 was China's largest online store, with several hundred million products. In order to increase traffic on the website, Alibaba has a business model where it is free to sell products through the platform. The main source of income is advertising revenue from companies that want to have a more prominent place on the pages.

Tmall was established in 2008 and is an upmarket B2C platform that caters to the growing Chinese middle class. This platform sells branded products and has linked up with companies such as Nike and Apple. Alibaba's revenue is based on a mix of deposits, fees, and sales commissions. This platform is similar to Amazon and eBay, but unlike Amazon, Alibaba does not have its own physical distribution apparatus on any of the platforms.

In addition to its trading platforms, Alibaba has established a network of complementary companies that support the main business. These complementary companies have been absolutely essential for growth in the trading platforms. In the first period, it was payment that represented the bottleneck in the ecosystem; later it was the logistics operations (Tsai, 2016). Therefore, to create growth in the ecosystem, it has been important to increase the capacity of these components. In 2021, in the wake of Covid-19, again it was the logistics operations that represented the bottleneck.

Alipay is a payment platform for third parties established in 2004. This platform was essential to establish a functioning payment system that was trusted by both sellers and buyers online; without Alipay, it is likely that the growth of trading platforms would quickly have come to a halt.

> Alipay was absolutely critical in the development of Taobao. Even if the buyers see a seller with a high rating, lack of trust would still be a big challenge. Alipay removed the settlement risk. The payment mechanism itself is not important. Payment is easy in China. People are used to sending money, also via the Internet. But banks cannot handle settlement risk. That's where Alipay comes into the picture. (Porter Erisman, former Vice President for international relations, referenced in Wulf, 2010, p. 5)

Alipay was spun out of the Alibaba Group in 2010 but is still a key component in Alibaba's ecosystem. In 2015, Alipay changed its name to Ant Group. Ant was the original name of Alibaba's microloan division, aimed at small and medium-sized businesses. Ant was important in securing funding and thereafter growth opportunities for the key segment in Alibaba's business vision. After seven years of operation, Ant Microloans had provided loans of less than one million yuan to almost three million small and medium-sized enterprises (Zeng, 2018).

To speed up its logistics operations, in 2018 Alibaba established China Smart Logistics (now Cainiao Smart Logistics Network) together with eight other companies. The goal was to provide real-time information about buyers and sellers to streamline package deliveries. The rapid growth of the company made Cainiao one of China's biggest unicorns in 2018.

In 2008, Alibaba established a platform for cloud services – Alibaba Cloud. To increase distribution of the cloud services, Alibaba Cloud offers partner agreements through which companies can become distributors of Alibaba Cloud's products alone or in combination with their own products. Companies that become partners are offered training and various types of support services. By 2020, Alibaba Cloud had 9000 partners and the business had invested significant funds to develop the partnership and ecosystem. To speed up the network effects in the ecosystem and tie the players together, Alibaba Cloud organizes the annual Apsara conference where thousands of researchers, technologists and companies meet. Over 10 000 programmers attended the 2020 conference. The conference is primarily a playground for programmers, but also a place where companies can recruit technologists and software developers (Source: Alibaba Cloud homepage, October 2020).

The competition between Alibaba and Tencent

Alibaba's biggest competitor is Tencent, which has developed a competing ecosystem. Tencent has a different starting point for developing its ecosystem, as it is founded on the gaming industry and social media (Buche & Cantale, 2018). Tencent was established the year before Alibaba, in 1998, by founders Ma Huateng (better known as Pony) and four friends. In 2021, the platform company was the world's largest supplier of games, and this is also what constitutes the main revenue stream for the company. From having launched its first instant messaging product, QQ, in 2001, Tencent has grown to become one of the largest companies within social media through services such as WeChat and Qzone. In addition, it has expanded into payment processing and Internet commerce, segments that directly challenge Alibaba's position.

Tanya Van Gastel (Content Commerce Insider, 2021) described the competition between the two ecosystems as follows:

> Alibaba and Tencent can be compared to two CEOs behaving like fighting cocks in a conference room. You don't really have anything to contribute – and you can't break them up. They gobble up all the oxygen in the room and you're just left hanging.

The background for the above description is an exclusivity requirement that Alibaba and Tencent places on the third-party suppliers. This has forced the companies to choose sides – a practice the Chinese call *erxuanyi* (choose one of two). If the companies fail to conform to this practice, they may be banned from both of the dominant players' platforms. One of the few companies that has dared to challenge this practice and go to court is the Galanz Group, the world's largest microwave oven manufacturer. It was hit hard when its CEO visited Tencent's growing Pinduoduo platform company and signed a partnership agreement. Shortly after, Alibaba's algorithms began to divert traffic away from the Tmall platform and Galanz's sales on the platform halved in a year (McMorrow & Liu, 2020).

This exclusivity practice has been maintained as a reason why Tencent did not gain momentum in its sales of fashion clothing through the JD.com platform; but the growing Pinduoduo platform is now a bigger threat to Alibaba, and in 2019 had a customer base of over half a billion. Moreover, Tencent has also shut Alibaba out of its platforms, making it difficult for users to share Taobao and Tmall links over WeChat.

However, there are clear signs that Chinese competition authorities have begun to take an interest in the business practices of platform companies, and new legislation is on the way addressing platform companies and the ease of consumers switching platforms. On Christmas Eve 2020, Alibaba's share price fell by 8% on the stock exchange when it became known that the competition authorities had started investigations into possible competitively harmful monopolistic behavior; the competition authorities were also investigating Tencent's dominance within IM (instant messaging or direct messaging).

As often happens when there is a negative spotlight on the companies, there are signs that the practice is changing. Alibaba's Ele.me has made WeChat pay available on its app, and Meituan, which has been part of the Tencent sphere, has also allowed Alipay. At the same time, both Ant Group's Alipay and WeChat pay feel that the Chinese central bank has threatened to stop the companies from exploiting their dominating position or, in the worst case, to break up the companies if they "represent serious hindrances to a healthy development for the payments market". (Draft of new competition rules discussed by Thomas Peters, Reuters, January 2020)

Covid-19

Paradoxically, the Covid-19 pandemic has also been a shot in the arm for the large Chinese platform companies and demonstrated their ability for quick and creative problem solving, as shown in table C9.1.1 from the consulting company BCG.

Three weeks after the Chinese authorities confirmed the presence of a new coronavirus in January 2020, Ant Group and Alibaba launched a series of new services together with partners. Live maps were created showing the locations of contagion, free online medical consultations were offered – at times there were up to 100 000 consultations each day – and free insurance coverage for medical personnel fighting the pandemic, in addition to subsidies for small businesses that used the Alipay platform, online teaching and virtual career days for recent graduates and the unemployed. On top of this, Alibaba organized a crowdsourcing event where it got the help of more than 4000 developers and software providers to create programs that addressed the pandemic.

Alibaba also helped businesses transition from brick-and-mortar sales to online commerce and offered people temporary jobs in its growing network of related businesses for industries affected by the pandemic. But Alibaba's competitors did not slacken off either.

Tencent launched a new international platform with the aim of helping companies, health institutions and governments cope with the pandemic. Services on the platform included a handbook on how to protect the population, an AI-based service called check-the-symptoms, online health consultations as well as a service that collected articles and videos on how to avoid infection.

LAUNCHED NEW, CUSTOMIZED OFFERINGS AND INTERFACES IN RECORD TIME
Example: AliPay released around a dozen new features fand services within three weeks of the outbreak.

LAUNCHED NEW PLATFORMS WITH ADDITIONAL AND EXISTING PARTNERS IN ONE TO THREE WEEKS TO ADDRESS BUSINESS AND CONSUMER NEEDS
Example: Tencent launched a health care platform with four subplatforms providing COVID-19 information and screening.

BROADENED EXISTING DIGITAL ECOSYSTEMS AND STANDARIZED DATE-SHARING AGREEMENTS THAT ENABLED QUICK ONBOARDING OF NEW PARTNERS
Example: FreshHema grocery chain "borrowed" 5000 workers from 40 other companies whose business were affected by lockdowns.

RAPIDLY DEPLOYED NASCENT TECHNOLOGIES, INCLUDING AI CHATBOTS, 5G, AND TELEMEDICINE
Example: Baidu's intelligent robocall platform made more than 3 million automated phone calls requesting travel history and other information and handled over 15 million COVID-19-related inquiries by mid-March.

HELPED TRADITIONAL OFFLINE BUSINESSES RAPIDLY SHIFT SALES AND SERVICES ONLINE, ALLOWING THEM TO MITIGATE THE EFFECTS OF THE DOWNTURN AND EVEN GROW
Example: Alibaba launched an app enabling consumers to buy directly from factories

PARTNERED WITH PUBLIC-SECTOR ORGANIZATIONS TO DISSEMINATE INFORMATION AND MIGRATE SERVICES TO ONLINE CHANNELS
Example: Social media and e-commerce platforms helped the Chinese Electronics Technology Group and health and transportation authorities quickly launch a close-contact system that served more than 450 million people and identified 160 000 close contacts.

Table C9.1.1 Response of Chinese ecosystems to Covid-19. Source: Chan, Lang, Modi, Tang and von Szczepanski (2020).

Baidu, the search engine platform that Alibaba blocked, also launched a number of new technological innovations. It shared its deep learning and image segmentation platforms, PaddlePaddle and PaddleSeg, with developers of Covid-19 applications. As a result of these collaborations, secondary RNA structures were analyzed which provided insight into how the virus jumped between different species. Further CT images were analyzed so that the virus could be detected in less than a minute. Baidu also made available an infrared sensor system based on AI that could measure the temperature of many people at the same time and quickly detect fever. This service was put into use at Beijing's Qinghe Railway Station to test two hundred people per minute without disrupting traffic.

On top of all this, the platform companies and the authorities collaborated to create an infection app that could track people who were infected and inform people who had been in contact with infected people. The app was also used to check that people moving in public spaces were not infected.

What can others learn from Alibaba?

What does the Alibaba case tell us about ecosystems and how they can be developed? Compared to the Norwegian technology-based ecosystems such as Vipps and Finance Innovation, the Chinese ecosystems appear considerably more mature. Of course, they also have a much larger domestic market to address.

One of the characteristics of Alibaba is its openness to the outside world. New services are developed in partnership, and the ecosystem grows rapidly by mobilizing other actors in the environment. Not only does Alibaba invite partners in to sell and distribute its products, it also allows them to be sold alongside its own products, and it actively support partners by offering technological and administrative support and training, and it invests in the collaboration. It develops new services in close collaboration with independent developers, a trend many of the new platform companies have also adopted. Alibaba is adept at managing emerging bottlenecks and developing support functions for new business opportunities. Clearly, Alibaba has understood what creates healthy dynamics and growth in ecosystems.

At the same time, Alibaba is aware that the goal is to drive traffic to its own platforms and not others, and that it wants to create a community that commits other actors to its ecosystem. Alibaba uses its power to create as much traffic as possible on its own platforms and attempts to shut out competitors like Tencent or Baidu through demands for exclusivity or through blocking. Paradoxically, the company that was founded on the idea of helping small and medium-sized companies compete with the bigger ones is now limiting the growth of these companies through demands for exclusivity.

The competition and blocking may prove detrimental to Alibaba's continued growth, not only because the competition authorities are breathing down its neck, but also because Alibaba may push customers away if it goes too far in blocking others from showing their own content. The fact that Alipay and WeChat pay are now becoming available on competitors' platforms is a sign that things are changing – even in the dominant Chinese ecosystems.

The external transparency is closely connected with management of the ecosystem. Since the beginning, Jack Ma has emphasized that the company must sacrifice synergies in order to grow quickly, and that it is better to let the various business units develop and grow at their own pace rather than have to coordinate and protect the individual units from internal competition. He has avoided the temptation to create centralized technological platforms and insisted that it is best to decentralize. That does not mean that he is not concerned with creating a common platform in the Alibaba group, and the rotation of directors and the investment in HR and building shared values are signs of this.

So far, we have focused on the development of individual ecosystems and looked less at competition between ecosystems. In this case, there is clearly a battle between the two dominant ecosystem actors in China: Alibaba and Tencent. In the Western world, there are clear parallels to what is happening between Apple and Google and their battle for customers.

Finally, the Alibaba case illustrates how external shocks can bring new opportunities. The Covid-19 pandemic affected the business world very differently, and many platform companies experienced unprecedented growth when physical development was limited, and trade, services, teaching, internal and external meetings moved to virtual platforms. In this shock, technological development allowed some firms to leapfrog the competition, and the large platform companies, especially the Asian ones, have been important contributors to this transformation.

Part 4

Innovation by spinning out and establishing anew

In this part of the book we look at innovation that occurs by moving out parts of the business or establishing something anew, for instance through relocation. This can, for example, occur through intrapreneurship that starts in the established firm and is later spun out, such as Storm in TV 2. In order for this to build innovation capacity in the established firm, benefits beyond financial rewards must be ensured. In the example of TV 2, spinning out and changing ownership provided new possibilities in terms of a broader, global market, ultimately resulting in higher quality services for TV 2. In our second case, we show how new establishments in the form of a new location can foster innovation, such as when the National Library located a branch in Northern Norway.

Chapter 10

Spin-outs and new establishments

In this chapter, we examine when growth and development opportunities might be better outside the established firm, either by inviting other owners in or establishing business in a new location. Previously we described how established firms can renew themselves and allow innovations to grow stronger through the ambidextrous solution. This was the case with Vipps. However, after its initial success, Vipps was eventually spun out entirely from the established firm DNB. In this chapter we describe the rationale underlying spin-outs and new establishments. We start by presenting perspectives on this from the research literature, and then we look at two cases – TV 2 and the National Library – which illustrate the point in different ways.

The act of spinning out and establishing a new unit with other owners strengthens the ability to *sense* and *seize* new opportunities. The spin-out can have a sharper focus and does not need to contribute to the established firm. Different *complementary capabilities* can be developed as the spin-out becomes liberated from the established firm, at the same time that full focus on the innovation can create *collective engagement* among the spin-out's employees.

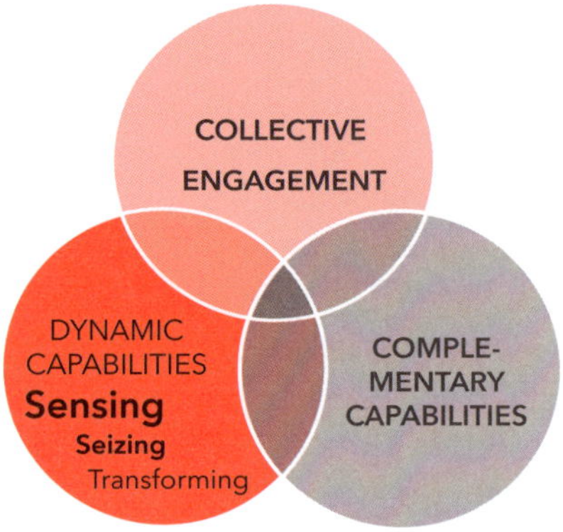

Figure 10.1 How spinning out contributes to innovation capacity

To describe the innovation of spinning out or new establishments, we draw on three different research streams: the spin-out/spin-off literature, corporate strategy, and value chain analysis. While the latter two are well-established research areas within strategy, the literature dealing with spin-outs is newer and thus more fragmented. Therefore, we will use most of the space to present research-based knowledge about spin-outs.

Spinning out from established firms

When a new business is formed on the basis of an innovation or activities that have taken place in an established business, we use the terms spin-off or spin-out. The two terms are often used interchangeably in the research literature. There are various reasons underlying the decision to spin out. In some cases, activities are separated in order to compete with the established actors (including the parent company), while in others it is about non-core activities that are considered to have better conditions for growth outside the established firm.

Starting a competing business

If employees of established companies form a spin-out that competes in the same market as the established company, the established company will usually not have ownership in the spin-out (Agarwal et al., 2004). This type of spin-out has particularly been studied in high-tech industries where employees take ideas from an established company to start their own competing company. According to Agarwal et al. (2004), these spin-outs will have knowledge advantages relative to other start-ups. Consequently, the knowledge that the founders bring with them from previous employment in the established company could pose a major threat to the established business.

Starting a complementary business

According to Chesbrough (2011), employees who leave established companies to start their own competing business (as described above) were previously seen as traitors, while today it is more common to think of these as the established business's best and strongest ambassadors.

This is particularly the case if the companies that are spun-out maintain a close connection to the established company with the purpose to create value for both the established firm and the new company rather than to compete head-on. While Agarwal and colleagues (2004) studied spin-outs that competed directly with the core endeavors of the existing business, Chesbrough (2003) studied technology-driven spin-outs where the purpose was to commercialize an R&D innovation that lay *outside* the core business of the company. In this case, it is more natural to take on the ambassador role. In such cases, the parent company often maintains ownership of the spin-out company. These spin-outs are established with two objectives: to create value for the new company (Garvin, 1983) and to ensure growth and entrepreneurship within the established company (Block & MacMillan, 1993).

In the research on complementary spin-outs, the established firm tends to be a university or a large commercial player with R&D activities. While internal R&D activities are important for the renewal of the established firm, it is also important to have good selection processes that effectively distinguish which innovations should be invested in further (and these should be aligned with the business's strategy) from those that should be spun out or terminated (Burgelman, 1983a; 1983b).

When should innovations be spun out?

In his research, Christensen (2000) found that established firms have an advantage when it comes to incremental innovation that does not challenge the core business, while they have a clear disadvantage regarding disruption and ground-breaking changes; here, newcomers have an advantage. According to Christensen, an innovation should be spun out of the established firm if:

1. It requires a completely different cost structure than the established business. A business that has specialized in luxury goods with a differentiation strategy will face challenges if it starts delivering on a cost strategy. Typically, there will then be a poor match between the innovation and the established company's core values and processes.
2. The new opportunity is minimal compared to the need for growth in the established business. Then, the new service will not be able to receive sufficient resources and attention within the established one.

Christensen is clear that a spin-out will only be effective if one of these two criteria is met. If there is a good match between core values and processes and the new opportunity is of a certain size, then other alternative forms of organization, such as the ambidextrous model, will be more effective.

An important element that also underlies value creation and positive results from complementary spin-outs is knowledge. In technology-driven innovations, a distinction is often made between technological knowledge and market knowledge. Market knowledge will be particularly important in technological spin-outs because it involves considerable uncertainty (Chesbrough, 2003). Spin-outs bring technological know-how from the parent company (Sapienza et al., 2004). While that knowledge can constitute a competitive advantage, both too much and too little overlap in knowledge between the established firm and the spin-out could inhibit value creation. If there is too little overlap, they will not understand each other, and if there is too much overlap, there will be an insufficient influx of new information. In order to ensure sufficient new information and knowledge, it can therefore be valuable to reach out to external owners, employees and/or collaboration partners.

Chesbrough (2003) has studied the ownership and management of spin-outs. In studies of Xerox, he found better financial results in the technological spin-outs that included start-up capital (venture capital, VC) on the owner's side and an external senior manager (rather than board members and CEO from the established business). Chesbrough explains this through the vast uncertainty that new technology entails and that external help (VC or CEO) brings new knowledge and information about the market. The study only measures results for spin-outs, but qualitative data from the study suggests that Xerox was equally concerned with how the spin-out also created value for Xerox. Although Chesbrough maintains that this was the case and that the spin-out resulted in a win-win situation, neither the researchers nor Xerox had good indicators of the value creation at the established firm.

Corporate strategy – How to create corporate advantage

Theories about corporate strategy can also be relevant to understanding and explaining value creation through new establishments and spin-outs. In contrast to business strategy, which is about how and where a company should compete in one product market, corporate strategy concerns which product markets the corporation should be present in. Corporations operate in more than one product market; for example, Norsk Hydro previously operated in aluminum, but also oil and gas, and fertilizer. Thus, a central question in corporate strategy concerns the questions: What should the company own? Furthermore, how broad should the portfolio of business areas be? How should the corporation (parent) create value, and which business areas should it invest in or possibly divest? There are several ways the parent company can create value (for a thorough review, see Lien & Jacobsen, 2015), but the decisive factor is that the parent company must be the best owner. If other owners would be able to create more value than the parent company, then the business unit should be separated, possibly sold or spun out.

What is spun out? Core activities vs. support activities

Classical strategy theory on value chains can also be useful to understand new establishments and spin-outs (see for example Lien et al., 2016, or Porter, 1985). According to this theory, an established firm should assess the need for control and the costs of coordination. Usually, it would make sense to ensure control over core activities, especially those that form the basis of the company's competitive advantage. Activities that are not defined as core, but instead constitute support, such as administrative IT services, cleaning, cafeteria management and the like, can be set aside for others, spun out, or contracted out in the market, especially if there is less need to maintain (inhouse) control and the coordination costs are not too great.

New establishment through relocation

Hitherto, we have focused on activities that are spun out of an established business, but new establishment can also take other forms – for example, a new form of establishment through relocating a firm or parts of it. We have particularly seen this in the public sector when public offices are moved out of the capitol. The organization persists, but due to relocation, many employees resign, and the organization will practically be established anew. Initially, the objective may not be innovation, but rather political motives to secure jobs and build up strong pockets of competence outside the capital. While not the initial intent, relocation and new establishments can lead to innovation. This applies, among other things, to parts of the National Library that were moved from the capitol Oslo to Mo i Rana in Northern Norway. After the relocation, digitalization accelerated.

Established firms, perhaps particularly in the public sector, may also experience that new competing firms are established in order to speed up both innovation and efficiency. Nye Veier (New Roads) was established as a competitor to the Norwegian Road Administration on the basis of a political desire to speed up road construction. Nye Veier was tasked with working in a faster and more cost-effective way than had previously been the case in Norwegian Road Administration, and the newly established firm was equipped with a new set of tools to speed up the pace and increase its power against key stakeholders.

CASE 10.1
TV 2[15]

TV 2 was established as a commercial challenger to NRK, the state-owned national broadcasting company, and a number of entrepreneurial businesses have been spun out of the TV 2 corporation. Several of these have developed into global successes. This applies, for example, to Storm and Vizrt. Common to these is that they were started within TV 2, but as they took shape and gained momentum, they were spun out as separate businesses, often with TV 2 on the ownership side.

In this case, we focus on four spin-outs from TV 2; all of these involve innovation of processes that were defined as outside TV 2's core business, yet extremely important to the core. These can be seen as complementary businesses that do not compete in the same product markets as TV 2. All are also technology-driven innovations that have renewed and improved important support processes in TV 2. Just as Schibsted and VG have developed an innovation muscle based on the ambidextrous model, TV 2 has developed an innovation muscle around spinning out technology-driven process innovations. In this case, we take a closer look at the factors that have contributed the success and describe how spinning out and inviting more owners on board can create value both for the spin-out and for the established firm TV 2.

Four companies that have been spun out from TV 2

Mosart Medialab AS

Mosart Medialab develops digital automation systems that enable companies such as TV 2 to save costs by standardizing media production. The system allows one to two employees to do the same job that six employees previously did. The idea came from an employee at TV 2 who worked on this innovation for almost four years alongside his job at TV 2. He spent much of his free time on this innovation. Together with another TV 2 employee, he started Mosart Medialab with TV 2 as the owner. An important reason why Mosart Medialab was spun out was that potential customers of the automation system were skeptical about buying the solution from a competitor (TV 2). They were afraid that the solution would lose focus if it remained in TV 2 and that potential setbacks might cause skilled resources to be pulled back into the core business of TV 2. The spin-out reduced these risks.

15 This case builds on research in RaCE and consists of conversations with John Kjellevold in TV 2, and Justin Harlan's master's thesis, which is based on interviews with several central people.

Vimond Media Solutions AS

Vimond started as a unit of TV 2 that offered online media products developed by the company. The company was spun out and 100 per cent owned by TV 2. The online offer was originally developed in a separate unit in TV 2 (the ambidextrous solution) that was established to meet the company's needs for online products. Such a unit still exists within TV 2. However, like Mosart, Vimond was spun out to be able to serve a number of international media companies in addition to TV 2. The services they deliver allow global actors (like TV 2) to operate their own online services.

Publish Lab AS

Publish Lab started by developing software to help TV 2 make its products available faster and more cost-effectively. Eventually, it began to approach large media companies that had a demand for such software, but a number of competitors who did exactly the same thing sprung up, and it became difficult to succeed in the competitive environment. Then, Publish Lab sharpened its delivery to focus on workflow and logistics with the aim of increasing production speed and reducing the need for the number of employees. The company was spun out and today TV 2 owns approximately 50% of it.

Electric Friends AS

Electric Friends develops automated camera robot products. The purpose is to improve the visuals of TV 2's media products and reduce the need for the number of employees. The idea came from a consultant hired by TV 2. He sold the idea to the management and then received funds to explore the possibility in his own company. Electric Friends differs from the other three companies, which had progressed further in idea development, testing and commercialization before being spun out. There have been a number of challenges both financially and for product development, but Electric Friends has now sold its new products to TV 2, SRF, the BBC and four other media players.

Innovation initiative bottom-up, while facilitated from the top

There are a number of common features of the four abovementioned spin-outs. In addition to the fact that they were originally developed within TV 2, the innovations are technology-driven and mainly had the aim of improving and streamlining processes in the company. The innovations emerged to meet a concrete need in TV 2, but it is important to note that this need was not stated by the management.

None of the four innovations was planned or driven forward by senior management; there were people in operational positions with technological expertise who sensed the need and opportunity to improve and streamline the processes. But even if senior management was not an original driving force or had a stated strategy around this, senior management played an important role as a facilitator.

Management provided support in the form of resources – financial and organizational – and allowed employees to use part of their working time and TV 2's equipment to innovate. The employees appeared to be driven by an inner motivation to accomplish innovative ideas, because they also used a good part of their free time. The management argued that if you give motivated and capable people a small amount of resources, it's amazing what they can achieve. The management provided support, but also a large degree of freedom. However, they did not uncritically support absolutely everything. They made two clear demands:

1. There must be a genuine need in TV 2 for innovation that it is not just innovation for innovation's sake.
2. The innovation must not be available on the market; then it is better to buy it.

When the innovation had been tested in TV 2 and had become mature, it was spun out and organized into a separate company where TV 2 typically became the owner, sometimes together with the founders or other owners, other times alone. For the spin-out, this provided a certain financial security, access to TV 2's network, and access to a large, established media company through which the innovation could be showcased to other media companies. Being able to show that the innovation actually works and how it works can be important for attracting new customers (Rogers, 2010). TV 2 became a valuable "showroom" for the spin-outs.

By disconnecting the innovation from TV 2 and establishing a separate company, the innovative services could also be offered to media companies internationally, so that the spin-out was presented to a much larger market than it could have achieved internally in TV 2. The national market, in which TV 2 operated, was limited. As mentioned, several of the spin-outs that came from TV 2 have become global players and today serve media companies all over the world. This would not have been possible if the innovation had remained within TV 2, not only because the national market TV 2 operates in was limited in size, but also because there could then be a battle for resources and the ventures would not receive the same attention.

In TV 2, it is emphasized that a combination with many creative souls who sensed opportunities and a management that was able to balance support and autonomy, is the key to success. Perhaps the media industry also attracts particularly creative people? In addition, the founders who were behind these four innovations described the role TV 2 was given as a challenger when it was first established. Many creative people came together to run something they had never done before, and together they created a very special culture in TV 2.

The founders also pointed out a strong, strategic CFO as a central player in the innovation processes we have described above. He seized opportunities when they arose and bet on many small experiments. The CFO himself says that "... it is the easiest job in the world as a CFO to say no, CFOs usually do that. But the culture in the organization was such that you didn't stop all ideas that came ...". In other words, he also indicated the culture was important, but in addition he mentions the function-based structure, which he believes made organizational slack possible because no strict requirements were set for earnings for each department.

A final point that is highlighted as a success criterion is the strong relationships the founders have with each other because they come from the same environment in TV 2. A larger network has also emerged through the media cluster NCE Media/Media City Bergen.

How and why spinning out innovation can create a win-win situation

The four above innovations had better conditions for growth and further development outside TV 2. Extended ownership and a separate legal entity opened up new market opportunities for the spin-outs. But how was value created for TV 2 beyond potential financial gains as owner of the companies that were spun off?

Three of the four innovations had the aim of providing cost savings, so that by supporting and facilitating the innovation, value was created in the form of lower costs and more efficient operations. The CFO further explained that when the newly established companies brought in large global customers, in reality this contributed to the development costs for TV 2 being shared by several and in some cases almost zeroed out. Moreover, this led to quality improvements also within TV 2. The global customers made strict demands on quality, and as the start-up companies further developed their innovations, the quality of the services they provided to TV 2 became even better.

Similarly, the CTO of Fox (USA) described that while in the past Fox was concerned with ownership rights and royalties when it contributed to technology development in a supplier company, today Fox would rather say "good luck" and "sell it to as many people as possible". Consequently, when the supplier (in this case the spin-out) makes development part of its standard product range, the established firm is assured of continuous improvement through updates and upgrades. For software products, only one-sixth of the development has been carried out when the innovation goes into production with the first customer, hence continuous development becomes key.

What can other businesses learn?

According to corporate strategy theory, the question established firms should ask themselves is: Are we the best owner? How do we (as a parent) create value for this business unit? Are there others who could create more value? If the answer to the last question is yes, then the unit should be sold or separated, and the established firm should then buy the services in the market instead. In the TV 2 case, we see that there are some clear advantages to spinning out innovations as this facilitates growth and commercialization.

Strategy theory also points to the need for control. A company will want to control activities and services that are considered to be critical and part of the core business, particularly those which provide a competitive advantage. The innovations in TV 2 were not considered core business; rather they were support processes, which are considerably simpler to spin out. In TV2 this also allowed the innovations to be commercialized and further developed.

Spinning out a core activity is riskier because then the newly established company could quickly become a competitor. A feature of the media industry that can make it less risky to spin out activity is that it has largely been geographically separated, so that actors such as TV 2 have traditionally not been real competitors to global actors such as the BBC or CNN. It may therefore be simpler and less risky to spin out support processes and offer these to competitors in a geographically divided market. However, in the longer term, geographic boundaries will probably a become less important in the media industry – we already see that with streaming and new global players such as Netflix and HBO, who offer their services and retrieve content globally and completely independent of national borders.

CASE 10.2
THE NATIONAL LIBRARY OF NORWAY[16]

In this case, we want to illustrate an organization that has gone through a fundamental digital transformation, facilitated by establishing a new location, namely Mo in Rana. Interestingly, digital transformation was not the reason for a new location; it was related to the need to replace jobs in the Northern Norway region after the closure of cornerstone companies. At the same time, the National Library had a management that seized the opportunity and managed to bring the institution to a high international level.

From traditional library to digital public information

The MET and the Smithsonian visit the National Library of Norway to see and learn how artificial intelligence is used in its work. The Library of Congress and Stanford University are some of the institution's close collaboration partners. The library's databases will soon catalogue all the country's books, newspapers, periodicals, digital documents, film, video, photographs, maps, broadcasts, audio books, music, sheet music, postcards, posters, small print, and theater material. The library has been completely digitalized for a long time. Best of all, most of the material is freely available to everyone.

How is it that this old but also new institution sees no need to discuss digitalization at seminars and conferences? "We never talk about being digital. It is something we use, and here we are miles ahead of other national libraries. Digital is simply a tool to deliver on our social mission. We are a public information provider for our entire cultural history," says Aslak Sira Myhre.

What allowed the National Library of Norway to achieve this position? What organizational and managerial steps were taken along the way? What societal benefits and user experiences do the National Library provide? And what have been the challenges? These are just some of the questions we seek answers to in this case.

A young institution with a long history

The National Library was a part of the University Library in Oslo until 1999. Its roots stretch all the way back to the Royal Frederick University's beginnings in 1811. The start of the great digital transformation can be traced back to an important decision in the Norwegian parliament in the 1980s. Ever since 1815,

16 This case is primarily based on an interview with Aslak Sira Myhre, the head of the National Library, but also on documentation from the media and from the National Library's website. The case has been written for this book, and the authors would like to thank Aslak Sira Myhre for coming forward and sharing his knowledge so generously.

anyone who published something that was intended to be distributed beyond a purely private circulation was obliged to hand it over to the University Library's collections. In 1989, the Act for the obligation to submit publicly available documents was extended beyond printed media including sound recordings, photographs, films, and digital documents, among others.

As a result of the Rana reform[17], the state decided in 1988 to provide funds for the creation of an extended national library. The department in Mo i Rana was established the following year with around thirty employees. The handover duty was transferred to the depository library in Mo i Rana. At the same time, the National Library added new services and job authorizations. At the time there was great skepticism about transferring such tasks to a small municipality in the north. What competence did this local community have at that time to protect these exacting cultural-historical tasks? In old news clips, one can study reports of the demonstration against the relocation of these national responsibilities.

Over the next ten years, new tasks were added and major organizational changes were executed. Different cultures were brought together under a new institutional superstructure.

In 1999, the National Library was also tasked with assuming the bibliographic functions from the University Library, and the public department at Solli plass in Oslo was opened. Criticism had gradually subsided. The experience of competence sharing and the creation of task functions at several geographical locations turned out to work well.

A new, young institution had been created. This mix of product, cultural and organizational changes in the last decade of the last millennium is probably one of the main reasons for the National Library's position today.

The digital shift

The common opinion seems to be that things move slowly in the public sector. The perception of quantum leaps and innovative change processes is more often linked to private companies with weighty technological expertise. The National Library (NB) has proven that the opposite can just as well be the case.

Aslak Sira Myhre was appointed as the new National Librarian in 2014. He was previously the general manager of Litteraturhuset (the House of Literature) in Oslo from its founding in 2007 until he got the position at the National Library. He was given a monster task in the summer of 2018: "Create a plan to digitalize everything that exists of documents, images and film in Norway. Not just for what is found in the country's libraries, no,

17 Norsk Jernverk (Norwegian Ironworks) was Mo i Rana's cornerstone company from 1946 to 1988. Norsk Jernverk was closed along with Norsk Koksverk (Norwegian Coking Works) in 1988, and 1500 jobs were lost. As compensation, the municipality received 500 million in restructuring funds and the state added 600 jobs in Mo i Rana, including a department of the National Library.

include all museums and private institutions as well. Make sure you do a proper survey beforehand. Based on what you come up with, then we will press the state budget button," said the Minister of Culture in June 2018. A committee was appointed.

Exactly twelve months later, the proposal from the committee was delivered. The process for surveying and planning was thoroughly described in the committee proposal, which Sira Myhre led. Budget funds for 2020 were thus secured. A significant amount – NOK 87.2 million – was set aside that year. In an astonishingly short time, one of the largest digitalization operations ever in Norway had begun.

Millions of documents, images and film clips have already been processed. Valuable rarities that were previously hidden in a safe or were gathering dust on inaccessible bookshelves have now been opened up to the public. Forgotten letters and historical accounts are therefore only a few keystrokes away. Historical treasures have been preserved for eternity.

This may sound too simple. It is, of course. The project itself will continue for decades to come. There are unimaginable amounts of material that have to last forever, housed in a digital cloud-based solution. Digitization is much more than scanning an analog document. There is scanning, too, but the process is immensely extensive and complex. If we look at the *entire* value chain, it is longer than what we find in most industrial companies.

First, an agreement has to be entered into between the National Library and the institution that owns the material. Afterwards, preparatory work related to the objects must be performed. Registration must be done. Packing must be carried out. Transportation must be planned and completed. After the material has been received, it needs to be proper prepared before the actual transformation to electronic format. Next, post-processing must be carried out, before the actual storage takes place. Finally, the analog material is returned or preserved in the National Library's warehouses.

Although impressive journey has been covered, the institution has a never-ending mission. Not only must new works be registered, digitized, and made available – whatever is produced and published online must also be archived. The National Library has shown the way for many others in both the public and private sectors. But how was this formidable challenge solved? How did the institution build innovation capacity? What obstacles were encountered on the way? And which experiences are relevant for other organizations facing a comprehensive digital transformation? Through conversations and review of relevant material, we will try to provide some answers.

Accidental or intentional? Luck or skill?

Behind a success there is always a certain amount of luck or coincidence, but the decision to extend the purpose for the National Library to also include sound, images and digital documents was not a coincidence; it was, rather, a conscious, thoroughly investigated and deliberate decision by the Ministry of Culture. The decision to invest in the northern part of the country, where there were large and vacant areas, available industrial expertise, and a need for new investments was a political choice. "Engineers from the smeltery came and started working at the National Library", said Myhre, "the industrial thinking became part of the development work in the organization".

Nevertheless, it is a managerial triumph to succeed in the integration of very different professional and geographical traditions. Librarians, sound and film engineers, computer programmers and industrial workers would build this national culture and knowledge base together. It would include all the physical materials that were available, but they would be made available digitally as well.

Industrial thinking was also important for the roboticization of the depot. Auto-storage was applied to the book collections in the same way as in wholesale warehouses in other industries. The organization began to think about production lines. Its large stores were well suited as physical and highly efficient storage areas. Now there are three mountain stores.

Giant robots run in and out on rails. The carts are remote-controlled and the process is digitalized. These logistics processes are constantly becoming more efficient and accurate. Contents in boxes that are not already digitized are registered when other contents are ordered from external users.

The job of restoring films and music was/is being done for film and record companies. "Almost all Norwegian music on Spotify which is older than CDs, comes from us." But CDs have also found their way to Mo i Rana. When the national broadcaster NRK got rid of its entire music collection of more than 100 000 CDs following a decision in 2009, there were major protests from NRK employees. They claimed that this would hit music journalism negatively, limit listening opportunities, and remove information about musicians involved in a recording (Klassekampen, March 22, 2014).

Today, the criticism has subsided and the availability is praised. "We are the ones who digitize [Norwegian classics such as] old Åge Aleksandersen songs, we are the ones who ensure that Ole Paus's first records are found on Spotify. They got this from us. We have digitized and restored the reel-to-reel material, the tape, and the master. The record companies have made their own material available. They cover the cost of the upgrade; we keep this forever. The film and record companies, the newspapers, NRK and TV 2 are our partners," said the National Library's librarian.

The strategy from 2005 – the third oldest website in Norway

A strategy sets the direction of an organization. The strategy that the National Library formulated in 2005 has had a great impact on the results in later periods. There were two important theses that particularly shaped the strategy. The first was that in the future most people would *expect* to find the information they were looking for online. The second was that if the library's collection was to be relevant in the future, it had to be found online.

Although these two theses seem simple and logical today, we must not forget that the "web" is a fairly young worldwide digital network. It was in the period right after 1995 that the web first saw an explosive increase in traffic and distribution, but as late as the year 2000, there were no more than 250 million users globally.

Therefore, embarking on a strategy whereby the entire National Library's collection was to be made available online was both a radical and innovative decision. Physical books, video cassettes, vinyl and CDs were still prevalent. Spotify had not been invented, and Netflix as a service was available in Norway first in 2012.

The National Library was the third website in Norway. Those who created it were also developing ISP services in their spare time. The new organization also introduced an entrepreneurial culture in Mo i Rana. "That's why nb.no is not Norges Bank [the Central Bank of Norway], but Nasjonalbiblioteket [the National Library]. If we had continued as a function of the University Library in Oslo, then little or nothing would have happened and we would have been left far behind", said Sira Myhre.

It wasn't just books and newspapers that had to be published online. The purpose was that "everything between heaven and earth should be made digitally available, church membership magazines, advertising, political leaflets and posters, music, film, porn magazines, photographs, maps – yes, all the printed word that could be found from our long literary history", said Myhre. It was a gigantic ambition that led to an industrial organization and operationalization of the work.

It had to be digitized en masse. This was the major change that came as a result of the revised strategy. Selection and demanding priorities were of no use. If the goal was to digitize everything, then production lines had to be built that aimed at maximum volume, not niche-by-niche. Academic communities and cultural preservation organizations are used to working in a hierarchical manner. What is most important? What is the most valuable material? What is the most central? What should we take first? The new strategy broke with these principles.

"We received a lot of criticism because we took Hallbing before Hamsun, *El Gringo* before *Sult*, but this was not about order. It was about quantities. It's about making *everything* available. Only NB and Google thought this way at the time. Today, we're being followed by the national library in Poland," Myhre emphasizes. "It's also part of history that the criticism from academia had largely died down by the time I took over as NB director in 2014. This is because the user-friendliness spoke for itself. Just like today, they could sit and search digitally in their offices, the sources quickly became enormous, and they were available around the clock. Moreover, the Bookshelf agreement had been put in place. It meant that all books published before the year 2000 were made available to all citizens of Norway."

Our service is to be a library – no more, no less

Every organization experiences being asked critical questions. They come from within and they come from the outside. In the case of the National Library, there have been many objections to the processes underway. Why digitize bad books? Is it possible to digitize everything? Is it desirable? Why spend money on this? When it is done at an industrial scale, will it be good enough? Why not process the material and create services on top?

The starting point has been that the digitalization task in itself is enough to take on. Fancy websites and fine exhibitions are relatively easy to produce for just a few works. Even the most skilled museums have more than enough to handle with 500–1000 works. "We have digitized more than 500 000 books, in addition to everything from audio, film and photos. We are a library, others can build services on the top," Myhre stated. This also shows that the National Library makes available a basic infrastructure that other players can utilize to create their own services.

Along the way, traditional library thinking and academic thinking have worked side-by-side with technical and industrial expertise. There is little doubt that there have occasionally been different views and contradictions, but the different capacities have created an enormous base of digital cultural history. Institutions on the outside, such as archives, museums, and others, have at times viewed developments in the National Library with envy. Nevertheless, the institutions faced the same type of requirements in the budget letters. Streamlining and digitization offer opportunities, but they also bring about changes in work tasks.

There has been a clear line from the National Library's leaders, Roger Jøsevold, Vigdis Moe Skarstein, and Aslak Sira Myhre that budget cuts should not come from the outside. "If it needs to be cut, we will cut it ourselves." It is advantageous to be at the forefront, so that the feeling of success is not taken away by outsiders. If you ask what you no longer need to do in five, ten or fifteen years, then you can turn the resources in the direction that best serves the purpose. "When we hire, it must be done strategically. We constantly ask ourselves what we'll be doing in the future. That's where the focus should be."

It is only human to defend one's job and thereby one's own work duties. Myhre talks a lot about changes with his employees. About the cuts they are going to make. About the algorithms that make certain functions, but not people, redundant. "You will work for the same purpose, but your tasks will be different and more high end." While other managers talk a lot about up-skilling and re-skilling, the National Librarian prefers to talk about the roles that will still be there even if the tasks change. "Our job is not to store things in the mountains, physically or digitally. Our job is that people out there use what we have stored, and make it known."

Traditionally, the library has been a service provider, a respondent, who preferably answers the questions that land on its desk. Myhre wants to make the library a public informant, a kind of "first mover" for cultural history, cultural heritage, and history as such. It is this mindset Myhre wants his employees to convey. The tasks change, but the role is the same. During the last decade, the union's resistance to making work more efficient has also changed significantly. Myhre feels that there has been a greater degree of job security and development opportunities in the organization, and consequently, employees are also more willing to change.

On a purely practical level, this means that history can be mirrored and experienced anew without hours of searching and endless hunting for source material: it ought to be easy to find. Immediately. By future generations and by those who shared the experiences there and then.

The long lines in strategy and management philosophy

There is no doubt that the digitalization journey has given the employees pride in what they have accomplished. In the administrative part of the public sector, it is rare that restructuring leads to extensive downsizing. At the same time, we have seen that more radical change with significant downsizing has taken place in wholly or partly state-owned companies such as Posten and Telenor.

The National Library has had forward-looking managers who have developed strategies that have proven to be robust over time. These strategies have instilled confidence in users, employees, and owners alike. An ever-increasing number of users have become more and more satisfied with its services. The responsible politicians have seen that the ambitions in the budget letters have not only been met, they have been exceeded. At the same time, internal resistance among the employees has decreased over time. Digitalization has threatened neither the number of jobs nor their professional quality. On the contrary, the scale of production and the *diversity of competences* have generated new and exciting tasks. The institution has also gained several new partners who support various projects financially.

Although the location of a branch of the National Library in Mo i Rana has subsequently been a blessing, it was not a given that it would turn out this way. The fact that the National Library today stands out as one of the world's most modern libraries is due to its leaders who had the ability to *seize the opportunities* and saw that the expertise in Mo i Rana could be transformed into something very valuable for the future National Library. It would have been far more difficult to bring about this conversion if a department of the library had not been established at this time.

The ability to listen to professionals, but at the same time turn a deaf ear when needed, is also something that has characterized the leadership of the National Library. Academics are not known for being the most forward-thinking and progressive types, and the National Library's leaders had the ability to stand firm on new principles that have promoted digitalization when this was necessary. Production orientation and all material being treated equally are not exactly catchwords for academics and librarians, but absolutely essential to bring about large-scale digitalization.

The interview with Myhre also illustrates that the leadership of the National Library has been and is concerned with continuous development and does not rest on its laurels. The *innovation capacity* that the *institution has built up must not be lost* but must be kept alive by constantly developing the organization and the social mission, and not waiting for the grants to go to waste. Last but not least, the management of the National Library has been conscious of *interacting with actors outside* the National Library who can enrich the mission, whether they are Spotify or other private or public actors.

Part 5

Final reflections

In this final part, we will tie together the previous chapters, compare and contrast the different organizational solutions, and discuss how they can be used in combination. Instead of drawing any solid conclusions about which solution is most effective, we will discuss some important questions managers need to consider if they aim to build innovation capacity.

The first question concerns *identifying the problem* the firm has with innovation. We point to specific problems each solution addresses and provide an overview of how each solution builds innovation capacity. In the previous chapters we have shown how some of the solutions primarily strengthen the ability to *sense* new opportunities, while others help to *seize* new opportunities more quickly. Some organizational solutions enable an established firms to quickly develop *complementary capabilities* while others primarily contribute by creating *collective engagement* among employees, fostering motivation and confidence in the organization. An overview of key points including similarities and differences is provided in table 5.1.

A second question concerns *the firm's legacy and to what extent the legacy hampers innovation*. Moving in a new direction also implies leaving something behind. For technology-driven innovation, IT systems can constitute baggage (or legacy) that the business needs to get rid of in order to be able to renew itself. Legacy can also be in the form of having developed a culture, identity, or skill set that restrains innovation and renewal.

A third question managers aiming to build innovation capacity must consider concerns how to handle *dependencies within and between organizations*. Drawing on the cogwheel model we introduced in Chapter 2, managers should reflect on whether there is a need to tighten the cogwheels to ensure that they pull in the same direction, or whether it might make sense to loosen the cogwheels by introducing changes in some cogs to create room for innovation? There can also be important dependencies between organizations, making it challenging to develop an innovation muscle alone. If there are major dependencies, then different types of collaboration and partnerships should be considered. They should be aware though that too strong interdependencies across firms can become dysfunctional.

A fourth question concerns the possibility of mobilizing several organizational solutions at the same time and *evaluating the timing and sequence* of these. While researchers often deal with single solutions, our cases show that most established firms adopt several different organizational solutions. What starts as an ambidextrous solution can shift into another solution, for example by the innovative unit being spun off into a separate company with different ownership. An important detail is therefore the time dimension and the question of which organizational solution will work best at a given timepoint and acknowledging that this can evolve over time. Assuming that early success creates confidence and positive experiences, it may be wise to carefully consider where one should begin.

Finally, we reflect on the role of serendipity and luck. We ask if big is always beautiful, or if the innovation muscle can become too bulky.

What is the innovation problem, and what kind of capacity is needed?

The different solutions we have presented address different innovation problems. In this section, we identify the specific problem each solution addresses and summarize how capacity is developed. We draw on the three dimensions of innovation capacity that we introduced in Chapter 1:

1. Dynamic capabilities (sensing, seizing, transforming)
2. Complementary capabilities
3. Collective engagement

If the innovation problem involves a lack of space for renewal, the *ambidextrous solution* will be suitable. The classic situation is that the established firm dominates and stifles any attempt at innovation outside its own areas. The ambidextrous solution builds capacity by enabling new opportunities to be seized. Because a separate unit is established with a specific mandate to innovate, complementary capabilities will also be acquired or developed. We have shown examples of how ambidexterity can become a renewal engine and used again and again – which implies that dynamic capabilities and the ability to transform the entire firm can be developed.

Innovation at the edge also addresses the problem of limited room for renewal. In addition, this solution embraces challenges linked to a lack of understanding of the need for change. Because it so clearly involves external actors, the solution will strengthen the abilities to both sense and seize new opportunities. It can also create collective engagement among employees, partly because it does not threaten the established unit, but also because motivated employees with different capabilities can be recruited to the edge.

Revolutionary transformation addresses the problem of need or desire for rapid radical change. This means that all cogs are reassessed and transformed. The solution develops capacity along three dimensions, helping to quickly seize new opportunities, rapidly scale complementary capabilities, and if successful, build dynamic capabilities to also transform the organization in the future.

The agile organization will also be effective if the problem with innovation has to do with a lack of speed and tempo, but this solution is typically linked to a concrete product or service. We have not seen evidence of radical change à la Ørsted using the agile solution. The interdisciplinary teams will be able to solve tasks quickly, but this requires well defined tasks and autonomous teams. Through the agile organization, the capacity for innovation will be built along three dimensions. First, the ability to seize opportunities will be strengthened by increasing the pace. Second, it can create collective engagement among employees. Third, agile organization can strengthen the ability to sense new opportunities if the entire organization is mobilized. In particular, employees who are closest to the customers and the market are essential as they can pick up other signals than managers further up in the hierarchy.

Collaboration with start-ups can be effective when the innovation problem is lack of knowledge about how the environment is changing. Such collaboration enables the established unit to sense what is happening in the surroundings. Given the size difference of the partners, start-up collaborations often have relatively little influence over the capabilities in the established firm. However, some established firms seek collaboration with start-up companies in order to change the culture and work processes to become more entrepreneurial and thus increase collective engagement for innovation. This requires significant support from the top of the established firm.

Partnerships among established firms will often be more demanding than collaboration with start-up companies and also involve a larger part of the business. Partnerships can be effective if the innovation problem concerns lack of ability, resources, or competence to propel innovation on your own. It can also be a mechanism for spreading innovation risk. In order for partnerships to be successful, a significant investment of resources is required from the established firm. If there are several partnerships, there may be a need to create a systematic approach with an infrastructure that enables the established firm to seize new opportunities. Collaborating with external parties on innovative solutions can trigger collective engagement among employees involved in the collaboration, but if this is to spread to a larger part of the organization, it requires systematic mobilization work beyond those directly involved in the partnership.

Innovating through an *ecosystem* requires a willingness to open up the organization and its value chains, for example by letting other suppliers into the platform or selling products and services through other firms' platforms. Similar to partnerships, the ecosystem approach can be effective if there is a lack of capacity, expertise and resources to innovate alone, or if new business models emerge that require collaboration between several actors. Becoming part of an ecosystem means that being more open to stimuli from the other actors in the ecosystem and seizing opportunities by specializing or creating value together with others. Most often, this solution will require transforming the established firm and orchestrating resources in new ways.

If the challenge with innovation involves a lack of attention and lack of resources and space to grow, it might make sense to *spin out* or establish anew. External environments sometimes provide better growth opportunities for the innovation. While it can liberate and benefit the innovation, it does not automatically build innovation capacity in the established firm. For this to happen, there must be structures and incentives in place in the established firm that continue to stimulate intrapreneurship. It is also important to mitigate potential loss of skillful people and expertise. This was a challenge when Vipps was spun out. By maintaining close relationships between the established firm and the spin-out, both may strengthen their innovation capacity, as we have seen in the TV 2 examples.

Table 5.1 is an overview of the various organizational solutions, the innovation problem each addresses and how capacity is developed. It also summarizes the organizational measures that are needed in the form of the cogwheel model, and which conditions must be in place for the solution to work effectively.

Table D5.1 Overview of organizational solutions that contribute to innovation capacity

Organizational Solution	Innovation problem the solution addresses and how the solution contributes to capacity	The solution involves organizational measures (the cogwheel model)	Conditions for the solution to work
Ambidextrous organization	Addresses lack of resources and space for renewal. The established company dominates, and stifles attempts at innovation. Contributes to innovation capacity by: • Strengthening the ability to seize new opportunities and building up new, potentially competitive, propositions based on completely different business models. • Creating opportunities to recruit distinctly different skills which, in the longer term, are scaled and become ordinary capabilities. • Potentially developing into a renewal engine that is used again and again.	Structure: Establish separate entity within the established firm. Culture: New entity develops distinct, innovative culture. Competence: Specialization. Established units focus on improving existing deliveries, while new unit recruits other expertise Work processes: New unit often adopts distinct work processes. Governance and management: New unit has an entrepreneur-based management style, while established units have a more traditional management style. Senior management must be able to handle tensions. Incentives and KPIs: Linked in the new unit to innovation, growth, and progress rather than profit.	Can function if there is both great uncertainty about the future and there is a clear vision/mandate. Requires senior management to protect and secure resources for the new entity. Requires senior management to handle tensions in the organization in an effective way.
Innovation at the edge	Addresses lack of understanding of the need for change and lack of room for renewal. Contributes to innovation capacity by: • Strengthening the ability to sense and seize new opportunities. • Potentially creating collective engagement since it does not threaten the established entity, but instead strengthens the established firm and is based on an emerging desire in the established firm to move towards the edge zone.	Structure: Establish activity at the edge of the firm (rather than at the core) – preferably geographically separated, but not necessarily. External relationships: Edge largely orients itself outwards and builds relationships. Culture: Edge develops a distinct culture, amongst others, by having external relations. Governance and management: Edge has large degree of freedom in governance and management. Incentives & KPIs: Linked to new thinking, growth in new areas rather than profit.	Functions particularly well when there is substantial uncertainty about the future. Requires senior management to protect and secure resources for the edge zone, but resources are of a limited scope. Does not involve direct competition with the core.

Organizational Solution	Innovation problem the solution addresses and how the solution contributes to capacity	The solution involves organizational measures (the cogwheel model)	Conditions for the solution to work
Radical transformation of the core	Addresses need or desire for rapid radical change. Contributes to innovation capacity by: • Being quick to seize future opportunities. • Potentially helping build skills related to transformation that can also be valuable in future changes. • Rapid scaling of complementary capabilities.	All cogs are reassessed and changed drastically, expertise in particular.	Requires success in creating a new income stream quickly.
Agile work processes and agile organizations	Addresses lack of speed/pace Contributes to innovation capacity by: • Strengthening the ability to seize new opportunities more quickly • Creating collective engagement among employees • Potentially also strengthening the ability to sense new opportunities by mobilizing the teams for this.	Structure: Interdisciplinary teams, possibly the entire business is organized in teams. Alternatively in hybrid forms. Work processes: Empower the teams, tight deadlines, trial and error. Competence: General competence and understanding of the whole (in the team's task and the company's task) instead of specialization. Leadership and management: Management must relinquish control and management to the teams and instead act as a facilitator that removes obstacles so that the teams can solve the tasks. Incentives and KPIs: Autonomous teams are measured on the delivery of clearly defined tasks within tight deadlines.	Requires a clear vision/mandate of the job to be done. Handles uncertainty about how the job should be done. The team must have the freedom to solve this as they think is best.

Organizational Solution	Innovation problem the solution addresses and how the solution contributes to capacity	The solution involves organizational measures (the cogwheel model)	Conditions for the solution to work
Collaborating with start-ups	Addresses a lack of good ideas and insight into what is possible. Contributes to innovation capacity by: • Strengthening the ability to sense future opportunities. • Potentially pairing its complementary capabilities necessary for scaling innovations in start-ups. • Potentially helping build collective engagement.	External relations: Strengthened. Ownership: Investments in start-ups. Competence and work processes: Build up internal competence and processes (and possibly structures) that contribute to the development of good collaboration with start-up companies.	Requires the ability to handle collaboration with a small firm that is typically less mature and more impatient. Requires the ability to handle the back-end problem and mobilize expertise in one's own organization. It may be easier to collaborate with start-up environments consisting of many start-up companies.
Partnership	Addresses lack of resources and expertise, desire to spread risk. Contributes to innovation capacity by: • Strengthening the ability to seize new opportunities. • Potentially strengthening the ability to sense future opportunities. • Potentially helping to ensure access to complementary capabilities necessary for future operations/core business.	Structure and ownership: Collaboration involving two or several organizations, which can go across sectors, and which often involve ownership. External relations: Strengthened. Competence and work processes: Build up internal competence and processes (and possibly structures) that contribute to good collaboration with different types of partners in different forms of partnerships. Governance and management: Partnerships require other forms of governance than hierarchical control. Culture: Openness to the outside world and willingness to share. Incentives: Create incentives that encourage the partners to invest and use their best resources in the collaboration.	Requires management of proprietary rights. Requires ability to build trust and deal with "frenemies".

Organizational Solution	Innovation problem the solution addresses and how the solution contributes to capacity	The solution involves organizational measures (the Cogwheel model)	Conditions for the solution to work
Ecosystems	Addresses lack of opportunity (capacity, competence, resources) to deliver alone. Value creation and scaling require collaboration or co-existence with many other players. Contributes to innovation capacity by: • Strengthening the ability to seize new opportunities. • Contributing to ensuring access to resources, expertise and ordinary capabilities that are necessary for effective delivery.	External relationships: Strengthens and creates dependencies. Competence and work processes: Build up internal competence and processes (and possibly structures) that contribute to the development of collaboration and co-existence with other actors where the purpose is to create value together. Ecosystems provide opportunities for established firms to specialize. Governance and management: The central actor, for example a platform owner, has a role as orchestrator for the other actors in the system. Culture: Openness to the outside world. Incentives: Will be different for different roles.	The orchestrator must develop the ecosystem in a way that makes the system grow and create and capture network effects. The producers and the complementary actors must cultivate their uniqueness. Bottlenecks need to be resolved for the ecosystem to prosper and grow.
Spinning out and establishing new	Addresses limited ability to commercialize good ideas and scale these in-house and/or the lack of understanding of the need for renewal. Contributes to innovation capacity by: • Strengthening the ability to seize new opportunities. • Strengthening the ability to sense new opportunities. • Ensuring access to other resources and expertise, including from new owners and customer segments among others. • Potentially creating collective engagement among employees in spin-out/new establishment. Can also trigger renewal in the established entity.	Ownership: Separated out by spin-out, invite others into the ownership side. Establish anew, for instance by relocating the firm.	Requires an efficient and effective separation process, especially new establishment will create tensions. In the case of a spin-out, it is required that not only is financial value created through ownership, but that it also contributes to renewal/innovation in established company. With a new establishment, sufficient distance is required, and competition can be allowed.

What about legacy?

When an established firm renews itself, the capabilities we have discussed above (dynamic, complementary and collective engagement) will be important, but renewal as a rule also means leaving something behind. According to Schumpeter, innovation means that something must be destroyed; innovation occurs through creative destruction. For established firms, leaving behind something that has previously been important and valuable can create resistance. As mentioned initially, the established firm, for better or for worse, brings with it a lot of history and legacy; it has likely developed both structural and cultural inertia. So how can an established firm deal with legacy that can hinder renewal?

The organizational solutions for innovation deal with this in different ways. In the ambidextrous solution, the new is built beside the old, so that there is no talk of destruction. The new unit grows next to the old and can potentially take over after a certain time, but that is not a given. Coexistence can effectively function over a long period of time. Innovation on the edge does not imply any immediate destruction either. Here as well, the new is built next to (in the peripheral zone of) the established firm, and if it gains the right to exist, it will help to pull the core and the established in that direction. These types of renewal processes evolve gradually and allow for development take its course. The radical transformation we described in Ørsted, on the other hand, was a significantly faster process where the organization left behind or rid itself of previous expertise, technology, and strategy by developing a completely new set of cogs.

Partnerships, spin-outs, and new establishments on the outside of the firm does not immediately involve leaving something behind. It can facilitate developing something new, based on new technical solutions where customers can be gradually migrated to the new platform. This was one of the solutions DNB explored when they established a joint venture with the British fintech company 11:FS. The idea was to establish a new and more modern technological platform, but this partnership was ultimately deemed too risky for DNB to proceed.

In the research on organizational changes, there is broad support that established culture and identity must be shaped and developed over time. Although one might wish that this could be changed quickly, it often works best to build on the existing culture and identity (Reger et al., 1994; Stensaker et al., 2015). This requires a good understanding of values, norms, and identity carriers so that these are acknowledged, while they are also challenged and further developed. Some of the solutions we have described accomplish this by building up alternative cultures and identities in delineated units or outside of the established firm, to serve as inspiration which can be followed-up for the entire established business.

If legacy concerns technology or IT systems, such a gradual adjustment can be more difficult because the systems are linked to the work processes in such a way that a small change could have major consequences. Complex legacy systems can thus become a real obstacle to renewal. Attempts to tackle the problem at its root and replace the entire IT platform and associated work processes are perceived as both risky and expensive. In our studies, we have seen that established firms often work with several alternative solutions to handle their technological legacy. It could be that they are trying to work around it by avoiding the problem. This happens, for example, when they establish APIs for the organization, but still have to have intermediate levels to communicate with the core systems. The companies can also try to reduce the technological legacy by removing the least critical pieces – almost like a game of Mikado. And they can try to take a piecemeal approach and replace piece by piece. The point here is that there are no simple solutions – and given that IT systems are closely linked to work processes, they will also often involve major organizational changes (Gooderham et al., 2021).

Tightening or loosening the cogwheel?

In Chapter 2, we introduced the cogwheel model as an overall framework for how established firms can develop innovation capacity. We described how one can "turn" the cogs to implement a new strategy, which aims to renew. We also described how the different elements are connected and can drive each other and how traditional organizational and change theory has been concerned that the cogs must be consistent. This implies a need to consider the whole "system" and how it is connected. To ensure efficient organization and implementation of strategy, the cogs should support the strategy. The traditional thinking within strategy and implementation is that the organization (and the cogwheel) should be tightly connected so that all cogwheels pull in the same direction.

But how does the cogwheel model function if the goal is innovation and renewal? Some of the organizational solutions we have presented follow the traditional strategy implementation perspective aiming to ensure good consistency and power to achieve the goal of innovation through creating close links. This applies, for example, to agile organization and spin-outs. But most of the solutions we have presented really are about the opposite – namely, dissolving a tightly interconnected organization and introducing something new. In established firms, the cogwheels can be tightly connected and fully coherent, but rather than connecting the cogs even more tightly together, there may be a need to loosen up a little and to introduce alternatives, for instance by introducing a new set of cogs, as the ambidextrous solution and innovation at the edge suggest, or by connecting external actors through the partnership solution or an ecosystem approach. Organizational solutions involving external partners bring in an extra layer of dependency and complexity, while the internal solutions can create tensions – but it is exactly these tensions and new challenges that also create opportunities. Allowing the cogs to move in slightly different directions (i.e. purposefully introduce inconsistencies) can also trigger new opportunities. Successfully doing so requires leaders who can handle paradoxes.

Dependencies in and across organizations

The strategy field is based on an underlying premise that organizations must adapt to their external environment in order to have legitimacy and survive. Of course, they can also proactively try to influence the environment, but the point is that if there is not a good match between the environment and the organization, the business will not survive. Correspondingly, there is an underlying assumption that the internal elements of the organization support the strategy and contributes to achieving the strategic goals. In other words, there are both external and internal dependencies.

The various solutions we have presented are based to varying degrees on such dependencies. While some of the solutions seek to ensure innovation within the organization's boundaries (agile, ambidextrous, radical transformation) thus foremost addressing internal dependencies, other solutions (collaboration with start-up companies, partnerships, ecosystems, and spin-offs) create dependencies to the external environment. Internal dependencies are easier for management to control and coordinate but can be limiting in terms of new input and inspiration. Solutions based on external dependencies are more difficult to control and will typically require more coordination, but on the other hand, these can be an important source of new input and inspiration. These solutions tend to emerge because the established firm lacks the means to renew itself. It needs impulses or resources from other actors around it.

Although we have divided the solutions into two broad categories, within or across the organization's boundaries, this division is not always crystal clear. Innovation at the edge, for example, is positioned within the established firm boundaries but has strong external dependencies and will not be able to survive without resources, support, and input from external players.

Many of the organizational solutions involve a trade-off between autonomy and integration. On the one hand, ensuring renewal requires a certain distance and autonomy; on the other, a certain degree of integration and interaction is necessary. A pattern we observe across solutions within the organization's boundaries is that the established firm must ensure that the innovative milieus have a large degree of autonomy at an early phase. This is because people can become locked into existing ways of thinking and it can be difficult to come up with ground-breaking ideas in the established firm. Autonomy in an initial phase will contribute to this. But as the innovation gains momentum, an increasing degree of integration and collaboration will often be required. It is therefore important that those involved in innovation and renewal are aware that while they can be rebels initially, in the long-term they must build their legitimacy towards the larger system.

The organizational solutions that cut across organizational boundaries will also experience trade-offs between autonomy and integration. Large established firms can come to dominate and sometimes swallow up small start-ups, and then some of the values that lay in the collaboration might disappear. On the other hand, too little integration can hinder the benefits of collaboration from spreading to the rest of the organization. Integrating and coordinating too much can also delay development and growth in the ecosystems, in which case it may be better to let go of the integration synergies and allow for competition.

Temporal aspects – the innovation journey

An important point that we have returned to several times throughout the book is the time dimension and the "journey" that many of the established firms describe. In Chapter 1 we referred to different types of innovations, portfolio thinking and options thinking, which implies that established firms can work along several parallel tracks at the same time. Here, we take a closer look at the trajectory and explore where it may be natural to start for the established company that wants to build its innovation muscle. Because established firms work along several tracks, it can be difficult to measure the effects of a specific solution in a precise and reliable way, but as we described at the beginning, our perspective is that continuous training of the innovation muscle will increase the *likelihood* that the established firm is ready for and can succeed in renewal.

Our introductory case about DNB illustrates the possibility of many parallel tracks. At the same time that Vipps was developed through the ambidextrous solution, DNB opened up more to the outside world and initiated collaborations with start-up companies. The ambidextrous solution coupled with agile working methods helped Vipps to develop quickly. After the mobile payment service was on the market, the innovation problem shifted to how to grow and expand, and the need for external partnerships with competitors and complementors emerged. This shows how a given organizational solution can contribute along some dimensions of the innovation muscle, but it will also be accompanied by a new set of challenges, meaning that the problem of innovation shifts. Building the innovation muscle therefore requires the ability to assess and adjust organizational solutions as needed.

In this sense, there is no single recipe for the correct sequence – it will always depend on the problem to be solved and the organizational context and situation. Nevertheless, change theory contains a clear recommendation: Start where results can be achieved. Some refer to this as picking the low-hanging fruit first: the probability of success will be greater when beginning with something relatively simple. Success increases confidence and collective engagement, fostering further innovation. In addition, skeptical employees will have had the opportunity to see that innovation can work. By starting with organizational solutions that seem simple and address the current innovation problem, the established firm can thus also build the third innovation capacity component – collective engagement.

It can be useful to maintain a perspective on innovation and change as a journey rather than a race or a portfolio of different initiatives, especially if the journey is expected to continue and is not just a matter of getting from A to B. A portfolio perspective on innovation illustrates the various types of innovation an established firm can pursue, but includes no time dimension. The perspective of innovation as a race the established firm must win is all about getting to the finish line first. A journey, on the other hand, can take place at a varying pace and contain different stops – some may be more exciting than others. With each new stage of the journey, useful knowledge is accumulated that can be employed in the future. In the same way, experiences and learning points from an attempt at renewal will form input for the next initiative. On a journey, the landscape outside will change, and one is likely to study this and adapt rather than rushing to the finish line ahead of the competition.

However, it is one thing to build innovation capacity in a group of enthusiastic and competent employees who are eagerly searching for new and innovative solutions that can renew the business; maintaining that capacity over time is something else entirely. Pisano (2019) has said that this is often where established firms fail. At the start of an innovation journey, it is easier to create engagement. If results take a long time (as they often do) and some innovations flop, patience and engagement begin to wane. If operational staff become impatient, the CFO demands results, and the owners express concern, the scope for building innovation capacity can quickly shrink.

Senior managers aiming to build innovation capacity must therefore secure support and legitimacy and point to any previous successes on which these can be built. There is little doubt that the success of developing Vipps was important in getting DNB's employees on board for the innovation journey. Likewise, DNB's New Tech Lab is keenly aware that they must also support operational work to maintain the good will to drive innovative projects. Long-term innovation capacity development thus demands a good relationship with extensive dialogue between senior management, the board, and the owners.

The role of chance and serendipity

In the introductory chapter we argued that the aim of building innovation capacity was to increase the probability of winning, while there is no guarantee. A bit of luck along the way is often necessary to succeed. Vipps wanted to beat Denmark's MobilePay in the Norwegian market and spent five months developing its new payment solution. But this could have gone wrong. The mobile payment solution could have faltered along the way and MobilePay could have been launched earlier, with the result that Vipps would have been launched as number two in the market. This would have substantial consequences due to the network effects and first-mover advantage in this market. No doubt there was some chance and luck involved.

Ørsted had plans to transform the company from black to green in thirty years, but it only took ten. The fall in gas prices and poorer credit ratings forced the company to sell off assets at a rapid rate. In this sense, one could say that there was a dose of luck (or coincidence) involved. But the fact that the company chose to go in a clearly green direction with higher risk cannot be said to be luck or coincidence.

Coincidence also came into play when the National Library's new digital department was established in Mo i Rana. The goal was to establish new jobs after the cornerstone companies Norsk Jernverk and Norsk Koksverk were closed down. The result of the decision to locate parts of the National Library here, however, was the start of one of the world's most modern digital library collections.

Scientists often seek simple explanations for what happens. This can lead to an underestimation of the role that chance and luck have on companies' success or loss. The airline Norwegian could have been one of the airline industry´s most environmentally friendly and innovative companies in 2022. Although its founders' willingness to take risks made the company vulnerable, few would have predicted all the events that caused Norwegian to almost disappear from the market. In this case, there was a good dose of bad luck. It started with technical problems with the Dreamliner airplanes that it had bought, then two Boeing 737s crashed, and investigations revealed that Boeing had cheated to try to win the competitive race against Airbus. The result was that of all the Boeing 737s that Norwegian had (which were many) were grounded. And as if that wasn't enough, the Covid-19 pandemic came and put a stop to almost all air traffic. Despite this, Norwegian recovered, and one year after the pandemic restrictions were lifted, the firm is making a profit and scoring among top 25 Norwegian firms on technological innovation.

Despite luck and chance, building innovation capacity will only increase the probability of succeeding in launching a new product or service or new method. As such, it is appropriate to repeat the athlete Kjetil André Aamodt's statement that "the more I train, the luckier I get."

Innovation overload?

Throughout this book, we have talked about building innovation capacity and given examples of various organizational solutions that foster innovation capacity. At the same time, there is little doubt that carrying out innovation work – especially at the radical end – is risky, and it is far from certain that it will generate any new income streams. If the operative business is starved too much, the inability to create sufficient income streams to cope with the transition can cause problems. It is also easy to underestimate how long it takes to close down a business, even when everyone is aware that it is heading off into the sunset. Telenor's copper network, which was described as obsolete in 1990, was only discontinued in 2021, and many older people miss their fixed phoneline. Preparations for dismantling the FM network in Norway were made for many years (and it was doomed), but it was only switched off in 2017, and even then niche radio stations in the big cities can still transmit over FM until 2027. In 2014, DNB's management was certain that large parts of its income were in danger of being lost as a result of new fintech and big tech players, but these changes appear to have happened slower than expected, although in some countries – Ireland is one example – the prophecies have come true. As of 2021, Revolut, one of the challengers to the traditional Irish banks, had 1.3 million customers.

It is also easy to become overenthusiastic and overexcited about dynamic capabilities. A one-sided focus on recruiting people with the ability to sense and seize can be completely wrong. Innovation takes time, and today's business often also demands attention and resources too. Building innovation capacity implies that dynamic capabilities are needed – not instead of, but in addition to, the ordinary capabilities associated with current operations. If a firm only targets dynamic capabilities, it can end up being vague and "hyperactive" – a firm that pursues every new trend, but never manages to deliver properly on anything.

Concluding remarks

Building and maintaining innovation capacity in an established firm is a long-term, systematic endeavor that has no end date. For some firms, getting started on building innovation capacity will be the challenge. In this book we have outlined many different organizational solutions for how to speed up innovation. For some firms, separating the innovative work from the daily operations and allow innovation to gradually emerge. For other firms, it will be easier to create enthusiasm early on by mobilizing more broadly, but this can backfire later if the breakthroughs are slow to come. Managers then need to cope with uncertainty, dare to make decisions, and carefully manage tensions between different parts of the organization.

Innovation involves uncertainty, trial and error, and an ability to learn from mistakes and adjust the course along the way. Innovation is thus fundamentally different from efficient operations. It is of little use to have detailed five-year plans; the only certainty is that it will never turn out as planned. An overarching vision or goal allowing for flexibility will be more appropriate if the context is highly uncertain.

We have argued that there are many paths to the goal and shown that established firms can adopt a variety of organizational solutions for innovation. This requires an understanding of the different cogs that make up an organization, and the connections between these. It may be futile to just turn on one cog – competence, for example – if the incentives still lag behind the detailed measurement of results. Then the collective engagement for innovation can easily crumble. In all the different organizational solutions, we have therefore outlined which cogs are most relevant.

Unfortunately, systematic attempts at building innovation capacity provide no guarantee for the successful launch of new products and services, but a stronger innovation muscle will increase the probability for innovation success – and not just once, but again and again.

References

Abrahamson, E. (1991). Managerial fads and fashions: The diffusion and rejection of innovations. *Academy of Management Review, 16*(3), 586–612.

Ackerman, F., & Eden, C. (2011). Strategic management of stakeholders: Theory and practice. *Long Range Planning, 44,* 170–196.

Adner, R. (2006). Match your innovation strategy to your innovation ecosystem. *Harvard Business Review, 84*(4), 98.

Agarwal, R., Echambadi, R., Franco, A.M., & Sarkar, M.B. (2004). Knowledge transfer through inheritance: Spin-out generation, development, and survival. *Academy of Management Journal, 47*(4), 501–522.

Aghina, W., De Smet, A., Lackey, G., Lurie, M., & Murarka, M. (2018). The five trademarks of agile organizations. *McKinsey & Company Report.* Retrieved from https://www.mckinsey.com/business-functions/people-and-organizational-performance/our-insights/the-five-trademarks-of-agile-organizations

Altman, E.J., Nagle, F., & Tushman, M.L. (2020). The translucent hand of managed ecosystems: Engaging communities for value creation and capture. *Academy of Management Annals, 16*(01). Retrieved from https://www.hbs.edu/faculty/Pages/item.aspx?num=60253

Anand, N., & Daft, R.L. (2007). What is the right organization design? *SSRN Electronic Journal.* Anand, N. and Daft, Richard L., What is the Right Organization Design? (December 7, 2006). DOI: http://dx.doi.org/10.2139/ssrn.961013

Annosi, M.C., Foss, N., & Martini, A. (2020). When agile harms learning and innovation: (And what can be done about it). *California Management Review, 63*(1), 61–80.

Baldwin, C.Y. (2012). Organization design for business ecosystems. *Journal of Organization Design, 1*(1).

Bang, H. (2013). Organisasjonskultur: En begrepsavklaring. *Tidsskrift for Norsk psykologforening, 50*(4), 326–336.

Barney, J.B. (2020). Measuring firm performance in a way that is consistent with strategic management theory. *Academy of Management Discoveries, 6*(1), 5–7.

Beck, K., Beedle, M., Van Bennekum, A., Cockburn, A., Cunningham, W., Fowler, M., Martin, R.C., Mellor, S., Thomas, D., Grenning, J., Highsmith, J., Hunt, A., Jeffries, R., Kern, J., Marick, B., Schwaber, K., & Sutherland, J. (2001). *The agile manifesto.*

Bercovitz, J., & Chesbrough, H. (2020). Hopping tables – An introduction to the SMR special issue on open innovation. *Strategic Management Review, 1,* 207–222.

Bergerskogen, V.A.R. (2021). *Organizational legitimacy in innovation units with radical mandates. An exploratory case study unpacking the role of New Tech Lab in the DNB organization.* Master's thesis in Strategy and Management, Norwegian School of Economics.

Birkinshaw, J., Foss, N.J., & Lindenberg, S. (2014). Combining purpose with profits. *MIT Sloan Management Review, 55*(3), 49.

Block, Z., & MacMillan, I. (1993). *Corporate venturing: Creating new businesses within the firm.* Harvard Business School Press.

Bogers, M., Chesbrough, H., & Moedas, C. (2018). Open innovation: Research, practices, and policies. *California Management Review, 60*(2), 5–16.

Bogers, M., Chesbrough, H., Heaton, S., & Teece, D.J. (2019). Strategic management of open innovation: A dynamic capabilities perspective. *California Management Review, 62*(1), 77–94.

Bower, J.L., & Corsi, E. (2012). *DONG Energy: Clean and Reliable Energy. Harvard Business School Case 312–108.* Harvard Business School, January 2012. Retrieved from https://www.hbs.edu/faculty/Pages/item.aspx?num=41445

Brandenburger, A.M., & Nalebuff, B.J. (1996). *Co-opetition.* Currency.

Brandenburger, A.M., Nalebuff, B.J., & Gearon, T. (2021). The rules of co-opetition. *Harvard Business Review, 99,* 48–57.

Brynjolfsson, E., & McAfee, A. (2014). *The second machine age: Work, progress, and prosperity in a time of brilliant technologies.* WW Norton & Company.

Buche, S., & Cantale, I. (2018, 22 January). *How Tencent became the world's most valuable social network firm with barely any advertising. The conversation in Smart Company.* Obtained from https://www.smartcompany.com.au/marketing/social-media/tencent-worlds-most-valuable-social-network-firm

Burgelman, R.A. (1983a). Corporate entrepreneurship and strategic management: Insights from a process study. *Management Science, 29*(12), 1349–1364.

Burgelman, R.A. (1983b). A process model of internal corporate venturing in the diversified major firm. *Administrative Science Quarterly, 28,* 223–244.

Bushe, G.R., & Marshak, R.J. (2009). Revisioning organization development: Diagnostic and dialogic premises and patterns of practice. *The Journal of Applied Behavioral Science, 45*(3), 348–368.

Cagan, M. (2017). *Inspired: How to create tech products customers love.* John Wiley & Sons.

Capgemini Invent (2019). *Design thinking is dead. Long live design thinking.* Idean Publishing.

Ceccagnoli, M., Forman, C., Huang, P., & Wu, D.J. (2012). Cocreation of value in a platform ecosystem! The case of enterprise software. *MIS quarterly, 36*(1), 263–290.

Chang, T., Lang, N., Modi, S., Tang, T., & Szczepanski, K. von (2020, 22 July). How Chinese digital ecosystems battled Covid-19. *BCG-report.* Retrieved from https://www.bcg.com/publications/2020/how-chinese-digital-ecosystems-battled-covid-19

Chesbrough, H. (2001). *Assembling the elephant: A review of empirical studies on the impact of technical change upon incumbent firms.* Emerald Group Publishing Limited.

Chesbrough, H. (2003a). *Open innovation: The new imperative for creating and profiting from technology.* Harvard Business Press.

Chesbrough, H. (2003b). The governance and performance of Xerox's technology spin-off companies. *Research Policy, 32*(3), 403–421.

Chesbrough, H. (2010). Business model innovation: Opportunities and barriers. *Long Range Planning, 43*(2–3), 354–363.

Chesbrough, H., & Bogers, M. (2014). Explicating open innovation: Clarifying an emerging paradigm for understanding innovation. In: H. Chesbrough, W. Vanhaverbeke, & J. West (Eds.), *New frontiers in open innovation* (p. 3–28). Oxford University Press.

Christensen, C.M. (1997). *The innovator's dilemma: When new technologies cause great firms to fail.* Harvard Business Review Press.

Christensen, C.M., & Overdorf, M. (2000). Meeting the challenge of disruptive change. *Harvard Business Review, 78*(2), 66–77.

Christensen, C.M., Ojomo, E., & Dillon, K. (2019). *The prosperity paradox. How innovation can lift nations out of poverty.* Harper Business.

Christensen, C.M., Raynor, M., & McDonald, R. (2015). The big idea: What is disruptive innovation. *Harvard Business Review, 93*(12), 44–53.

Cooperrider, D., Whitney, D.D., & Stavros, J. (2008). *The appreciative inquiry handbook: For leaders of change.* Berrett-Koehler Publishers.

Cox, E., Katila, R., & Eisenhardt, K. (2014). *Who takes you to the dance? How funding partners influence innovative activity in young firms.* Working Paper. University of Washington, Washington, D.C., and Stanford University, Stanford, CA.

Davis, J.P. (2016). The group dynamics of interorganizational relationships: Collaborating with multiple partners in innovation ecosystems. *Administrative Science Quarterly, 61*(4), 621–661.

Diestre, L., & Rajagopalan, N. (2012). Are all 'sharks' dangerous? New biotechnology ventures and partner selection in R&D alliances. *Strategic Management Journal, 33*(10), 1115–1134.

Doz, Y.L. (2019). Governing multilateral alliances. *California Management Review, 61*(3), 93–114.

Dushnitsky, G., & Lenox, M.J. (2005). When do incumbents learn from entrepreneurial ventures?: Corporate venture capital and investing firm innovation rates. *Research Policy, 34*(5), 615–639.

Edmondson, A. (1999). Psychological safety and learning behavior in work teams. *Administrative Science Quarterly, 44*(2), 350–383.

Eisenmann, T. (2021). Why startups fail. It's not always the horse or the jockey. *Harvard Business Review*, May–June, 76–85.

Felin, T., & Zenger, T.R. (2020). Open innovation: A theory-based view. *Strategic Management Review, 1*(2), 223–232.

Fernandez, A.S., Le Roy, F., & Gnyawali, D.R. (2014). Sources and management of tension in co-opetition case evidence from telecommunications satellites manufacturing in Europe. *Industrial Marketing Management, 43*(2), 222–235.

Fosse, L.J., & Tønsberg, C (2019). *Håndtering av styringsutfordringer i et økosystem. En kvalitativ casestudie av PSD2-samarbeidet i Finance Innovation.* Master's Thesis in Strategy and Management. Norwegian School of Economics.

Freeman R.E. (1984). *Strategic management: A stakeholder approach.* Pitman.

Førland, I., & Klemp, S. (2021). *Agil organisering i et komplekst selskap med store avhengigheter: En kvalitativ casestudie om agil organisering i et veletablert finanskonsern.* Master's Thesis. NHH/SNF Race project.

Garud, R., Kumaraswamy, A., & Karnøe, P. (2010). Path dependence or path creation? *Journal of Management Studies, 47*(4), 760–774.

Garvin, D.A. (1983). Spin-offs and the new firm formation process. *California Management Review, 25*(2), 3–20.

Gawer, A., & Cusumano, M.A. (2014). Industry platforms and ecosystem innovation. *Journal of Product Innovation Management, 31*(3), 417–433.

Glesne, D., & Pedersen, M. (2020). *Strategic agility: Adapting and renewing strategic direction: An exploratory case study.* Master's Thesis. NHH/SNF Race project.

Gnyawali, D.R., & Park, B.J.R. (2011). Co-opetition between giants: Collaboration with competitors for technological innovation. *Research policy, 40*(5), 650–663.

Gooderham, P., Meyer, C.B., Sandvik, A.M., Stensaker, I., Elter, F., & Pedersen, T. (2021). *Legacy removal: Leading digital transformation of incumbent service firms.* Working paper.

Gray, B., & Purdy, J. (2018). *Collaborating for our future: Multistakeholder partnerships for solving complex problems.* Oxford University Press.

Gulati, R., Lavie, D., & Singh, H. (2009). The nature of partnering experience and the gains from alliances. *Strategic Management Journal, 30*(11), 1213–1233.

Gunasekaran, A. (2001). *Agile manufacturing: The 21st century competitive strategy.* Elsevier.

Hagel, J. (2019). Unleashing motivation for transformation. The power of scaling the edge. *Deloitte Insights.*

Hagel, J., Brown, J.S., & Kulasooriya, D. (2019). Scaling edges: A pragmatic pathway to transformation. Key design principles for scaling edges. *Deloitte Insights.*

Hallen, B.L., Katila, R., & Rosenberger, J.D. (2014). How do social defenses work? A resource-dependence lens on technology ventures, venture capital investors, and corporate relationships. *Academy of Management Journal, 57*(4), 1078–1101.

Hamel, G., & Zanini, M. (2020). *Humanocracy: Creating organizations as amazing as the people inside them.* Harvard Business Press.

Hannah, D.P., & Eisenhardt, K.M. (2018). How firms navigate cooperation and competition in nascent ecosystems. *Strategic Management Journal, 39*(12), 3163–3192.

Hauge, A.H. (2021). Gründer i blodet. *Magma,* 0421.

Hestad, S., & Solheim, L. (2021). *Spenningen mellom kaos og kontroll: En eksplorativ casestudie om hvordan etablerte selskaper kan lykkes med agil ledelse og organisering av agile team i reisen mot å bli smidige.* Master's Thesis. NHH/SNF RaCE project.

Hoffmann, W., Lavie, D., Reuer, J.J., & Shipilov, A. (2018). The interplay of competition and cooperation. *Strategic Management Journal, 39*(12), 3033–3052.

Jacobides, M.G., Cennamo, C., & Gawer, A. (2018). Towards a theory of ecosystems. *Strategic Management Journal, 39*(8), 2255–2276.

Jacobsen, D.I., & Thorsvik, J. (2019). *Hvordan organisasjoner fungerer.* Fagbokforlaget.

Jemison, D.B., & Haspeslagh, P.H. (1991). *Managing acquisitions: Creating value through corporate renewal.* The Free Press.

Kamath, S. (2020). *The influence of agile ways of working on change capacity: A case study exploring organizational agility in practice.* Master's Thesis. NHH/SNF RaCE project.

Kaplan, S. (2020). Beyond the business case for social responsibility. *Academy of Management Discoveries, 6*(1), 1–4.

Katila, R., Rosenberger, J.D., & Eisenhardt, K.M. (2008). Swimming with sharks: Technology ventures, defense mechanisms and corporate relationships. *Administrative Science Quarterly, 53*(2), 295–332.

Knight, E., Daymond, J., & Paroutis, S. (2020). Design-led strategy: How to bring design thinking into the art of strategic management. *California Management Review, 62*(2), 30–52.

Kolko, J. (2015). Design thinking comes of age. *Harvard Business Review,* September, 66–71.

Kuo, L. (2019, 10 September). Jack Ma, China's richest man, steps down as chairman of Alibaba. *Guardian.* Retrieved from https://www.theguardian.com/business/2019/sep/10/jack-ma-chinas-richest-man-steps-down-as-chairman-of-alibaba

Lavie, D., Haunschild, P.R., & Khanna, P. (2012). Organizational differences, relational mechanisms, and alliance performance. *Strategic Management Journal, 33*(13), 1453–1479.

Le Roy, F., & Fernandez, A.S. (2015). Managing coopetitive tensions at the working-group level: The rise of the coopetitive project team. *British Journal of Management, 26*(4), 671–688.

Lee, J. (2020). *Spotify's Failed #SquadGoals.* Retrieved from https://www.jeremiahlee.com/posts/failed-squad-goals/

Lem, C.H. (2018). Strategi har gått fra langdistanse til sprint. *Magma,* 0618.

LeMay, M. (2018). *Agile for everybody: Creating fast, flexible, and customer-first organizations.* O'Reilly Media, Inc.

Levine, S.R. (2020, January 15). Diversity confirmed to boost innovation and financial results. *Forbes.* Retrieved from https://www.forbes.com/sites/forbesinsights/2020/01/15/diversity-confirmed-to-boost-innovation-and-financial-results/?sh=efbc875c4a6a

Lien, L.B., & Jakobsen, E.W. (2015). *Ekspansjon og konsernstrategi.* Gyldendal akademisk.

Lien, L.B., Knudsen, E.S., & Baardsen, T.Ø. (2016). *Strategiboken.* Fagbokforlaget.

Lorenzo, R., Voigt, N., Tsusaka, M., Krintz, M., & Abouzar, K. (2018, 23 January). *How diverse leadership teams boost innovation.* BCG-report. Retrieved from https://www.bcg.com/publications/2018/how-diverse-leadership-teams-boost-innovation

Løvik, O.L. (2020). *Hvordan få til et godt samarbeid i den tohendige løsningen? En eksplorativ casestudie.* Master's Thesis. NHH/SNF Race project.

Manso, G. (2017). Creating incentives for innovation. *California Management Review, 60*(1), 18–32.

Marks, M.L., & Mirvis, P.H. (2012). A research agenda to increase merger and acquisition success. In: Y. Weber (Ed.). *Handbook of research on mergers and acquisitions* (p. 61–75). Edward Elgar Publishing.

McGahan, A.M. (2020). Where does an organization's responsibility end?: Identifying the boundaries on stakeholder claims. *Academy of Management Discoveries, 6*(1), 8–11.

McGrath, R.G. (2020). *Seeing around corners. How to spot inflection points in business before they happen.* Houghton Mifflin Harcourt.

McGrath, R.G., & MacMillan, I.C. (2000). *The entrepreneurial mindset: Strategies for continuously creating opportunity in an age of uncertainty* (Vol. 284). Harvard Business Press.

McMorrow, R., & Liu, N. (2020, 14 January). Sellers asked to choose in battle between Alibaba and Pinduoduo. *Financial Times.* Retrieved from https://www.ft.com/content/b55d0e0a-33a1-11ea-9703-eea0cae3f0de

Meyer, C.B., & Norman, V. (2019). *Ikke for å konkurrere. Strategi for fellesskapets tjenere.* Fagbokforlaget.

Meyer, C.B., & Stensaker, I.G. (2011). *Endringskapasitet.* Fagbokforlaget.

Miron-Spektor, E., Ingram, A., Keller, J., Smith, W.K., & Lewis, M.W. (2018). Microfoundations of organizational paradox: The problem is how we think about the problem. *Academy of Management Journal, 61*(1), 26–45.

Moore, J.F. (1993). Predators and prey: A new ecology of competition. *Harvard Business Review, 71*(3), 75–86.

Mutoloki, J. (2020). *Innovation through collaboration. An exploratory study examining the open innovation output created through strategic partnerships and the subsequent effect of ongoing change processes.* Master's Thesis in Strategy and Management. Norwegian School of Economics.

Nagji, B., & Tuff, G. (2012). Managing your innovation portfolio. *Harvard Business Review, 90*(5), 66–74.

Northouse, P.G. (2019). *Leadership theory and practice.* Sage.

O'Reilly, C.A., & Tushman, M.L. (2004). The ambidextrous organization. *Harvard Business Review, 82*(4), 74–83.

O'Reilly, C.A., & Tushman, M.L. (2013). Organizational ambidexterity: Past, present, and future. *The Academy of Management Perspectives, 27,* 324–338.

O'Reilly, C.A., & Tushman, M.L. (2016). *Lead and disrupt. How to solve the innovator's dilemma.* Stanford University Press.

Oreg, S., Vakola, M., & Armenakis, A. (2011). Change recipients' reactions to organizational change: A 60-year review of quantitative studies. *The Journal of applied behavioral science, 47*(4), 461–524.

Phillips, K.W., Medin, D., Lee, C.D., Bang, M., Bishop, S., & Lee, D.N. (2014). How diversity works. *Scientific American, 311*(4), 42–47.

Pisano, G.P. (2019). *Creative construction. The DNA of sustained innovation.* Public Affairs.

Podolny, J.M., & Hansen, M.T. (2020). How Apple is organized for innovation. *Harvard Business Review*, Nov.–Dec., 86–95.

Porter, M.E. (1985). Technology and competitive advantage. *Journal of Business Strategy, 5*(3), 60–78.

Prydz, N. (2020). *Startup-helvete: En svært personlig gründerhistorie.* NoBox AS.

Puranam, P., & Clement, J. (2020). *Why agile may be fragile. Insead Knowledge Edu.* Retrieved from https://knowledge.insead.edu.blog.insead-blog/why-agile-may-be-fraglile-10201

Quinn, R.E., & Thakor, A.V. (2018). Creating a purpose-driven organization. *Harvard Business Review, 96*(4), 78–85.

Rahause, S. (2020). *Developing sensing and seizing capabilities through interactions with external partners. An exploratory study of a major Norwegian Financial Institution.* Master's Thesis in Strategy and Management. Norwegian School of Economics.

Reger, R.K., Gustafson, L.T., Demarie, S.M., & Mullane, J.V. (1994). Reframing the organization: Why implementing total quality is easier said than done. *Academy of Management Review, 19*(3), 565–584.

Reguly, E. (2019). A tale of transformation: the Danish company that went from black to green energy. *Corporate Knights,* Spring Issue.

Ridley, M. (2020). *How Innovation Works.* 4th Estate.

Rigby, D.K., Sutherland, J., & Takeuchi, H. (2016). The secret history of agile innovation. *Harvard Business Review, 4.* Retrieved from https://hbr.org/2016/04/the-secret-history-of-agile-innovation

Rogers, E.M. (2010). *Diffusion of Innovations.* Simon & Schuster.

Røvik, K.A. (2007). *Trender og translasjoner: Ideer som former det 21. århundrets organisasjon.* Universitetsforlaget.

Sandvik, A.M., Whiting, S., & Seglem Larsen, A. (2019). Hvordan "mission" motiverer ansatte til gode prestasjoner. *Magma, 7,* 71–76.

Sapienza, H.J., Parhankangas, A., & Autio, E. (2004). Knowledge relatedness and post-spin-off growth. *Journal of Business Venturing, 19*(6), 809–829.

Schein, E.H. (2015). *Dialogic organization development: The theory and practice of transformational change.* Berrett-Koehler Publishers.

Schmeiss, J., Hoelzle, K., & Tech, R.P. (2019). Designing governance mechanisms in platform ecosystems: Addressing the paradox of openness through blockchain technology. *California Management Review, 62*(1), 121–143.

Seran, T., & Bez, S.M. (2020). Open innovation's "Multiunit back-end problem": How corporations can overcome business unit rivalry. *California Management Review, 63*(2). https://doi.org/10.1177/0008125620968609

Shipilov, A., & Gawer, A. (2020). Integrating research on interorganizational networks and ecosystems. *Academy of Management Annals, 14*(1), 92–121.

Skelton, M., & Pais, M. (2019). *Team topologies: Organizing business and technology teams for fast flow*. It Revolution Press.

Skogli, E., Stokke, O.M., Hveem, E.B., Aamo, A.W., Scheffer, M., & Jakobsen, E.W. (2019). *Er verdiskapning noe Norge kan leve av?* Menon-publikasjon nr. 88. Retrieved from https://www.menon.no/wp-content/uploads/2019-88-Verdiskaping-med-data.pdf

Smith, W.K. (2014). Dynamic decision making: A model of senior leaders managing strategic paradoxes. *Academy of Management Journal, 57*(6), 1592–1623.

Stensaker, I.G. (2018). Radikal endring og innovasjon: Et nytt blikk på den tohendige løsningen. *Magma*, 0718.

Stensaker, I.G., & Haueng, A.C. (2016). *Omstilling: Den uforutsigbare gjennomføringsfasen*. Fagbokforlaget.

Stensaker, I.G., Colman, H., & Elter, F. (2015). Jakten på effektiviseringsgevinster. Global integrering og standardisering. *Magma, 18*(7), 34–45.

Tan, B., Pan, S.L., Lu, X., & Huang, L. (2009). Leveraging digital business ecosystems for enterprise agility: The tri-logic development of Alibaba. *International Conference on Information Systems* (ICIS).

Teece, D.J. (1986). Profiting from technological innovation: Implications for integration, collaboration, licensing and public policy. *Research Policy, 15*(6), 285–305.

Teece, D.J. (2007). Explicating dynamic capabilities: The nature and microfoundations of (sustainable) enterprise performance. *Strategic Management Journal, 28*(13), 1319–1350.

Teece, D.J. (2020). Hand in glove: Open innovation and the dynamic capabilities framework. *Strategic Management Review, 1*(2), 233–253.

Teece, D.J., Peteraf, M., & Leih, S. (2016). Dynamic capabilities and organizational agility: Risk, uncertainty, and strategy in the innovation economy. *California Management Review, 58*(4), 13–35.

Teece, D.J., Pisano, G., & Shuen, A. (1997). Dynamic capabilities and strategic management. *Strategic Management Journal, 18*(7), 509–533.

Tsai, W.C. (2016). Analyzing the emergence of Alibaba Group from business ecosystem perspective. *The Journal of International Management Studies, 11*(2).

UN-GGIM (2018). *Future trends in geospatial information management.* UN-GGIM-report. Retrieved from https://ggim.un.org/future-trends/

Ungureanu, P., Bertolotti, F., Mattarelli, E., & Bellesia, F. (2019). Making matters worse by trying to make them better? Exploring vicious circles of decision in hybrid partnerships. *Organization Studies, 40*(9), 1331–1359.

Vuori, T.O., & Huy, Q.N. (2016). Distributed attention and shared emotions in the innovation process: How Nokia lost the smartphone battle. *Administrative Science Quarterly, 61*(1), 9–51.

Wagner, E.J. (2018). The relationship between a firm's ownership structure, governance, and innovation. *College of Business Theses and Dissertations, 1.* https://via.library.depaul.edu/business_etd/1

Watzlawick, P., Weakland, J.H., & Fisch, R. (1974). *Change: Principles of problem formation and problem resolution.* Norton.

Weiblen, T., & Chesbrough, H.W. (2015). Engaging with startups to enhance corporate innovation. *California Management Review, 57*(2), 66–90.

Wulf, J. (2010). Alibaba Group. *Harvard Business School Case, 710,* 436.

Zeng, M. (2018). *Smart business: What Alibaba's success reveals about the future of strategy.* Harvard Business Review Press.

Zobel, A.K. (2017). Benefiting from open innovation: A multidimensional model of absorptive capacity. *Journal of Product Innovation Management, 34*(3), 269–288.[start kolofon]

Index

G

H

I

L

M

N

O

P

R

S